To Leo,

even best profits in
hard times!

Jordan Goodman

FAST PROFITS
IN
HARD TIMES

FAST PROFITS
IN
HARD TIMES

10 Secret Strategies to Make You Rich in an Up *or* Down Economy

JORDAN E. GOODMAN

**BUSINESS
PLUS**

NEW YORK   BOSTON

A Lynn Sonberg Book

Business Plus
Hachette Book Group USA
237 Park Avenue
New York, NY 10017
Visit our Web site at www.HachetteBookGroupUSA.com.

Business Plus is an imprint of Grand Central Publishing.
The Business Plus name and logo is a trademark of Hachette Book Group USA, Inc.

Printed in the United States of America

First Edition: January 2008

10 9 8 7 6 5 4 3 2 1

Library of Congress Cataloging-in-Publication Data

Goodman, Jordan Elliot.
    Fast profits in hard times : 10 secret strategies to make you rich in an up or down economy / Jordan E. Goodman. — 1st ed.
        p. cm.
    Includes index.
    ISBN-13: 978-0-446-58156-1
    ISBN-10: 0-446-58156-9
    1. Investments.   2. Real estate investment.   3. Speculation.   4. Securities.
5. Portfolio management.   I. Title.
    HG4521.G556 2008
    332.6—dc22   2007033204

To my wife, Suzanne, whose patience and support throughout this project was never-ending, and my teenage son, Jason, who has learned far more about investing at his age than I ever did.

Acknowledgments

Fast Profits in Hard Times would not have been possible without the generous and skillful contributions and extremely hard work of many talented people.

Foremost among these contributors are the team of Lynn Sonberg and Roger Cooper, who worked with me to hone the original idea for this book. Lynn skillfully guided the work from the original proposal through the research, writing, and editing process, always staying on top of the many details and maintaining a high standard for accuracy and clarity in the work. Roger was also instrumental in framing the book's direction and was a key player in getting the book distributed to the wide audience that is benefiting from its message.

The writing and research team also did a remarkable job of combining skillful writing skills with exhaustive research on many complex financial topics. Minda Zetlin artfully wrote most of the text, weaving in real-life case studies amidst the explanations of the investing strategies. The writing and editing skills of John Downes and Ellen Neuborne contributed greatly to the chapters on bonds and options.

Many experts contributed their insights to make the descriptions of all these strategies understandable and accurate. This includes, among others, Larry Loftus on tax liens and deeds, David Early on real estate strategies, Carla Pasternak, Roger Conrad, and Richard Lehmann on income trusts, master limited partnerships and high-yield stocks, Vita Nelson on dividend reinvestment plans, Fred Rewey on cash flow opportunities, and Earle Pasquill on payday loans.

The team at Grand Central Publishing was also instrumental in making this project a reality. Executive Editor Rick Wolff immediately embraced the concept of explaining investments that thrive in an up or down economy that most investors had never heard about. Jamie Raab, publisher of Grand Central, was extremely supportive of the book from conception through publication. Flamur Tonuzi, art director, created the wonderful cover design. Robert Castillo was responsible for overseeing the production of the book, and Fred Chase undertook the meticulous copyediting of the manuscript. Herman Estevez skillfully took the photograph for the flap jacket. My thanks as well to Tracy Martin for her editorial assistance.

I want to thank the many people who volunteered their success stories that help illustrate that these strategies are working today for real people across the country. All of the stories told in the book are completely true, though I have changed the names and locations to protect their privacy. Finally, great thanks to the thousands of subscribers to my Web site, www.moneyanswers.com, and the many thousands of people who, over the years, have contacted me for ongoing financial information and advice. This book resulted from the many questions I get from subscribers on how best to invest their capital.

My hope is that you, the reader of *Fast Profits in Hard Times,* will indeed put some or all of these strategies to work and end up earning much higher returns than you ever could have from "safe" alternatives like certificates of deposit or money market funds. By combining the knowledge you learn from this book with all of the resources I put at your disposal here, you should be able to earn significant profits, no matter what the economy does in the future.

Jordan E. Goodman
January 1, 2008

Contents

FAST PROFITS
IN
HARD TIMES

INTRODUCTION

You *Can* Profit in Hard Times

Ten years ago, the stock market was right in the middle of its biggest run-up of all time. The Dow Jones Industrial Average rose an average 25 percent per year from the beginning of 1995 to the beginning of 2000. Real estate saw a parallel boom, as home values rose 18 percent between 1990 and 2000, after adjusting for inflation. Internet trading took off. A television ad at the time showed a beauty parlor full of manicurists gleefully day trading as their customers' cuticles soaked. It had never seemed easier to make money, and millions of people did just that.

Economists have a phrase for times like these: *A rising tide lifts all boats.* That is, when the stock market is on an upsurge, when real estate prices are climbing, when profits are high and the economy is flying along, everyone benefits. The thing about tides, though, is they always turn, and as surely as the tide will rise, sooner or later it will sink again. In times like those, many investors see their good-time gains evaporate. They find themselves buckling down, trying to preserve their assets, borrowing to get along, and hoping for better times to come.

It doesn't have to be that way. In my more than thirty years helping people understand their finances and watching the markets rise and fall, I've learned one thing: It's possible to make money, and make it fast, whether the economy is up or down. I wrote this book to help you do the same. The investment strategies I will teach you in this book earn returns in the range of 5 to 10 percent at the low end and often much higher—20 to 100 percent at the high end regardless of whether the Dow is up or down, and whether the economy is growing or shrinking.

In the following chapters, I'll let you in on ten little-known strategies for making money in good times or bad, strategies you need in times like these when you can't count on a rising tide to carry you along. All you need is a willingness to try some strategies most ordinary investors have never used—and probably don't even know about.

Why Haven't I Ever Heard of These Opportunities Before?

That's a good question. The answer has to do with how most people approach investing. Afraid they aren't smart enough to beat the markets—or even fully understand them—they depend on advisors or fund managers at big investment firms to figure it out for them. With stocks or funds available in every conceivable industry, investing with big investment firms would seem the smart way to grow your money, spreading the risk over many different markets and types of investments.

The only problem with this approach is that brokers don't actually present their clients with the full range of investment opportunities that exist, only the ones their firm is selling. These are the products that will earn them the commissions or management fees on which their livelihood depends. And, because they're generally making the same investments as everyone else, they tend to do about as well as the market at large. When the tide is rising, things are great, and investors love their brokers and fund managers. When the tide is sinking, they aren't so happy. That unhappiness can turn to anger as investors contemplate the commissions and/or management fees they must pay, even when their accounts are heading south.

There's a better way. The strategies outlined in this book are investments anyone can make, on their own behalf, without help from a broker and without going through a mutual fund. The reason you've never heard of them is that the big brokerage houses aren't selling them—because they don't stand to earn their usual hefty commissions and management fees. That's a good thing: The commissions they're not earning means you get to keep more of your profits to reinvest and earn even higher returns.

I first began learning about these secret investment strategies after I left my job at *Money* magazine, where I'd been a correspondent for eighteen years. During my time at *Money,* I'd been very much steeped in traditional investment thinking: blue chip stocks and Treasury bills and mutual funds. *Money* never covers unorthodox investment strategies, so I never learned anything about them. My own investments followed the same conventional lines, and the returns I earned were okay, but never spectacular. I began wondering whether it was possible to do better.

I left *Money* to pursue my own career teaching investors to make the most of their money. But it was also a chance to begin finally exploring the wider range of investment options I knew must be out there. I began reading, going to seminars, signing up for newsletters, and consulting with expert investors who'd done it themselves. I soon discovered there was a whole world of investment choices most individual investors never come across. I started trying out these strategies myself, and consistently earned much higher yields than I had been with my more traditional choices. In one case, I actually tripled my original investment.

I also learned that many of these alternative investments are in fact very well known—in certain circles. Large institutional investors, such as banks and insurance firms, had been using them to make huge, market-beating profits for decades. They simply hadn't been available to individuals with thousands, not millions, of dollars to invest. But this has changed dramatically in the last few years, thanks to the wide availability of personal computers and high-speed Internet connections. This is a huge new opportunity you can profit from. The Internet allows you to follow the options and foreign exchange markets minute by minute. It allows you to research companies and real estate that may be thousands of miles away. It has leveled the playing field between big investors, who have the time and money to fly cross-country to check out properties at a tax deed auction, and everyone else. Throughout this book, I will show you how to use the Internet to make smart investment choices from your own living room or home office.

Today, thousands of real-life individual investors are using each of these approaches to earn better-than-market returns year after year, and you'll meet many of them throughout this book. I've used some of these strategies myself, and I'll tell you exactly how I did it. In every case, I'll give you step-by-step instructions on getting started and lots of resources where you can go for more information, or to actually start investing.

Going Against the Cycle

Although many investors feel trapped in the boom-and-bust cycle of market fluctuations, the moneymaking strategies in this book will help you defy the ups and downs of the markets, earning that 8 to 10 percent or better return whether the economy is booming, stagnating, or even sinking into a recession. How is this possible?

Noncyclical Strategies

Not all investments rise and fall with economic ups and downs. Many investment strategies I teach in this book are *noncyclical*—that is, completely unaffected by the state of the market, or the economy in general. For instance, you can make money fast by trading options whether the market is up or down, or both, and this strategy works just as well when a stock is losing value as when it's gaining. Foreign exchange is another good way to make a fast profit that's noncyclical—you can make money off the differences in currency values whether the economy is strong or weak, and whether the dollar is rising or falling, compared to other currencies. Vending machines (a form of passive income) are another great noncyclical investment: People eat snacks in good times and bad.

Also, keep in mind that hard times here in the United States may not necessarily mean hard times elsewhere in the world. There is always a bull market *somewhere*. When the U.S. economy weakens, the dollar often falls in price against other currencies. You can take advantage of that drop by investing in foreign bond mutual funds, whose already impressive yields are bolstered by significant capital gains as the dollar continues to decline. That's because when you buy bonds from foreign governments and corporations, you are actually converting your money into the local currency (yen, yuan, euros, etc.) to do so. If the dollar goes down, then 100 euros (for instance) will buy more dollars than it did before, and you can reap the benefit.

Countercyclical Strategies

Other strategies I will teach you are *countercyclical*—that is, you can actually make more money when the economy is weakening than when it is strengthening. Hard times are a great time to invest in tax liens and deeds: When people are struggling financially, they're more likely to have trouble paying their real estate taxes, which means more liens and deeds are available for investors to buy, and you can thus have more of a chance of buying property way below market value if you end up foreclosing. Bad economic times are also good times to invest in payday loans. When people are economically stretched, more need to borrow in order to get from paycheck to paycheck, and payday loan profits increase.

Some investors tell me they're uncomfortable at the thought of using countercyclical strategies such as these because it seems too much like taking advantage of someone else's misfortune. This is a perfectly understandable first reaction. But let's take a closer look at, say, investing in tax liens and deeds. True enough, the only reason they are available for sale is that unfortunate homeowners have found themselves unable to pay their property taxes.

In many cases this is a temporary situation, and after a while, the homeowners get back on their feet, borrow, sell assets, or otherwise manage to get the tax money together. At that point, like it or not, they will owe interest—at rates that are legally mandated by the community where they live. It won't make much difference to them whether it's the municipality receiving the back taxes and interest, or an investor who bought the lien.

It may, on the other hand, make a big difference to the municipality. Cities and towns put tax liens and deeds up for sale because they desperately need cash to meet payroll, keep the streets in good repair, and provide a variety of services for their citizens. That's what your investment in tax liens and deeds helps to do.

The fact is that all countercyclical investments, from tax liens to below-market-value real estate, to funding payday loans, provide cash to people who really need it when they need it most. Borrowing money from a payday loan store might seem like an awful thing to have to do, but it can be a blessing to the borrower, if the alternative is being evicted.

Picking Strategies to Start With

There are dozens of different strategies in this book, so you will need to pick a few, or even just one, to get you started. Each chapter will offer detailed advice and how-to information, including:

- How much time and effort the strategy takes
- Any special skills required (though most strategies are easy for anyone to follow)

- Minimum investment to "get in the game"
- The upside—good reasons to consider this investment
- The downside—possible drawbacks to consider before you jump in
- How to minimize your risk
- Resources if you want to learn more, as well as lists and ticker symbols for actual investments to buy
- How to get started—what to do if you want to give it a try

Here's a quick overview of how each of the strategies works:

1. Tax Liens and Deeds

When property owners fail to pay their taxes, those unpaid taxes accrue interest and penalties and the owner has a certain period, ranging from six months to five years, in which to pay up.

In lien states, the municipality then places a lien on the property and may sell the lien to investors. The price of the lien is based on the taxes owed. If the owner pays up during the redemption period, the investor collects the interest—which may be as high as 25 percent. If the owner does not pay up within the redemption period, the lien holder can foreclose—which means you can wind up owning a property for the price of the taxes, a tiny fraction of its market value.

In deed states, municipalities skip the first step and proceed directly to selling the deed once a property is ready to be foreclosed. Again, it's an opportunity to buy a property for much less than its actual worth.

2. Below-Market-Value Real Estate

In this chapter, I'll introduce you to ways of acquiring real estate at a fraction of its worth, besides buying tax deeds. These include:

- *Pre-foreclosures*—identifying properties about to be foreclosed on by lenders, when you can make a deal to the owner's advantage;
- *Probate*—buying properties whose owners have recently died and whose heirs would otherwise have a long wait until the property is disposed of;
- *Pre-construction*—Buying properties such as condos that are under construction.

I'll tell you exactly how to get started with each of these techniques and how to pick the best investments, as well as how to determine what price you should pay, depending on how you plan to use the property once you've acquired it.

3. Income Trusts and Master Limited Partnerships (MLPs)

These two types of investment are similar in concept. Most companies earn profits and then decide whether and how much to distribute to shareholders as dividends. But income trusts and MLPs have little corporate structure and are required by law to distribute virtually all their profits directly to shareholders. This means they can often offer double-digit yields.

Income trusts usually produce a natural resource, such as oil or natural gas. On the other hand, most MLPs can be found in the pipeline industry, an especially attractive sector because pipelines make money as long as demand for oil or natural gas remains steady, whether oil or gas prices themselves are high or low.

4. High-Yield Stocks

Many investors evaluate stocks only based on capital growth, and overlook many investments that offer returns in the form of dividends rather than capital gains. High-yielding stocks tend to be more stable, and can be a safer investment than other equities, since dividends don't evaporate the way capital gains do if stock prices go down.

5. DRIPs

Dividend reinvestment plans are commonly known as DRIPs. These are special programs offered by some companies to allow investors to buy shares directly from the company, and automatically reinvest the dividends their shares earn into a purchase of more shares. One advantage is you can make very small investments—sometimes as little as $50 or less, which can be automatically deducted from your bank account—and can be used to buy a single share or even a fraction of a share without a profit-killing brokerage commission. Some companies even offer a discount off the market value of their shares for DRIP investors, making them an even more attractive investment.

6. Bonds

Most investors don't think of bonds as a way to make fast profits, but the right ones can be. Bond mutual funds based in foreign countries can take advantage of falling dollar values to create double-digit returns. Bond funds based in the emerging markets of Asia and Eastern Europe can offer particularly spectacular returns. High-yield bonds (also known as "junk" bonds) are another way to grow your capital, and you can lessen the risk by investing via mutual funds.

7. Options

An option is the right (or "option") to buy or sell a stock by a given day at a given price. Most small investors avoid options because these are considered an extremely risky investment. But I play the options market all the time, and vastly reduce the risk by using software to select which options to buy, and taking advantage of price movements rather than waiting and exercising options. I'll teach you how to do the same.

8. Foreign Exchange

This is an area that, until recently, has been completely unavailable to all but the big institutional investors. Foreign exchange is a classically risky investing area, but, as with options, trading software can help you analyze the market, vastly reduce the risk of large losses, and take advantage of trends to make fast profits whether the economy is up or down.

9. Selling or Brokering Cash Flow

Cash flow refers to providing immediate cash in return for an antici-pated payment at a discount off the expected amount. It might work like this: A doctor's office has invoiced an insurance company $10,000, but the insurance company may take several months to pay. Meanwhile, the office has payroll and overhead expenses to meet. It might be worth it for the doctor's office to accept your immediate payment of $9,500 in return for transferring the $10,000 payment to you when it arrives. They get to keep meeting expenses without taking out an expensive bank loan. And you get a better than 10 percent annualized rate on your investment.

10. Passive Income Strategies

I'll show you a whole variety of strategies designed to produce a steady flow of income while you do as little as possible. Investing in vending machines, timeshares, and debit card swiping machines can create income with virtually no effort, once you have a system in place. I'll teach you how to set up income-generating investments that will keep money rolling in for years to come.

Which Strategies Are Right for Me?

Each of the strategies comes with different advantages and drawbacks, and I'll give you a quick snapshot of the pros and cons when I describe each of them. You can also use the chart on pages 15–18 to compare the different strategies to see how each of them lines up with your particular goals.

To get you started, here's a look at which investment options work best for specific investing concerns:

If you want something easy to understand and execute:

First of all, none of the strategies I'll teach you here requires any expertise in finance or investments. If you made it through junior high school math, you'll be able to master every technique in this book. If you want, though, you can make it easiest on yourself by starting out with investment strategies that take the least know-how. Consider discount DRIPs, which take little study time, and are easy to understand. Bond mutual funds, where a fund manager does the homework for you, might be another good choice.

Or, you might consider some of the below-market-value real estate strategies I'll teach you in Chapter 2. If you find the idea of studying the financial markets intimidating, buying a house or condo at less than its market worth, and then either selling it at a profit or renting it out, might be less intimidating.

Ultimately, though, I encourage you to at least take a close look at all the strategies in this book. None of them is difficult to understand or put into action. And, the more you learn, the better able you'll be to use your capital to create both fast profits and lasting growth.

If you have little time to spend investing:
Having little or no free time to spend managing investments is a big problem for many people. Keep in mind you'll be able to do all the work you'll need on most of these investments from a home computer, over the Internet, at your convenience. Take options trading for instance, which I teach you to do in Chapter 7. The days of having to watch the market every second so as to buy or sell are over: Now you can program options trading software with stop-loss triggers that will sell your options for you at just the right moment, even if you're busy doing something else.

You can do this work in your spare time, according to your own personal schedule. If the only time you have is after 10 P.M., that's still a great time to troll municipal listings for tax liens or probate records for real estate opportunities, as well as set your options strategy for the next day. And late at night is the perfect time if you decide to invest in the lucrative, fast-moving foreign exchange market. No matter what time it is where you are, it's business hours somewhere in the world. So this is a market that almost never shuts down.

If you don't want to have to watch your investments:
You might be a good candidate for DRIPs. The whole point of these programs is that they do the investing for you, building your stock holdings while you attend to the rest of your life.

Other good choices include income trusts and master limited partnerships, two types of stock structured to provide income to shareholders, rather than grow in value. That means that, unlike traditional stock investments, you don't need to sell the shares to derive a benefit from them: Payments keep coming in for as long as you own the stock. Also, take a look at some of the bond strategies I teach you in Chapter 6.

But there's also a whole assortment of passive investment opportunities that I'll explain in Chapter 10. Investments in timeshares and debit card machines pretty much take care of themselves. Once you've put them in place, there's little more for you to do but collect the earnings.

Any of these set-it-and-forget-it strategies can be a good choice for those too busy to even think about their investments.

If you want to start with a small investment:

Many of the strategies I'll teach you don't require a big up-front outlay of cash. In some, you can start out with as little as $500 to $1,000. Consider buying tax liens, which can be surprisingly inexpensive. Or try bond mutual funds, where the minimum investment is $1,000 and earnings can be reinvested. Discount DRIPs are another good option, with a minimum investment of $500, which you can easily add to later as you go. And because these are structured to continue buying shares as dividends roll in, your small investment can soon turn into a bigger one. Trading options is another strategy with a modest minimum investment. If you want to use software for trading options, most Web sites will let you get started with an investment of only $1,000. And if you have the time to spend watching the options market and making trades, you can build your small investment into a bigger one in a hurry.

If you need your investment to be liquid:

This is a common concern. It makes excellent sense to plan for your expenses as much as possible, and also have money quickly available for expenses no one can plan for.

How much liquidity do you need? It may be tempting to say "all of it," but that would prevent you from investing in some of the highest-yielding choices. Real estate, for instance, has offered phenomenal rates of return over the last few years, and many a fortune has been made buying and selling homes and other properties. But real estate is illiquid: You can't buy a house today with the assurance of selling it tomorrow. A more effective strategy is to carefully review your financial position, consider any upcoming expenses you know about, and any expenses you can conceivably see on the horizon (such as the trip you and your spouse always said you'd take for that big anniversary). Use these figures to give yourself a rough idea of how much of your investment really needs to be available at a moment's notice, and how much you can commit for the longer term.

Whatever you decide, there are plenty of strategies in this book that will work for your needs. Trading in options, for instance, is very liquid; indeed if you follow the option strategies in this book, you'll be buying options and selling them again in a very short period of time, sometimes less than a day. Discount DRIPs, bond mutual funds, income trusts, and master limited partnerships all allow you to cash out whenever you need to.

Some of the investment strategies I will teach you in this book are highly liquid, but volatile. Foreign bond funds are a good example of this. The bond interest payments themselves may be stable, but the value of your investment will rise and fall rapidly, not only based on the market price of the bonds, but also on the fluctuating value of the dollar. Your best bet is to use investments like these when you're planning to leave your money in place for a while, or at least when you will have some leeway when picking the moment to sell. Otherwise, though you can always get your money back in an emergency, you may have to risk taking a loss. Which brings us to the most common concern of all:

If you want to avoid risk:
This is a huge issue for many people. Ask investors what kinds of returns they want and they'll answer "As high as possible." Eight percent, 10 percent, 15 percent—whatever they can get. But then ask them how much risk they're willing to accept, and the answer will be, "None."

Unfortunately, you can't have it both ways. How much risk to take on is something each investor must decide for him- or herself. As a general rule, it's wiser to make risky investments when you're younger, because you'll have more time to recover from a loss, you can hold an investment longer (sometimes they bounce back over time) and chances are you have less to invest, and a greater need to increase your net worth. Less-risky investments are often recommended for older people, who may soon need to draw on the investment money to sustain them during their retirement years.

But this is a very general guideline that completely fails to take into account individual circumstances, work histories, plans, or temperaments. Ultimately, it is this last issue—your particular personality—that more than anything else will determine your ability to handle moderate- or high-risk investments. (If you want to learn more about how your money personality can influence your investment choices, and how to choose those that best fit your personality, take a look at my previous book, *Master Your Money Type: Using Your Financial Personality to Create a Life of Wealth and Freedom*.)

All of the strategies I teach in this book are designed to maximize profits while minimizing risk. Some are very low-risk strategies, such as investing in bonds, bond funds, or income trusts. Others, like playing the options market or buying real estate, are slightly higher in risk, though they also offer the potential for very large returns. Use whichever strategies are most comfortable for your particular level of risk tolerance—or try a combination of strategies to get both the safety of low risk and the benefits of huge rewards that come with higher-risk investments.

Whatever strategy or strategies you choose, I urge you to try *something*. Too many people let their fear of risk push them to spend their lives investing in blue chip stocks or mutual funds, earning less than half the returns of even the simplest and safest of these secret strategies. It's a shame, because if they were willing to give some of these more unorthodox investments a try, they might be able to build their investments into lifetime wealth. Which makes sticking with these "safe" investments the biggest risk of all.

Are You Ready to Try Something New?

It's never easy to set aside one's preconceptions about the best and safest way to invest and try unusual strategies for making faster and bigger profits. It means abandoning conventional "wisdom" about how to invest. Even harder, it means leaving the herd behind, and going off in your own new and different direction. Herds exist for a reason, both in nature and among people: There appears to be safety in numbers, and if you're making the same investments as everyone else you know, then you probably won't get into too much trouble. It's this kind of thinking that's helped keep the large investments houses' profits high for many decades, and helped banks sell millions of CDs.

The problem, of course, is that if you invest like most other people, your investments' performance will be...the same as most other people's. That means great in good times, when the markets and the economy are on the rise, and not so great in hard times, when the economy and the markets are on the decline. Just like mine were, back when I was at *Money*.

If you're willing to leave the herd behind, you can beat the whole crowd of investors, and the market itself, with consistent returns of 8 to

10 percent or more, whether in good times or bad. Even if all you can invest is a few hundred dollars and you have almost no free time in which to learn new investment strategies.

The choice is yours. If you're ready to start earning higher rates of return than most investors you know, then read on. I did it myself, and I will show you step by step how you can too. And remember: The reason most investors aren't using these strategies is not that they're ineffective or hard to implement, it's just that the big investment houses and banks aren't selling them. Which means you're already a step ahead of most investors, who will never even get to know about them.

Pick Your Strategy!

Every investor is different, and so are investor goals and priorities. As you go through this book, you will learn about a wide range of strategies for achieving fast profits. Some will be a good fit for you, others less so. Each has its upsides and downsides, which I'll list for you along the way.

This chart is intended to give you a quick start, comparing some of the most important aspects of each strategy. It's designed to answer common questions, such as: How much do I have to invest? What returns can I expect? How much work is involved? Do I have to commit for the long term, or can I get out quickly? How risky is it?

In some cases, the answers are more complex than will fit in a sentence or two: Bond investing, to take just one example, can be very low-risk, or very high-risk, depending on how you do it. So think of this chart as a starting point to help you determine which strategies might work for your goals, and then read on to learn the details—and unique benefits—of each.

	Minimum Investment	Typical Return on Investment	Easy to Do?	Do It from Home?	Risk Profile	Easy to Cash Out?	Performance in Down Times
Tax Liens	$100	8–25% (or you could wind up with property)	No, research required	Yes, in most cases	Very low, if you select liens carefully	No: You have no control over when liens are paid.	Good
Tax Deeds	$1,000	20–100% or more	No	No, site visits required	Moderate to high	No	Excellent: More deals available
Below-Market-Value Real Estate	$10,000	20–100% or more	No	No, site visits required	Moderate	No	Good
Income Trusts	$500	10% or more	Yes	Yes	Moderate, legislative initiatives can affect price and performance	Yes	Fair: Many trusts depend on energy usage
Master Limited Partnerships	$500	5–8% or more	Yes	Yes	Low to moderate	Yes	Usually unaffected
High-Yield Stock	$200	5% dividends plus possible capital gains	Yes	Yes	Low to moderate (high-yield stocks can be volatile in price)	Yes, but plan for long term because of price volatility	Can be affected

	Minimum Investment	Typical Return on Investment	Easy to Do?	Do It from Home?	Risk Profile	Easy to Cash Out?	Performance in Down Times
DRIPs	$100 can get you started, add over time	5% or more	Fair, requires some research	Yes	Very low (plan for long term)	Yes (but makes most sense as long-term investment)	Usually unaffected (dollar cost averaging compensates for ups and downs)
Bonds	$200	3–10%	Yes	Yes	Low to moderate (depending on type of bond)	Yes, but price fluctuation can create loss	Good: Bond prices rise as interest rates fall
Options	$500	8% or more	Fair, must watch markets	Yes	Moderate to high	Yes	Unaffected: You can profit from rising or falling prices
Foreign Exchange	$1,000	10–25%	No, must study markets	Yes	High	Yes, but price fluctuation can create loss	Excellent, you can profit even if U.S. economy weakens

Cash Flow (Brokering)	$5,000 (for course materials and American Cash Flow Association membership)	Earn fees or commissions of 5–20% of loan for brokering deals, with only your time invested	No, takes months to learn	Very low	N/A	Excellent: Bad times mean more people need alternative funding
Cash Flow (Investing)	$5,000 (for course) plus $10,000 for investment	8–20%	No, takes months to learn	Low to high, depending on cash flow type	No	Excellent: Bad times mean more people need alternative funding
Vending Machines	$500	Machine may return $1–10/day	No, must fill and service machines	Low	No	Unaffected: People snack in good times and bad
ATM/Debit Swipe Machines	$10,000 if investing with company, less if placing own machines	20–30%	Yes, if investing; no, if placing own machines	Moderate	No	Not usually affected

	Minimum Investment	Typical Return on Investment	Easy to Do?	Do It from Home?	Risk Profile	Easy to Cash Out?	Performance in Down Times
Timeshares	$15,000	10% or more	Fair: Must plan rental of timeshare weeks in advance	Yes (unless used for vacation!)	Low to moderate	No	Can be affected
Payday Loans	$20,000	13%	Yes	Yes	High	No	Good: More people need loans in hard times
Internet Advertising	$3-15/month (for Web site hosting)	Earn from ads with only your time invested	No, must create and update compelling Web site	Yes	Very low, since there's little investment	N/A	May be affected

CHAPTER

1

Profit from Unpaid Taxes: Investing in Tax Liens and Deeds

Investing in tax liens and at tax deed auctions are both great ways to make fast profits, and few investors know about them. Since I first learned about these investment opportunities a few years ago, I've been studying the process and attending auctions to see what kinds of deals investors can get. But I'm not a lien and deed investing expert, so I've turned to some of the most experienced experts in the field to bring you the best information about these lucrative opportunities. In particular, Larry Loftis, author of *Profit by Investing in Real Estate Tax Liens: Earn Safe, Secured, and Fixed Returns Every Time* (Kaplan, 2007, 2nd ed.), has shared his invaluable expertise for this chapter as someone who's spent many years investing in both liens and deeds all across the United States.

This chapter will teach you how to take advantage of these great investing opportunities for making fast profits with little risk.

Before we get started, I want to make sure you understand the difference between investing in tax liens and tax deeds. Though part of the process is the same—you research properties and then bid at auctions—these are two completely different investment approaches, with completely different results.

With liens, you're buying a low-risk interest-bearing instrument that pays a much higher interest rate than bonds or CDs. Assuming you buy wisely (this chapter will teach you how), your investment will most likely pay off at the interest rate you purchased, but it is secured by real estate in case it doesn't.

What you're actually doing is paying off a property owner's delinquent tax debt and collecting the interest he or she owes to the municipality. If he or she doesn't pay, you have the right to foreclose and take the property—which may be worth hundreds of times what you've invested. Of course, that's the catch—few people will let good real estate go just for the cost of the taxes, so the overwhelming likelihood is it will pay off and you will simply collect the interest.

Investing in tax deeds is a completely different matter. In this case, the municipality has already foreclosed on the delinquent taxpayer, so you're buying the property outright. It's a riskier-than-usual way of buying real estate. Why? Because you won't be able to do the research careful purchasers usually do before they close on a property. However, it's one of the best ways there is to purchase real estate at significant discounts, sometimes half or less of its real market value.

Which is right for you? It really depends: Are you interested in placing your money in safe investments and watching it grow with little effort from you, or do you want to get out there and play the real estate market? While it's possible to invest in both deeds and liens, most investors choose one or the other and stick with that investing strategy.

Let's begin with a snapshot of each of these types of investments so you can compare them with each other, and with the other strategies throughout this book:

SNAPSHOT: Tax Lien Investing

How It Works:

When owners fail to pay property taxes, municipalities charge interest (and in some cases, a penalty). As an investor, you can pay those back taxes and then collect the interest when the property owners (or their foreclosing bank) eventually pay the municipality. If the owner fails to pay the taxes within their allotted time, you can foreclose yourself and wind up owning the property.

THE UPSIDE:

- High Interest: Interest rates vary but are substantially higher than CDs, bonds, or most other interest-bearing investments.

- You Can Hit the Jackpot: Though the vast majority of liens are paid off in time, there's always the chance that you could score big and wind up owning a property for a tiny fraction of its worth.
- It's Countercyclical: In hard times, more property owners cannot pay their taxes, and so there are more liens to invest in.

THE DOWNSIDE:

- Unpredictable Timing: Tax liens can be paid off anytime (within a statutory redemption period, which is typically one to two years, but could be as long as five years), and you will have no control over when this happens.
- Study Required: You will need to spend time contacting municipalities where you might invest, studying their procedures, researching properties, and bidding.
- Legal Procedures May Be Needed: If your tax lien remains unpaid after the redemption period, you will likely need to file for an administrative procedure with the municipality to foreclose on the lien. Once you own the property outright, you may need to have an attorney "quiet the title" so that you can sell it for full fair market value.

Who Should Invest:

Tax liens are a great choice for investors who want to get started with small sums, can devote some time to research, and are willing to trade liquidity for a safe investment with a high interest rate. "It's a fixed rate of return, and with penalties, a 10 percent rate on paper can give you a much higher yield," says Larry Loftis, attorney, tax lien and deed investor, and author of *Profit by Investing in Real Estate Tax Liens: Earn Safe, Secured, and Fixed Returns Every Time.* On the other hand, he says, "It's important to do your research. The only way to lose is if you don't know what you're doing."

SNAPSHOT: Tax Deed Investing

How It Works:

Rather than buy a lien, you buy the property itself, usually at auction after the municipality has foreclosed for delinquent taxes.

THE UPSIDE:

- Huge Profits: Buying a property through tax deed sales can mean getting it far below its market value.
- Quick Turnaround: Many buyers at auctions turn around and immediately resell the property on the regular real estate market at a substantially higher price.
- It's Countercyclical: In hard times, more people fail to pay their taxes, so there are more foreclosures and more properties to buy.

THE DOWNSIDE:

- Moderate Risk: Chances are, you won't be able to inspect a property thoroughly before bidding.
- Cash Needed: Most municipalities demand full payment at or near time of purchase.
- Study Required: You will need to spend time carefully researching and inspecting properties before you bid.

Who Should Invest:

You can make huge profits in tax deed investing, but it's not for everyone. You will need access to ready cash—either your own or borrowed—before you can buy. You will need to spend several hours per auction researching the properties for sale, and most of this research must be during business hours, as you will need to contact county tax assessor offices, visit properties in daylight, and bid at the auction itself. These are not the easiest investments in this book, but if you can meet these criteria, returns can be spectacular. "I've doubled, tripled, and quadrupled my money by buying at tax deed auctions, and I've had students who have done even better," Loftis says, "but it is very time-consuming and travel costs may eat into your return."

Lien States vs. Deed States

Twenty-one of the fifty states and the District of Columbia are *lien states*, meaning they sell liens on properties when taxes are delinquent. The remaining twenty-nine are *deed states* which sell properties after foreclosure. But wait! Like everything else involving state law, the picture is more complicated than it at first appears.

Some states have aspects of lien sales and also aspects of deed sales. Loftis calls these "hybrid" states. For example, Texas and Georgia are deed states *with redemption*. That is, the municipality forecloses and sells the property to the highest bidder, yet still allows the former owner who defaulted to buy the property back within a certain period of time (the redemption period), repaying the investor all costs plus a penalty. Redemption periods vary from state to state, but usually fall between six months and four years.

Some investors find deed states like Texas and Georgia particularly attractive because, after your purchase at the auction, you already own the property without the bother of foreclosing. Texas—where everything is said to be larger—has the biggest of these penalties: to redeem a property, the former owner must reimburse the price plus all fees and costs paid at auction, along with a whopping 25 percent penalty! This makes the state highly attractive to tax deed investors, but of course also means you will have more bidding competition there.

Finally, Loftis points out that several states don't fit neatly into their categories. New York, for instance, is a deed state, but the law allows counties in New York City to sell liens, though these aren't usually available to individual investors. The same goes for populous counties in Ohio. And Pennsylvania is a deed state that sells some properties on the redemption system. For a detailed list of lien states, deed states, redemption deed states, and the various exceptions see, pages 39–41.

Investing in Tax Liens

Understanding Interest and Penalties

Let's start with a closer look at tax lien investing. Interest on delinquent tax payments is set by law in each state (for a state-by-state list of interest rates, see pages 39–41). For example, the maximum interest rate in Florida is 18 percent per year. A property owner who doesn't pay his or her taxes could have to pay 18 percent interest on those taxes to avoid losing the property in foreclosure. If you hold the lien, that means you automatically collect that 18 percent return, right?

Wrong! Or at least, it's highly unlikely. Remember that most liens are bought at auctions, which means investors are bidding against one another. Loftis explains that there are five types of bidding methods used by lien states, some of them designed to select bidders at random and then offer them first refusal on a lien. Two of the most common bidding methods dramatically affect interest rates: bid-down-the-rate and premium bidding.

Bid-Down-the-Rate Method: In bid-down-the-rate bidding, which Florida uses, 18 percent is the statutory maximum interest for a lien. Bidders at auction then bid down the rate by offering to accept 17¾ percent interest, 17½ percent, and so on.

However, attractive properties in Florida are routinely bid down to ¼ percent. Why? As Loftis (who lives in Florida and has extensive experience buying there) explains, the state has a statutory minimum 5 percent penalty that an investor must get.

Please note: There is a big difference between interest and a penalty! Interest is calculated over time, and a 5 percent annual interest rate would mean that it would take an entire year to earn that 5 percent. An investment paying a 5 percent annual rate would thus yield 2½ percent if you held it for only six months.

Penalties, unlike interest, are a flat fee, not a pro-rated annual percentage. In the above example, instead of getting only 2½ percent if you hold a lien with a 5 percent penalty for six months, you will still get 5 percent—which amounts to a 10 percent annual yield. If you held the lien for one month, you'd still get 5 percent—which amounts to a 60 percent annual yield! Of course, if the taxpayer doesn't pay off the lien for the whole year, then that 5 percent becomes a 5 percent annual yield, which may not have you jumping for joy, but it's still respectable compared to CDs and bonds. Now, since Florida has a two-year redemption, your risk (if you bid only ¼ of one percent) is that the lien pays off in the 24th month, and your penalty has yielded you only 2.5 percent. But the law of averages will kick in. Some liens will pay off after one month (60 percent yield), some after two months (30 percent yield), some after six months (10 percent yield), some after one year (5 percent yield), and a few after two years (2.5 percent yield). Loftis has even had liens pay off before he actually paid the county's invoice (an infinite return). So your overall return will average out over time.

Premium Bidding Method: In states that use this method, bidding typically proceeds as at a traditional auction, with the face value of the lien being the starting bid, and bids going up from there. The amount over the face value is called a *premium*. In one state, the county does not return the premium, so you have to factor that into your calculations. If you buy a $100 lien at face value in a state with 20 percent interest, and bid up to a price of $105, you'll still receive $120 if the lien is redeemed at the end of a year. But now, instead of 20 percent interest, you've earned about 14¼ percent interest, because $120 is an increase of about 14¼ percent over $105.

Some states, such as Texas, collect a statutory penalty on the full amount of your investment, while others either pay interest on the premium at a different rate, or return the premium (with no interest) when the lien is redeemed. *It is very important to know what will happen to your premium before bidding at a premium auction!*

Note also that auctions are not the only way to buy tax liens. Counties in lien states occasionally have more liens to sell than they can at one auction. And sometimes a successful bidder can't pay for the lien after all. These all go back into the county inventory and are available for sale "over the counter" to investors who buy them directly. In this case, since there is no bidding, you will pay face value for the lien and get whatever interest rate the state is collecting. States with attractive interest rates rarely have liens left over (absent a few bidders who couldn't pay for their liens), but it does occur, especially with states with average interest rates. Buying liens over the counter is a hit-or-miss affair—you don't know what, if anything, a county might have for sale between auctions. But if you do find attractive liens for sale, you can get them at better interest rates compared to bidding at auction. The downside is that these liens are typically the "leftovers" (i.e., vacant lots and undesirable properties).

Will You Wind Up Owning It?

The reality is, probably not. The overwhelming majority of liens are redeemed before the lien investor forecloses on the property. Why? Because of one of the best aspects about tax lien investing: In almost all states, a tax lien is a first-position lien, taking precedence over all others. That includes mortgages. If the property has a mortgage on it, the bank holding the mortgage is virtually certain to pay off the lien—otherwise you could foreclose, leaving the bank with nothing.

Every once in a while, for whatever reason, a taxpayer—or the bank that holds the mortgage—fails to pay off the lien on a valuable house or commercial property before the deadline, and in that case, the lien investor hits the jackpot. The small possibility of making a big killing like this lends excitement to tax lien investing, and keeps some investors coming back for more. This occurrence is extremely rare, but it does happen every so often. (I'll tell you more about what to do if the property owner doesn't pay during the redemption period under the heading "If They Don't Pay Up..." just a little farther in this chapter.)

However, the reality is that most unredeemed tax liens are on properties no one would want: vacant lots that are partly or mostly underwater, empty parking lots in decrepit neighborhoods...you get the idea. This is why it's vital to do your research before you bid.

In an ideal world, you would be familiar with the neighborhood where your tax lien property is located, and actually visit the property before buying a lien. If you live in or can visit a state where you'd like to invest in liens, I absolutely encourage you to do this kind of on-the-ground research, the safest way to invest. But, in the real world, you may be investing in counties that are far away, and spending the time and money to travel cross-country to examine a property could cut into your earnings fast.

So, if you can't physically inspect a lien property before you buy the lien, what can you do to make sure your investment doesn't turn into a big disappointment? Loftis suggests a number of precautions to help protect you:

1. Stay away from industrial property, gas stations, former gas stations, and properties adjacent to gas stations. This is a good rule for all real estate investment. These properties could turn up with environmental problems, and your $2,000 tax lien could wind up costing you hundreds of thousands in cleanup costs.

2. Buy liens on homes. These are obviously the safest investments, as the incentive for a property owner (or bank) to pay off the lien is higher than on vacant land or commercial property. Even better, buy liens on homes with a *homestead exemption,* which means that the owner lives in the property as his personal investment. This designation is typically listed with the county's lien information.

3. Buy fewer larger liens rather than many small ones. Buying many small liens might seem like a smart way to reduce your risk by spreading it over several properties, and several property owners. But those "junk" liens you don't want, on vacant lots or underwater parcels, are likelier to be inexpensive. Since tax liens are based on taxes, and taxes are based on a property's assessed value, it seems clear that, say, a $2,000 lien is probably on a pretty valuable property, whereas four $500 liens probably are backed by four much less desirable properties.

Of course, there are disadvantages to this strategy: For one thing, instead of staggered redemptions, all your money will come in at once. Most lien investors prefer staggered redemptions: If a lien pays off too quickly, you may earn little money on it (especially if it's interest-only) and are faced with the need to buy another lien or otherwise reinvest those funds. Also, if something does go wrong, a bigger piece of your investment is compromised. Still, you're probably safest going with larger liens.

How to Research a Property

As you can see, most of the above strategies underscore the importance of researching a property before you bid on the lien. Realistically, you probably won't do as thorough a research job as if you were buying the property itself, at a deed auction, for instance. But do enough research to have a fair idea what you'll be getting if by any chance the lien isn't paid off.

How do you do this research, especially if you're bidding in places far away from you? Here are some ideas:

1. Start with the county offices. Chances are, you'll need to get in touch with them anyway for information about the auction, or after-auction lien sales (see "Tax Liens and Deeds Action Plan," on pages 36–38). You may need to talk to two or more departments to find all the information you need, such as any other liens on the property, its assessed value, and so forth. So the simplest approach may be to call a central information number, or county clerk's office, explain what you're looking for, and ask them to direct you to the correct departments. Your purchase of tax liens benefits the county, so they may be quite willing to help you. Some counties also list their departments and phone numbers on the Internet, so this may save you a step—but you'll likely have to get on the phone at some point.

2. Look for tax assessor's reports online. Many counties put property assessments online and you can search them to find detailed information about your property. This is where you can find out the property owner's name, which you may need for further research.

If They Don't Pay Up...

If the property owner (or a bank holding the mortgage) doesn't pay off the lien during the redemption period, then you will have the right to foreclose. If the state has a two-year redemption period and sold a second lien on the same property, you will first need to pay off any subsequent lien holders (just as a bank would have had to pay you off before it could foreclose). But even adding a second year's taxes and interest, you're still about to get a great deal on a piece of real estate that is likely worth many times more. Loftis points out that you may also have to pay off other county liens, such as "weed" liens, in case the property has been mowed by the county, and possibly water or sewer liens.

Depending on the state, there are two basic types of tax lien foreclosure: You will either simply foreclose on the property, and then take title to it yourself, or, in the case of Florida, you will file for the tax deed, triggering the county to sell it at a tax deed sale. In the case of Florida, your lien may be paid off, including interest, and whatever other charges you've paid to the county, plus reimbursement for any other tax liens you've paid off, before the tax deed sale. If it isn't, you can take the property as your collateral, just as a bank would in a mortgage foreclosure.

What if the property is occupied? This may seem like a logical question, but getting a house at a tax deed sale is unusual, and getting one that has people living in it is extremely rare. You could easily buy 10,000 tax deed properties and never see this situation. If you did come across it, the people living in it are most likely not the owners (would you lose *your* house over back taxes?), but renters or vagrants. Consult a local attorney for the eviction process for that jurisdiction.

Buying Tax Deeds

In deed states, rather than selling a lien on a property, the county forecloses and then sells the property itself at auction. The advantage is that the foreclosure is already done for you. Instead of buying an interest-bearing instrument, you are actually buying the property itself. Some counties require a minimum bid based on taxes owed (after all, collecting the taxes owed is the county's primary goal) and some require a percentage of tax-assessed value. But don't get too excited—remember you'll be bidding against other investors, who may be as able to recognize a property's real worth as you are. As one auctioneer puts it, "If your house was for sale for only two years' worth of property taxes, wouldn't there be a line of people waiting to buy it?" Chances are the price will be bid up well above the taxes owed—but still well below true market value.

Before you bid on a property, you should have a clear plan for what you will do with it: fix it up and either rent it out or resell it at or near market value, "flip" it by reselling it immediately well below market value, while still taking a profit, or live in it yourself. I'll tell you much more about how to profit from below-market-value real estate in the next chapter.

Since you're buying the property itself, it's even more important for you to research carefully before bidding than if you were buying tax liens. Remember that county tax authorities, unlike real estate agents, don't have to worry about keeping a good reputation or maintaining a relationship with their customers, so it may not matter to them how badly the property fails to live up to your expectations. In his book, Loftis gives numerous examples of properties for sale that were basically drainage ditches, off the edge of a mountain, or under a large utility tower. He describes how he bought a vacant lot fifty feet wide in a county in Kansas, only to find out later that the minimum legal requirement to build on the property was sixty feet. He's even seen counties offer "landlocked" plots, completely surrounded by other people's land, with no legal means of access except by helicopter!

Because such things are possible, wise tax deed investors have an absolute rule: Loftis advises strongly not to bid on a tax deed property until you've "put your feet on it." He once came very close to breaking his own rule. He was planning to bid on a Pennsylvania condominium unit for sale at a tax deed auction. Knowing how important it is to see the property, he drove to the address to check it out. It was a very nice looking building—with good security. There was no way to get inside and actually see the unit, since he did not have the code to get in the main entrance to the building.

It was obvious that this was an upscale building, and any unit in it would be well worth bidding on. He had probably learned all he was going to already, so the most logical thing to do would be to turn around and go home.

Being a lawyer, however, Larry is a stickler for rules, even self-imposed ones, so he stubbornly waited around until one of the building's residents left and he could sneak in before the door closed. Once inside he began looking for the unit, which was number 10. He found 1...2...3...4...must be the other direction. Okay, here were 5...6...7...8...9...and that was it. He walked up and down the hallway twice. Nope, there was definitely no number 10. The county was about to sell a condominium that didn't exist!

"That unit was probably in the original architectural plans that were filed with the county," he explains. "And then the builder changed the design for some reason." Meanwhile the county kept the fictitious unit on its tax rolls, and foreclosed when the taxes weren't paid.

It's important to remember that—even once you know for sure it exists—buying a property through a tax deed sale still carries many more risks than buying it from an owner or through a broker. The reason is you'll be dealing with incomplete information. Chances are you won't be able to get inside for a look around—unless the doors or windows are broken, and even then you would be trespassing. You certainly won't be able to conduct a structural inspection, as most home buyers do before closing. You won't be able to ask the current owners anything about the property, so your only sources of information will be county records, neighbors who may be willing to chat with you, and local real estate agents.

"The good thing is that all bidders are dealing with the same incomplete information," one auctioneer told me recently, and that's very true. Everyone bids accordingly, which is why properties at tax deed auctions often go for half or less of their market value.

If the property is improved (i.e., has a house or building on it), it's likely that an owner who couldn't afford, or didn't bother, to pay property taxes probably didn't keep the property in good repair either. So you should assume any property you buy at a tax deed auction will need a lot of work to restore it to good condition, and possibly to be habitable—even if it looks okay from the outside. Keep this in mind while calculating your bids, and also while planning what to do with the property once you've acquired it.

Buying Land at Deed Auction

As you might expect, the bulk of the properties sold at tax deed auctions are tracts of land. That makes sense, if you think about it. Imagine you were having trouble paying your property taxes on several pieces of real estate you owned. Which property would you choose to neglect? Probably not your house. And you might also try to hang on to any rental property that was earning you income and might have resale value. But an empty tract of land, for which you might have only paid a few thousand dollars, would be another story. If you had to, you might let that go.

Most improved properties (houses, condos, or commercial buildings) listed for sale at tax deed auctions will disappear (have their taxes paid) a day or two before the auction. That's why Loftis suggests doing your research on them the last business day before the sale. The reason is that if you search earlier, you will be spending valuable time driving around, looking at a lot of properties, only to see them withdrawn, one by one, as auction day approaches. By the time of the auction itself, about nineteen out of twenty remaining properties to be sold are vacant lots, many of which are unbuildable. What keeps people coming to these sales, of course, is the one improved property, and the several decent lots.

While this type of investing requires considerable work, there are some real advantages to buying land at a tax deed auction:

1. It's likely to be far less expensive. You may be able to buy yourself an attractive property without taking out a loan or tying up enormous amounts of cash.

2. Buying vacant land reduces the time pressure. When you buy an improved property, from the moment you close, the clock is ticking for you to make use of it. You must start renovations, rent it out, or put it on the market as quickly as you can. Leave a building sitting empty and it's prey to rodents, insects (including termites and carpenter ants), mold, burst pipes, vandalism, and squatters, to name just some of the dangers. Most unoccupied buildings lose value over time, and all will cost you money for maintenance.

Land is different. You can leave land unoccupied for a very long time, and the only cost you'll incur is property taxes and perhaps a monthly mowing. Indeed, many people buy land with the intent of hanging on to it for a few years and watching its value grow.

3. You can see what you're getting. Inspecting a house or even a commercial building offered at auction can be tricky. If the house is occupied, the current residents will likely be displeased if you start snooping around. If it's empty, it's sure to be locked. Either way, you can't go in to check for water stains, musty smells, termite trails, rickety heaters, or other signs of trouble. With land, there are few hidden surprises, especially if you stick with residential neighborhoods. Just be sure to check with the county to verify the lot is buildable.

Making Sure You Really Own It

Whether you wind up buying land, a house, or commercial property, you should be aware of one big difference between buying real estate at a tax deed auction and buying it through traditional means: You won't get the same kind of deed. The same will be true if you wind up foreclosing on a property where you held a tax lien.

In a traditional property sale, the seller guarantees you a clear and insurable title. Not so with a tax deed transfer. Attorney Loftis instructs us that, in a tax sale, you will get either a *tax deed, a sheriff's deed, constable's deed,* or similar deed of conveyance (see *Profit by Investing in Real Estate Tax Liens* for an example of a sheriff's deed). The bottom line is that the municipality is conveying its rights to the property to you. That's a far cry from the guaranteed title a purchaser or title insurance company will require from you. Loftis notes, however, that you could sell the property as is, without the typical title guarantees, by selling it at a slight discount with a *quit claim deed* (a deed of conveyance often used with related party transfers).

If you want to sell the property for full fair market value, however, you will probably need an attorney to "quiet" the title for you so that you can buy title insurance. This is another expense you should factor into your bidding. You may also need to pay off any prior tax lien (and possible "weed" or similar county lien) against the property before you can take clear title. But, because you'll have done your research with the municipality before you bid, you'll already know what liens these are, if any, and how much they will cost to satisfy.

Another issue is bankruptcy. In a tax deed sale, the county that foreclosed on the property has notified all lien holders, and should know about any bankruptcy proceeding involving the property. Having done your research, you will know too, and avoid bidding on any properties that are subject to bankruptcy proceedings.

Bankruptcy can also be a concern for tax lien holders, if the property owner declares bankruptcy during the redemption period of the lien. This is rare, but it does happen. Since you're a first-position lien holder, the court may well uphold your claim, but you may have to wait several months for a ruling, and you could wind up receiving only part of what's owed. This is one of the unavoidable risks of buying tax liens—since the bankruptcy won't have happened yet at the time you purchase the lien, research can't help you here. Some experts believe sticking with larger, more expensive liens reduces this risk, since the wealthier owners of valuable homes may be less bankruptcy-prone than the owners of more modest homes.

Bidding at Auction

You've done your research, picked out the liens or properties you want to buy, and now you're headed out to a local auction. Here are Larry Loftis's top tips for successful bidding:

1. Auctions can be fast-moving and confusing. If you've never bought this way, and you have the opportunity, it's a great idea to attend an auction or two as an observer, to get a feel for how things work.

2. Before the auction, decide what your maximum bid will be for each property or lien you want to bid on, and then stick to that price. It's much too easy to get swept up in the competitive action at an auction. (One auctioneer told me he'd seen a nice house sold at a tax deed sale that went for much *more* than its fair market value! Just because someone else is willing to pay a higher price for something doesn't mean it's really worth that price.)

3. Be assertive. Bidding at tax deed auctions is not for the timid. Sit close to the front. When placing a bid, yell loud and clear, and without hesitation.

4. Beware of late bidders. Loftis warns of auction experts who stay silent during the early rounds of bidding and suddenly, just before the auctioneer says "SOLD!," jump in with a big increase over the previous highest bid. This sometimes shocks the rest of the audience enough so that they stop bidding, and the new bidder wins the auction. This won't happen to you, though, because you'll be firmly prepared with your maximum number. If the late bid is still less than your ceiling, then you'll know to continue bidding.

One other note: Some auctions have a "buyer's premium"—which means your bid of, say, $1,000 is really a bid of $1,100. Make sure you know about any buyer's premium and don't be caught unawares.

Then again, you might not even have to go to the auction. More and more counties are accepting bids over the Internet for both tax liens and deeds. Bidding methods vary. In some cases, you'll be actually bidding from your computer during the auction itself. In others, you put in your maximum bid ahead of time, and the software bids for you until it reaches that amount. In other words, if the next highest bid is only half your maximum bid, your winning price will be only enough to beat out that bid. (Users of eBay should be familiar with this auction method.)

Whatever the case, make sure you know the details, and make sure you register well in advance and provide all the information and supporting materials the county requires. An auctioneer at a recent tax deed auction told me sixty-eight people had tried to register as online bidders, but only three could actually bid. The other sixty-five had failed to provide the required information in time. Contact the county where you'd like to buy property or liens to find out whether Internet bidding is available. (See "Tax Liens and Deeds Action Plan" on pages 36–38.)

Start Small

As with any new-to-you investment strategy, keep your first investments small and manageable. That means going to just one lien auction to start, perhaps buying two or three liens (remember, the bigger they are, the more solid they probably are). Then wait for those liens to play themselves out before diving in again.

Tax deeds, on the other hand, are much more complicated and labor-intensive. That's because you actually will be buying a property, and you should know what you are going to do with it. Even if you just plan to turn around and sell it through a real estate broker, getting the title ready for sale will demand some of your time and attention, and will tie up your cash until the deal goes through. If you're planning to rehab the property, sell it yourself, or rent it out, it will take even more of your time and cash before you begin seeing returns.

So, when it comes to tax deed buying, I recommend you start with just a single property, and follow the process to completion before investing in another. And if you're not sure what to do with a piece of property once you buy it, read on! I'll give you lots of suggestions and helpful information in Chapter 3.

Don't Forget to Have Fun!

Compared to most other forms of investment, investing in tax liens and deeds is a blast! Bidding at auction, whether live or on the Internet, is exciting and competitive, and it can give you a real rush to find you've beaten out everyone else to win a lien or piece of property.

Buying tax liens is one of the safest ways there is to earn better-than-market returns, especially in a down economy. Buying tax deeds carries more risk and requires more work, both researching the property and dealing with it after you've bought it. But there's the potential to double your money, or better.

So head to the nearest lien or deed auction that appeals to you, or to the Internet. You'll be glad you did.

Lower Your Risk—Tax Liens

1. Buy liens on homes designated as homestead.
2. Buy few, more expensive liens, rather than many less expensive liens (liens on more valuable property are less likely to default).
3. Buy liens in areas you know well, where you can judge by the address whether a property is in a nice residential neighborhood or a neighborhood you'd rather avoid.
4. Avoid buying liens on industrial property, gas stations, or property near gas stations.
5. Avoid buying liens on vacant land unless you know the lot is in a good location and is buildable.

Lower Your Risk—Tax Deeds

1. Do NOT bid on any property you have not visited.
2. Research the property with the county. Find out about any other outstanding liens and whether the property is part of any bankruptcy proceeding. If the property is vacant land, you may need tax or plat map numbers and/or the former property owner's name to find these records. In some cases, counties will provide this information by phone or Internet.
3. Buy property in areas you know well, where you will be able to assess how difficult selling (or renting) the property will be.
4. Use information about neighboring sales, tax assessments, and advice from a local real estate agent to try to determine a property's

true market value before you bid. Assume any building on the property will need work, and that you will also need legal help to quiet the title if you desire to sell it for full value. Make sure to factor in these extra expenses when calculating your maximum bid. Loftis suggests that a quiet title action may cost you around $1,500–$2,000, depending on your area.

5. Avoid buying industrial property, gas stations, or property next to gas stations.

6. When buying vacant land, make sure it is legal to build on (with regard to lot size and configuration, septic or sewer access, and so on). Make sure it has access to a road or street, either directly or by right-of-way over another property.

Tax Liens and Deeds Action Plan

Here's what Larry Loftis suggests to get you started:

1. Pick the right investment type for you. Do you prefer the security and high interest rates of lien investing? Or the higher risks but potentially huge payoffs of buying property directly through tax deed sales? Or maybe you'd like to invest some of your money in each. Decide which strategy best suits your investment objectives.

2. Pick a state or states where you'd like to invest. If you're buying liens, select a state where interest rates and terms are favorable (see list on pages 39–41). If you're buying deeds, pick a state where you can easily visit properties, either because you live nearby or travel there on a regular basis.

3. Once you've picked a state, select several municipalities that might fit your needs. If you're buying deeds, your *number one* consideration is whether you'll be able to visit properties for sale. Remember, you must never bid on property you have not actually visited. If buying liens, site visits are less crucial, but it's still a good idea to pick counties you are familiar with, so you can guess from the address what type of neighborhood a property is in and what it might be worth.

4. Contact the counties you've selected. Most counties have Web sites where you can register for a tax lien or deed sale and research properties. The National Association of Counties (www.naco.org) offers general contact information for most U.S. counties. Some counties provide much information, sometimes even their catalogue of liens or deeds for sale, on the Internet, but most don't yet. So you will likely wind up having to make some phone calls. When you call, you'll probably want the Delinquent Tax Department (for tax deed sales) or County Tax Assessor's or Treasurer's Office (for tax lien sales), but some states have different departments dealing with tax sales, so if in doubt, explain what you're looking for and let the operator direct you to the right department.

5. Ask questions and register for the auction. How long until the next auction? Does the county sell liens (or properties) between auctions? Will you be able to bid by Internet (or phone) or must you attend in person? What are payment terms at auction? What bidding method is used (if you're buying liens)?

Also, how many liens or deeds are typically for sale at an auction, and how many bidders usually show up? You may not get answers to these last two questions, but it's worth a try. In an auction situation, you're better off with more items for sale and fewer bidders.

Based on the answers to these questions, select one or two counties where you will attend the auction and bid. Remember to get, fill out, and return all registration forms the county requires. Some counties may require you to register days before the auction.

6. Review the list of liens or deeds. Once you've picked one or two counties, get a list of the liens or deeds for the next auction from the county (you may be able to see it online). Select liens or properties to bid on. If buying liens, look for larger, rather than smaller amounts and residential properties, ideally with homestead homes. If buying deeds, *make sure to visit the properties.* Remember what Larry said about deed properties set for auction—most decent properties will disappear from the tax deed list as owners pay their taxes at the last minute to avoid foreclosure. To avoid a wasted trip, remember to wait till a few days before the auction before making your site visits. Remember also that, before you bid on a property, you should have a plan for what to do with it—flip it, rehab it for sale or rent, or (in the case of land) hold it for future sale. In all cases make sure to *avoid* gas stations, former gas stations, properties adjacent to gas stations, industrial areas, and unbuildable or "landlocked" land.

7. Research the properties. Find out the property's assessed value from the county assessor's office. If buying a lien, look to see if it is a lot, a residential home, or a commercial property. If residential, look to see if it has a homestead exemption (identifying that it is the personal residence of the owner). If buying a deed, walk the property, look at the county's file on it (to check for a bankruptcy filing or any other tax or other county liens), and try to speak to a local real estate agent about a resale value.

8. Plan your bidding strategy. If buying deeds, decide on the maximum price you will bid on the properties you want to buy. If buying liens, make sure you understand the bidding method, and decide ahead of time how far down you're willing to bid the interest rate, or how much premium you're willing to pay.

9. Attend the auction in person or by Internet. Remember, many counties demand payment in full at auction or even a deposit before you can bid. They often accept only certified checks or cash, so come prepared to pay. How can you be prepared when you don't know what the final price will be? Loftis suggests bringing certified checks of various denominations, say $5,000, $10,000, and a few $1,000. Make sure the checks are filled out correctly per the county's instructions. Before bidding, review the bidding strategies on pages 33–34. After the auction, don't forget to return any unused certified checks to your bank so the money can be returned to your account.

10. Follow up. If you've bought tax liens, you should mark your calendar to make note of the end of their redemption periods, so you'll know if and when it's time to foreclose. You may also want to make note of any upcoming tax lien auctions. Why? Because if the lien is redeemed early, you will need to reinvest that money.

If you've bought property you may want to have an attorney quiet the title for you and buy title insurance so you know you can sell it for full market value. You've already planned what to do with the property if you got it, so now is the time to put that plan into action, and either start work rehabbing, prepare the property for rental, or put it on the market.

DOES YOUR STATE SELL LIENS OR DEEDS?
CHECK THESE LISTS TO FIND OUT

First, here is a list of the twenty-one states (plus the District of Columbia) that sell tax liens, along with the statutory interest on these liens. I have noted which states use penalties—flat fees that, unlike interest, are not calculated over time. See page 23 for details on the difference between interest and penalties. Also, please note these interest rates DO NOT take into account the possible impact of bid-down-the-rate or premium bidding, both of which can reduce the actual interest you earn. For more on how bidding methods can affect interest, see pages 24–25.

Lien States	Statutory Interest Rate
Alabama	12%
Arizona	16%
Colorado	9% plus Federal Discount Rate, rounded to nearest full percent
Florida	18%
Illinois	18% penalty every six months
Indiana	10–25% (depending on length of default)
Iowa	24%
Kentucky	12%
Maryland	6–24%
Mississippi	18%
Missouri	10%
Montana	10% plus 2% penalty
Nebraska	14%
New Hampshire	18%
New Jersey	18%
North Dakota	9–12%
Oklahoma	8%
South Carolina	9–12%
Vermont	6–12%
West Virginia	12%
Wyoming	18% plus 3% penalty
District of Columbia	12%

continued

Deed States:

These states are deed states. Go to a tax foreclosure sale in these states and you will be bidding on the deed to the property itself.

Alaska
Arkansas
California
Idaho
Kansas
Maine
Michigan
Minnesota
Nevada
New Mexico
New York
(New York City sells tax liens, but not to the general public)
North Carolina
Ohio
Oregon
Utah
Virginia
Washington
Wisconsin

Deed States with Redemption Periods

The following states fall somewhere between lien and deed states. You are purchasing the deed to the property itself, as in a deed state, but the former homeowner still has a redemption period within which to buy it back. If this occurs, the redeeming property owner must pay interest to the deed holder. Here is a list of deed states with redemption periods, along with their interest rates for repayment.

Connecticut	18%
Delaware	15% penalty
Georgia	10–20% penalty (20% after the deed holder has served notice of intent to foreclose on the redemption period)

continued

Hawaii	12%
Louisiana	12% plus 5% penalty
Massachusetts	16%
Pennsylvania	10%
Tennessee	10%
Texas	25% penalty every six months

RHODE ISLAND AND SOUTH DAKOTA OPT OUT OF THE TAX LIEN GAME

If you carefully read over the lists of states above, you may have noticed two were missing: Rhode Island and South Dakota. It's not that I forgot about them. While I was writing this book, both these states chose to take themselves out of the tax lien marketplace.

In February 2006, South Dakota passed HB 1069, prohibiting the state's counties from selling tax lien certificates. Then, in July 2006, Rhode Island passed what it nicknamed the Madeline Walker Law, after Walker, an eighty-one-year-old, was evicted from her home due to an unpaid sewer tax bill of about $500. Unlike the South Dakota law, the Rhode Island law doesn't outlaw the sales of tax liens outright, but when it comes to residential one- or two-family homes, it gives the Rhode Island Housing Authority first refusal. The idea is that the Housing Authority will buy the liens and work to help homeowners stay in their homes. Since residential homes are the most dependable properties for tax lien investing, the Madeline Walker Law makes Rhode Island a much less attractive place to buy liens.

Do these two new laws signal a national trend? Since I can't see into the future, I can only guess, but my guess is no. After all, counties and municipalities don't hold tax lien and deed sales for their entertainment. They do it because when property taxes go unpaid, they need to raise funds some other way. It seems doubtful that too many of them will be able to do without the influx of money that tax lien and deed sales provide.

Case Studies

To help show you how these strategies actually work, I've provided three case studies. The names and locations have all been changed.

Investor: Jared Brown
Investment: Tax liens
Investment Goal: Dependable interest
Investment Amount: About $8,000
Return: Over $287,000

Jared, an accountant who works in Pennsylvania, has been crossing the border into New Jersey and bidding on tax liens for about six years. "I love going to the auctions, and trying out different bidding strategies," he says. "Of course, this is mostly a way to earn high interest on my investments—but knowing there's always that chance, however small, that I could do a major deal keeps me coming back for more."

Jared knows firsthand the potential for huge payoffs in tax lien investing is real—because it's already happened to him. "My first year of buying tax liens, I happened on a $3,500 tax lien for a really nice-looking house. The assessed value was over $250,000." He knew this would be a very safe investment, so Jared bought the lien at a county auction.

Then he waited. With such a valuable property, the owners would make sure not to lose their house for unpaid taxes, even if they had to borrow to pay the lien off. Besides, a property that valuable is likely to carry a mortgage or a home equity loan (or both!) and the bank in question would never forfeit its right to foreclose on such a house for a measly $3,500.

But the redemption deadline arrived and the lien remained unpaid. Needless to say, Jared was on the phone with his lawyer bright and early the next morning, getting the foreclosure process under way. It cost about another $4,000 beyond his initial investment to get all the paperwork in order, but soon the house was his, free and clear. It was in very good shape, especially for a house with a tax lien against it, so Jared invested just a few hundred more in some minor cosmetic touch-ups, got himself a real estate agent, and immediately put the house on the market. It sold, within a month, for $314,000.

"I possibly could have made more by doing a major rehab, or by putting it on the market at a higher price and holding out," he says now. "But then I would have had to pour a lot of money into it. It was such an amazing windfall, I just wanted to take my profit and get out quick." Even so, after the real estate agent's commission, Jared got over $295,000 for the house. With an initial investment of around $8,000, that represents more than a 36 times return on his investment.

Jared remained curious as to why no one ever paid off the tax lien, so after the deal was done he began making inquiries, and eventually learned what happened. There had indeed been a mortgage on the property, and the bank holding the mortgage had begun the process of foreclosing against the previous owners, who had already moved out by the time Jared bought his lien. But the bank was in a merger with another bank.

"Have you ever tried to conduct a complex transaction with a bank that's in the process of a merger?" Jared says. "If you have, you know that nothing ever gets done. Apparently, there was a lot of confusion over exactly who was responsible for clearing liens on foreclosed properties. By the time they got it straight, they had missed the deadline."

"I know it's a fluke that it happened," he says now. "I'm not expecting anything like this will ever happen again. But meantime I'm getting great interest rates on my investments. And, there's always the chance…"

Investor: Sarah Cooke
Investment: Tax deed
Investment Goal: Quick profit on rural land
Investment Amount: $235
Return: $1,765

Sarah Cooke is an MBA student at the University of Minnesota. She learned about tax foreclosure sales as part of her coursework, and now often attends tax deed auctions in her spare time, especially in rural farming communities. "I'm an amateur photographer," she says. "So I love driving out into the countryside, finding these out-of-the-way properties, and also taking pictures of the farms. It's beautiful, in a stark, Midwestern way."

Also, she notes, "Rural communities are often the best for getting real bargains." Recently, Sarah attended a tax deed auction and found she was one of only two bidders on a one-acre parcel in a small farming village. After a few rounds of low bids, the other party dropped out of the auction, and she found, to her surprise, that she'd purchased the parcel for $235.

After the auction, she found out why. "It turns out the land had a drainage problem that would make it very difficult and expensive to put in any kind of septic system," she says. "It was the kind of thing you couldn't possibly know about in advance."

Sarah figured she'd be hanging on to the property for a while—fortunately she hadn't spent too much on it. But she decided to try for a quick sale by knocking on the neighbors' doors on either side to ask if either of them would be interested in buying the property. "One of them was," she said. "He hadn't heard about the auction till after it happened, and he was very concerned about the possibility of someone building there. He offered $2,000 cash, right on the spot.

"It was a small transaction compared to the big deals I hope to do someday. On the other hand, it was more than a 750 percent return on my investment, so I'm not complaining!"

Investor: Bill Gravini
Investment: Tax deed
Investment Goal: Vacation property
Investment Amount: $67,000
Return: $142,000 (estimated value)

Bill, a psychotherapist who works in New York City, likes to spend his winter weekends skiing in the Catskills. One year, he took a summer vacation there too. A friend told him about the local county tax deed auction, and he decided to go. He'd wanted to buy a place in the region, but couldn't find anything he could afford within a reasonable drive from the city.

One of the properties was a small log cabin, at the top of a steep hill overlooking one of the area's most popular tourist villages. Even better: It was right off the road to one of the biggest ski resorts in the Northeast. "As soon as I saw it, I knew it would be perfect for me," he says. "I could see it would need work, but it had a great view and lots of potential. And there was even a stovepipe poking out the roof, so I knew the place had a hookup for a wood stove."

Bill's bid of $67,000 won the auction that day, and he immediately hired a carpenter to spruce the place up. That was four years ago, and the cabin has since become a favorite winter retreat for Bill and his friends during ski season. Even better, he rents it out at $1,000 a month in June, July, and August, when the summer tourists arrive. "A few months ago, just for the heck of it, I asked a real estate agent what she thought it was worth," Bill says. After looking around, she said if she were selling it, she'd list it at $239,000. I probably paid about $30,000 for renovations. The rest is pure profit."

Resources

As I mentioned at the outset of this section, I'm not a tax lien or tax deed expert. This chapter is designed to give you an *overview* of tax lien and deed investing. If this area interests you, I would suggest that you do further study before actually jumping in. These are the sources I suggest:

Books

Profit by Investing in Real Estate Tax Liens: Earn Safe, Secured, and Fixed Returns Every Time, 2nd edition, by Larry B. Loftis (Kaplan, 2007). Having bought liens or deeds in ten states, and attended auctions in another four, Larry is most likely the top national expert who writes on this form of investing. His book lays out the entire process for tax lien and deed investing, how to do your research, how to avoid risks, addresses legal issues (he's an attorney), provides a comprehensive list of all fifty states (illustrating how each state runs bidding, the interest rate, redemption period, and sale dates), and provides an appendix with sample county registration forms and rules.

Web Sites

Association for Optimum Achievement: www.gettaxlien.com

This company offers a complete course on tax liens and deeds, including a guidebook, action manual, nationwide directory of tax liens by county, and an audio CD course. The company offers an online listing of upcoming auctions, including contact information at each county.

Taxlienauthority: www.taxlienauthority.com

This company offers a complete course about tax liens, including a reference guide on liens, deeds and forms, a DVD titled "Making It Big with Tax Liens," and an audio CD course. You can also find out more by calling 877-265-5580.

TaxSale.com: www.taxsale.com

This site is free to join and is an outstanding and reliable source for tax lien and deed information. It's an online community for both tax lien and deed investors and counties selling these products. Sign up to find information about sales near you and Internet sales across the country.

The National Association of Counties (NACo): www.naco.org

NACo's Web site is a convenient way to find contact information for most counties in the United States. From the home page, click on "About Counties" and then select "Find a County."

CHAPTER

2

Build Wealth Fast with Below-Market-Value Real Estate

One of the quickest paths to wealth is the real estate market—in fact, it's probably *the* quickest. Any smart investor looking to increase his or her net worth meaningfully should seriously consider buying real estate to resell, rent out, or offer as a lease-option.

But is it really smart to invest in real estate during an economic slowdown? In the 1990s and first few years of this century, buying and immediately reselling (flipping) houses was a standard way to achieve quick wealth. The underlying assumption was that real estate values would go up and up forever—with no ceiling in sight. In an environment like that, where every piece of property was nearly guaranteed to be substantially more valuable six months after purchase, it certainly made sense to buy... pretty much anything.

That's fine, as long as the economy keeps growing and growing—and also as long as your property value remains unaffected by such local factors as storms and local business closings. But of course, these things can and do happen. And, an economic slowdown, whether local or national, will inevitably bring down prices. In short, it's an unwise investor who takes it for granted that real estate prices everywhere will keep going up forever.

So how do you minimize risk while still taking advantage of the moneymaking power investing in real estate can offer? By making sure you buy properties *below their market value*.

This sounds paradoxical, I know: If something is available at less than its market value, isn't someone else likely to snatch it up before you? Yes and no. Buying real estate below market value usually means bypassing the traditional venues of real estate agents and bank financing. Be prepared to work much harder to find and pull together the right deal. You will also likely have to accept the property "as is"—which can mean a lot of effort and expense in terms of cleanup and refurbishing, and sometimes unexpected expenses for necessary repairs.

Not everyone shopping for real estate is willing to do what it takes, and many of those who are don't know the methods for finding real estate bargains I'll teach you in this chapter. But first, let's begin with a snapshot of below-market-value real estate investing.

SNAPSHOT: Buying Real Estate Below Market Value

How It Works:

Using the strategies in this chapter, you will be able to identify real estate sellers who are willing to accept less than their properties' fair market price. Most often, this is because they need to sell the property quickly or conveniently. Buying real estate below market value gives you a wide range of options, from reselling the property immediately at a higher price to rehabbing it, renting it out, or even living in it yourself. Best of all, you've reduced your risk, because even if prices fall or you find unexpected problems that need repair, the difference between what you paid for the property and its market worth provides a financial cushion.

THE UPSIDE:

- Huge Potential Profits: Buying real estate below market value is probably *the* quickest path to wealth.
- It's Countercyclical: In leaner times, more property owners run into trouble with debt and you can find more and better bargains.
- You May Actually Be Helping Someone: In many cases, you're buying from someone who needs to sell fast, either because they've fallen on hard times, have had a recent death in the family, or need to relocate on short notice. By crafting a win-win deal, you can profit *and* help someone who needs it at the same time.

THE DOWNSIDE:

- It's Labor-Intensive: You will have to work hard to find and put together the right deals for you.
- Moderate Risk: Though you can reduce your risk through financial analysis before you make an offer, buying real estate always carries some risk, especially at foreclosure, when you cannot inspect the home first.
- Cash or Financing Required: Many below-market-value deals require very quick turnaround. This means you will need cash on hand or access to financing to take advantage of these opportunities.

Who Should Invest:

Buying real estate below market value is a great choice for investors who want to dramatically change their financial picture, have the time and willingness to do the learning and the work required, and can tolerate moderate risk.

This is also a great field for you if you're outgoing and like to work with people. Buying real estate below market value is one of the most collaborative strategies in this book. You will need help from a wide variety of experts, from real estate agents to attorneys to building inspectors, lenders, and contractors. You'll also want to get to know the neighbors in the area where you're buying, as well as the sellers themselves. The relationships you build with all these contacts will be your single biggest asset as a below-market-value real estate investor.

There are many different methods of buying real estate, a wide variety of financing options, and a fairly wide range of choices for what to do with a property once you've acquired it. For the purposes of this chapter, though, I'm going to focus on some of the lesser known ways to acquire real estate at lower-than-market prices. The second part of the chapter will give you some guidelines to help you make sure the deal is right, no matter which technique you choose.

Put these pieces together, and follow my action plan to get started in the exciting world of buying and selling real estate. And believe me when I tell you that you never know where it might lead! Some investors I know are making enough off buying and selling properties that after the first year or two of investing, they've decided to quit their day jobs and focus full-time on real estate investing. This does not mean they're lounging by the swimming pool all day—they're working just as hard as ever—but they're making more money doing something they enjoy and being their own bosses.

This doesn't happen for everyone, of course. But I've noticed that the most successful investors in below-market-value real estate deals are self-motivated go-getters who love working with people, are great at building relationships, and look at these deals as shared projects where everyone benefits. If this sounds like you, then buying real below market value is one of the best investment choices you can make.

Finding Property

How and where do you find property available for sale below market value—before someone else finds it first? Many real estate investors find this aspect of the process daunting, and I can understand why. It certainly isn't as easy as calling up a real estate agent and heading out to visit available homes. But if you have a little time to invest, it's definitely doable. Here are some of the best strategies for finding discounted deals:

1. Lender Foreclosure Auctions

In Chapter 1, I discussed buying property deeds at tax foreclosure auctions. This is one type of foreclosure sale. A better known type of foreclosure sale is that conducted by a bank after it has foreclosed on a property where it holds the mortgage. These foreclosure sales are in some cases conducted on the courthouse steps, with buyers bidding against each other out in the weather. For properties backed by government loans (such as those from Housing and Urban Development or the Veterans Administration), the government agency in question may sell the property instead. The Veterans Administration (VA) sells properties through the Multiple Listing Service (MLS) used by virtually all real estate agents. Housing and Urban Development (HUD) conducts its own form of auction, and gives preference to buyers who intend to use the property as a home rather than an investment.

Lender foreclosure sales offer a definite discount off real market value, though not as deep a discount as tax deed sales. Look for discounts of 10 to 25 percent—depending on the economic health of the area where you're buying. The more the economy is down, the deeper the discounts are likely to be. You'll also likely find more selection than at tax deed auctions—again, the worse the local economy, the more borrowers will find themselves in foreclosure and thus the wider the selection is likely to be. Indeed, according to RealtyTrac, an online marketplace for foreclosed properties, foreclosure rates have more than doubled in the last few years, as more and more investors find they've gotten in over their heads with mortgages and counted on rapidly rising prices that didn't materialize.

Buying at a foreclosure auction has its downside, though. I discussed most of these in Chapter 1, but they're important, so let's go over them again. First, if the former homeowner was having trouble making payments, the mortgage may not be the only debt attached to the property. It's wise to check with the local county clerk for any other liens that may be recorded against a property before bidding on it. Also, because you're buying a house without its occupants' consent, you won't be able to have the house professionally inspected, or even take a look at the inside. Third, the previous owners may still be living there, and you may be stuck with the unpleasant and potentially expensive task of evicting them.

A further complication is that in some states borrowers have a redemption period during which they can buy back the property for the amount of the winning bid. Make sure you know what redemption rules are in place in your state before bidding on a foreclosure property, and especially before making expensive repairs.

LENDER FORECLOSURE AUCTIONS

Upside:

- 10 to 25 percent discount off market value
- Wide and growing selection of properties
- Countercyclical: the worse the economy, the better the discounts and selection

Downside:

- No chance to inspect property properly
- May have outstanding liens
- May require eviction

continued

- Former owners may have right to buy property back during redemption period

How to get started:

First, find the dates of upcoming foreclosure sales in the area where you'd like to buy. RealtyTrac (www.realtytrac.com) is one of the easiest sources for finding foreclosure sales throughout the United States. You should also check the legal notices in the local paper and inquire with local banks as to when they may be having sales. Keep in mind most auctions will require you to pay on the spot, with cash or a cash equivalent, such as a cashier's check.

2. Real Estate Owned (REO)

This highly uninformative term is commonly used to refer to properties offered but not bought at a lender's foreclosure auction—in other words, "real estate owned by lender." This happens for one of two reasons: Either no one bid on the property at auction, or the lending institution itself made the highest bid in order to avoid having a property sell for too low a price—in effect, its reserve was not met. (Lenders always want to recoup the outstanding balance on loans when they sell a foreclosed property, and, depending on market conditions, may try to get more.) The upshot is that after the auction is over, the lender still has properties for sale.

In many cases, the lender will now try to sell the property on the open market, using a real estate agent and MLS. But that means the lender can no longer sell the property as is, as it would have at auction. The property will now be subject to a structural inspection and title search before closing, so at this point the lending institution will probably make any necessary fixes, and clear the title.

Thus, buying an REO property means lowering your risk—you will have the same protections that you would if you were buying the property by traditional means. On the other hand, it will lower your discount too—look for only about 5 to 10 percent off market value. Is the trade-off worth it? It depends on your investment goals and resources, and how much risk you can handle.

The best time to make an offer on an REO property is immediately after the auction—especially if you would have been willing to buy the property at the price of the lender's winning bid, but could not come up with the cash (or equivalent) usually required at auction. At that point, the bank may be happy to get the property off its books and may still be willing to accept slightly less than full market value. Once the property is listed on the open market, you'll be competing against many more potential buyers, and you may not be able to get a discount of any kind. By the way, you may be able to sweeten the deal when negotiating for an REO property if you let the lender in question also write the loan for your purchase, so if you're interested in this kind of financing, be sure to include this information in your negotiations.

REO SALES

Upsides:

- Lower risk: You can inspect the home and demand a clear title
- Easier financing: Instead of needing cash on the courthouse steps, you can take the time to arrange a loan
- Better buying process: Instead of bidding against others in a frenzied auction, you can make offers in the traditional way

Downsides:

- Discounts of only 5 to 10 percent off market value
- You may have to compete against many real estate buyers if bank offers the property on the open market

How to Get Started:

To find REO properties for sale in the area where you want to buy, begin by checking with local banks to see if they have any properties for sale. You may find that the banks in your area have a real estate agent or agents handling their properties; get to know them. This is where your skill-building relationships can really help.

You may, however, be able to get some particularly good deals if you can catch a property before it goes to an agent. How? One way is to attend the auction—even if you don't have the cash to bid—and making note of any properties that fail to sell or are bought by the lender. If there are any that seem like a good fit, let the lender know as soon as possible that you're interested.

3. Pre-Foreclosure

Sometimes the best time to buy a property is right before it goes to foreclosure auction. Before foreclosing on a property, a lender must file a notice of default with the county. Auctions usually take place about ninety days after the notice of default is filed, and are usually scheduled about three weeks in advance. This time period is a defaulting owner's last chance to sell the property, pay off the loan, and perhaps walk away with some cash. Otherwise, the owner will lose the property outright, and will also have to contend with having a foreclosure on his or her credit record. Most defaulting owners are highly motivated to make a deal at this stage. However, they may have been approached by a variety of disreputable real estate investors or "credit counselors," so be prepared for a little wariness when you approach them.

One thing I really like about buying real estate in pre-foreclosure is that, rather than only profiting from the previous owner's misfortune, you actually have the chance to make money while helping them out of a bad situation. Since foreclosure would leave them without even enough money to relocate, you may be able to buy the property by assuming the loan (or loans) and providing cash to help them start over in a new place. But it's important to remember that, while the owners may be in deep financial trouble, they likely are well aware of their property's market value. They are also in the middle of what is probably the most humiliating experience of their lives. Take all this into account as you structure your offer.

Another huge advantage is that, unlike buying at a foreclosure auction, you are now buying the property with the consent and cooperation of its owners. This means you can go inside the house to look around, order an inspection, and ask questions about the house's particular quirks. Depending on when you make the deal, you may have a little time to research the property properly and arrange the best possible financing. On the other hand, I've heard of fantastic deals pulled together at the last minute, when desperate owners figured out they really weren't going to be able to get enough money together to keep the house. This is where having the right contacts and relationships will really help—because the ability to make a deal happen quickly is a huge asset in this business.

PRE-FORECLOSURE

Upsides:

- Buying with resident's cooperation allows for inspections and no eviction needed
- You're helping people out of a tough situation
- Long notice for foreclosures may give you more time to put together a deal

Downsides:

- Discounts generally not as good as at foreclosure auction
- Deal can fall apart if seller finds other source of funds
- Sellers may be mistrustful if they've been solicited many times already

How to Get Started:

As I noted before, RealtyTrac (www.realtytrac.com) lists properties in pre-foreclosure, as well as foreclosure. You can also check with the local court or county clerk's office for notices of default, since the lender will have had to register the default legally, before it can foreclose. You can then contact sellers directly to let them know you're interested in buying.

A second approach, which can be equally effective, is to let the community at large know you're interested in buying houses and can close a deal quickly if they're under threat of foreclosure. For more on getting the word out, see "Buying Before Property Hits the Market," pages 56–58.

4. Buying at Probate

When property owners die, their homes are usually sold, with the proceeds to be divided up as part of the estate. It sounds ghoulish, I know, but this situation often spells great opportunity for real estate investors. Discounts off market value may vary, but when a home is part of an estate its owners are nearly always motivated to sell. First, unless the deceased had many other assets, the heir or heirs will likely need to spend their own money—if they have it—to settle the estate expenses.

Meanwhile, with the house sitting empty, they still have to cover maintenance costs and make sure the property remains in good order.

This alone is enough to make many inheritors willing to sell. They may be downright eager if they live far away from the property and need to get back as quickly as they can to their own busy lives. So buying at probate not only gives you the chance to buy real estate as much as 30 percent below market value, it also lets you help grieving family members put money in their pockets more quickly, and put closure to a difficult period in their lives.

This form of investing takes more research than foreclosure, pre-foreclosure, or REO sales, because you'll have to begin with a list of notices of recently deceased people whose estates are in probate, and then review the probate paperwork to see whether the estate includes real estate. If it does, and if you're interested, your next step is to contact the estate's personal representative (or executor, in some states), and inquire whether the property is for sale. Perhaps because it takes a little more work, real estate investors often find they have less competition making offers on properties in probate than at foreclosure auctions and other real estate sales.

Chances are you'll be talking to one of the deceased's family members, so be thoughtful in how you approach him or her. Try something like: "I'm so sorry to bother you at what must be a very tough time. I understand your late mother owned a house at XYZ address, and I'm very interested in making an offer. Whenever you feel the time is right to discuss this, can I ask you to give me a call?" Some investors note that the fact that a family has filed probate paperwork is in itself a sign that they've moved past the initial grieving process and are now ready to begin dealing with the estate.

One especially good thing about buying real estate at probate is that you may well be able to buy the house with its contents, particularly if the heirs live far away. I realize it may be a daunting prospect to find yourself the proud owner of a houseful of personal effects that belonged to someone you never met. But there are legendary stories of bond certificates, priceless paintings, even a classic car on the premises of a deceased's house that became the property of the purchaser. These are, of course, very much the exception, buy you may find a few valuable antiques or collectibles among the leftovers. If you don't mind sorting through the former owner's possessions (or inviting a few dealers in antiques and secondhand items to do it for you), it's great to buy a house with its contents because you never know what you might discover.

BUYING AT PROBATE

The Upsides:

- Discounts of 15 to 30 percent off market value are often possible
- Less competition from other investors
- May be able to buy house with contents

The Downsides:

- More research needed to find available properties than other methods
- Contacting grieving relatives to inquire about purchase requires extreme tact
- Study required: You will need a basic understanding of probate law and common practices in your area

How to Get Started:

Check local weekly and community papers under legal notices for notices of death or probate, and in particular, notices alerting the deceased's creditors of his or her passing. Another way to find estates in probate is to check at the local courthouse or clerk's office where they are filed. Learning whose estates are in probate is only the first step, though. You'll then need to review the filing to determine whether the estate includes any real property.

5. Buying Before Property Hits the Market

This approach is sometimes referred to as "FSBO," as in, "For Sale by Owner." The idea behind the term is that investors scout the neighborhood, looking for "For Sale by Owner" signs in order to find properties not represented by real estate agents and thus available at a discount. This is only one of many approaches investors have used effectively to identify properties for sale before they turn up in the MLS.

How else do you find properties for sale before they are offered on the open market? Seasoned real estate investors report that they learn to look at places differently while going about their normal routine. If a house has been noticeably vacant for a while, for instance, they may ask neighbors or check at the county courthouse to find out who owns it, and whether the owner might want to make a quick sale. They'll do the same if a house is visibly unkempt and neglected, which may mean residents are having financial trouble and in need of cash. Likewise, if they see a moving van in front of a house, they will knock on the door and ask if the house is for sale.

An equally effective way to find homes for sale by their owners is to put the word out that you're looking for them. Some investors offer finders' fees to neighborhood acquaintances who alert them to homes for sale. Others advertise in a local paper or post on local Web sites and message boards (as well as physical bulletin boards in grocery stores and post offices) that they're looking to buy homes for quick cash.

The advantage to these strategies is that they're easy to do in between other real estate investment tasks or your daily routine. And, some investors and home buyers have gotten very good discounts this way. On the other hand, you're not guaranteed a motivated seller, as you would be with foreclosure and pre-foreclosure sales. So, even after you've identified an attractive property for sale, you may wind up walking away from the deal.

BUYING PROPERTY BEFORE IT'S ON THE MARKET

Upsides:

- You're buying with owner's cooperation and can inspect the property
- Usually less time pressure than with pre-foreclosure or foreclosure deals
- Depending on why property is for sale, it may be in better condition than a foreclosed property

Downsides:

- Seller may not be motivated to make a deal
- Potential expenses for finders' fees, newspaper ads, and so on
- You may need to review a lot of properties before finding one for sale at the right price

continued

How to Get Started:

While driving or walking around the area where you'd like to buy, keep a sharp eye out. You're looking for "For Sale" signs that list only a phone number, or specify that the property is for sale by its owner. You're also looking for properties that appear unoccupied, unkempt, or where there are signs of departure such as a moving van. If you find any of the above, knock on the door and ask if the property is for sale, or ask neighbors for information about the property. You can also inquire at the local municipality or county offices to find the owner of record for the property.

Don't forget to let your friends and neighbors know you're looking for properties to buy. Offer a reward (cash, a bottle of wine, or lunch in a favorite restaurant) to those who help you find good prospects. You might also consider placing an ad in your local paper or shopper and/or posting on local Web sites—as well as bulletin boards in local businesses—to get the word out that you're looking to buy.

Making the Right Deal

The five strategies above can help you find properties below their market prices. But that won't be true of every property you find. And just because a property is available below market value doesn't necessarily make it the right deal for you. So how do you determine if a deal is right?

First of all, let me stress that, unlike selecting a home to live in, you're now buying real estate as an investment. Investment success is a function of numbers, nothing more. If the numbers are bigger at the end of the process, you've made a good investment, if they're smaller, you've made a bad one. A one-room shack with a tin roof that you buy for $20,000 and sell two months later for $35,000 is an excellent investment. A charming home with a fireplace, large yard, and in-ground pool is a poor investment if you buy it for $400,000 but then can't sell it for more than $395,000.

Real estate is an emotional matter, and it's tempting to let your desire to own a beautiful home or transform a misused property into a lovely one rule your decisions. Don't give in to that temptation! Whether a deal is right for you has little to do with how nice the property is, and much to do with the market forces at work, the price and terms you can get, and how you'll earn profits on the property. So, to get a preliminary idea if a property you've found is a good investment, consider the following questions:

1. What will you do with the property? "I'll see" is not an acceptable answer. From the moment you close on a real estate deal, you should hear the loud ticking of your financial clock. Why? First, because the longer a house sits empty, the more maintenance it will need. More important, when you close on the loan that will pay for the property, you immediately start paying interest. If your monthly mortgage payment is $1,000, you're spending more than $250 for every week the place stays empty. If it's empty because you're in the process of making improvements, or showing the house, or looking for a buyer or tenant who will meet your price, that $250 may be a worthwhile investment that will be paid back in a higher sale or rental price. But don't spend that $250 a week waiting till you have enough free time to focus on what to do.

As a practical matter, there are only three choices once you buy an investment property (whether or not you fix it up): rent it out, resell it, or—a combination of the two—lease-option, in which renters pay a down payment up front and a premium over their rental that are credited against the purchase of the house after a set period of time (usually two to three years). You should decide which of these three things you're planning to do before making an offer on a property. Why? Because these plans will dictate what kind of deal you need. Read on to learn more.

2. Do the numbers make sense? Your first task when looking at a property is to figure out its approximate market value. There are many different sources you can use to try and determine this number. They include:

- Opinions from experienced real estate agents working in the neighborhood (but keep in mind they may aim high if they are trying to get you to list with them).
- A professional appraisal of the property.
- Prices of other nearby properties that have recently sold (compare the price per square foot to your prospective property).

Each of these methods may yield a completely different number, but together they will give you some idea of what a reasonable price should be. (You should also know the assessed value for tax purposes, but this has little to do with a property's actual value and is often absurdly low.) Take into account any intangibles, such as whether the house borders a park, or is too close to the street. Also, take into account any expensive repairs you know the house will need.

Once you've determined the property's approximate value, you can figure out how much of a discount you need to make this a good deal. Here's where you need to know your plans for the house.

If you're buying a property in order to resell it (with or without renovations), look for a price at least 25 percent below market value, advises Andy Heller, a real estate investor and co-author of *Buy Even Lower: The Regular People's Guide to Real Estate Riches.* "Keep in mind you'll likely have to pay a real estate agency commission and closing costs both buying and selling," he says. That 25 percent also gives you a bit of a cushion in a down market—values can fall quite a bit and you should still be able to sell at a profit.

If you're buying a property with the intention of offering a lease-option, he says, you don't need as much of a discount. "That's what my business partner and I do, and we usually buy at a discount of 15 to 20 percent," he says. "We make additional money by getting renters committed to a long-term lease, and we also get tax benefits. That's the beauty of rent-to-own."

If you're buying a property with the intent of renting it out (without a lease-option), that's a longer-term proposition, Heller notes. Getting a discount off market value loses importance, because chances are, by the time you sell, the market will have completely changed. Most real estate gains value over the long term, so chances are you will make a profit when you finally sell the property.

On the other hand, you need to make sure the property won't create negative cash flow in the meantime. That is, the rent or rents you receive should cover your loan, tax, and maintenance costs for the property, including any repairs you may need to make on an ongoing basis. At the same time, you want to minimize your cash investment in the property because that cash will be tied up indefinitely.

Making these numbers work can be tricky, and you may choose to focus your negotiation on terms. For instance, if you can get owner financing with a very low down payment and interest lower than the bank's, it may make sense to pay a higher price for the property.

3. What is the trend in the area? Different strategies make sense in different areas, and you need to understand those dynamics when planning your real estate deals. Is the neighborhood on the outskirts of a rapidly growing city with new residents arriving every day? Then chances are existing homes, especially those on large lots, will gain in value. Is the area one that appeals to weekenders and retirees? There again, you'll probably do well.

On the other hand, if a large local employer has recently relocated, or the neighborhood in general seems to be going downhill, properties may not be appreciating—but on the other hand, there are probably great deals available. This doesn't mean you shouldn't buy in the area, but it probably does mean you shouldn't plan on a quick flip. Instead, think in terms of lease-option, or straight rental.

4. Is it a good deal for everyone? The seller, the buyer or renter of your property, as well as the real estate agents and lenders who work with you should all feel they've gotten a good deal. Why should you care? Because to create wealth you need to do more than just one transaction. You need to continue buying real estate below market value and reaping the profits in both up and down markets for years to come. You're best off doing this in or near your own community, where it's easy for you to visit properties, and you're well acquainted with the market dynamics. And it'll be easiest to do when you build lasting relationships with real estate professionals, and leave the people you've bought from or sold to feeling happy about the experience.

"My partner and I have bought over 100 properties," Heller says. "We found more than half of them through just three sources." The bulk of their purchases were REOs, he notes, most of which were sold through real estate agents. Because they have built up good working relationships, the agents are happy to work with them in REO deals.

When David Seider, president of Seider Select Properties, did his first real estate deal in San Diego, he bought a house in pre-foreclosure, paid off some hefty loans, spruced up the property for a quick sale, and helped a family get back on its feet. The lending group that held the loans on the house was impressed, he reports. "They told me they had four other homeowners in similar straits. Would I be willing to talk to them and try to help them out?"

Of the four, he recalls, one was a solid prospect: a homeowner with a house worth at least $500,000 and only about $10,000 in arrears. Seider bought and resold that house as well, providing about $25,000 cash to the previous owner and clearing about $75,000 for himself—money that came directly from the good relationships he'd built.

Now Is the Time!

Now that the red-hot real estate market has cooled, many investors are leery of buying investment properties. They're wrong! This is a great time for getting real estate deals, for those who are willing to do their homework and find the right property for them. "Some of the greatest opportunities for wealth accumulation occur during economic down cycles," Heller notes.

The reason, he says, is a simple matter of supply and demand. With a cooling real estate market, some of the speculators of years past are now sitting on their hands. Meanwhile, with foreclosures reaching record numbers, banks have more and more properties to sell. "In the last five years, it was more challenging to find a property at a discount," he says. "Now it's getting easier and easier."

Use the first section of this chapter to pick which methods of finding below-market-value real estate work best for you—or try a combination of tactics. Then use the questions in the second part to help you determine if the deal really is a good one. You'll soon be on your way to your own profitable real estate deal.

Lower Your Risk—Below-Market-Value Real Estate

1. Focus on single-family or two-family homes.
2. Have a structural inspection and professional appraisal done before closing (may not be possible with foreclosure sales).
3. Always have professional third-party representation, ideally a lawyer, review all agreements before you sign, particularly if you are signing documents drafted by the seller.
4. Think exit strategy: Try to keep your initial down payment when signing the contract low enough that you won't be devastated if you have to walk away. In general have a plan for getting out of the deal, or quickly reselling the property, if things go wrong.

Below-Market-Value Real Estate Action Plan

1. Pick an area where you'd like to invest. Ideally, this should be close to where you live; if you plan to offer the property for rent or lease-option, it should be less than an hour away. It should also be an area you know well, so that you can quickly spot market trends.

2. Pick an investment strategy that will work in this area. If the local economy is in the doldrums, or a local employer is downsizing, don't plan on buying and immediately reselling a house. On the other hand, this could be a good market for lease-option deals, which can have real appeal to local residents without enough cash or credit to buy a home in the traditional way.

3. Get to know the local players. Try to meet and build relationships with local real estate agents, title companies, and lenders. Let them know you're on the lookout for below-market deals. Make it clear you're not a short-term speculator, but hope to continue investing in this area.

4. Pick a strategy or strategies for finding properties. You may want to try attending a foreclosure sale, checking out some probate files, and contacting banks to ask about REO properties. Always be on the lookout for homes that appear to be vacant, where occupants are moving out, or that have "For Sale by Owner" signs.

5. Select some properties that seem like good prospects. You should start with a few, because they won't all turn out to be good deals. Remember, you are looking for good financial deals, not necessarily the most appealing homes.

6. Research these properties. Using information from local sources, determine the approximate market value of each property.

7. Make a written offer. Real estate experts suggest putting a serious offer in writing. The exception, of course, is buying at foreclosure auction, where you will have to bid on the fly.

8. Plan your auction strategy. If you're planning to attend a foreclosure auction, you should still go in with a definite idea of how much the properties you will bid on are worth, and how high you can go before a good deal turns into a bad one. Keep in mind that you are buying the property "as is" and will have to pay for any needed repairs.

9. Follow through. Once you've found the right deal and have an accepted offer, it's time to spring into action. Order a structural inspection, if you haven't had one already. Begin preparation for any repairs or improvements so that work can begin immediately upon closing. Line up any needed financing, if not in place already.

10. Put it on the market. As soon as possible after you purchase a home, get it back on the market, either for sale, lease-option, or rent. The longer it sits unoccupied, the more likely it is to need maintenance, and the longer you'll be paying interest on a property that's earning nothing. The sooner the property is rented or sold, the sooner you can start collecting on this investment—and planning for the next one.

Case Studies

To help show you how these strategies actually work, I've provided three real-life case studies. The names and locations have been changed.

Investor: Joe Wiggins
Investment Goal: Build wealth for retirement
Buying Technique: Buying before property is on the market
Purchase Price (including repairs): $180,000
Sale Price: $265,000

Joe is a lawn and yard care professional who works in western Ohio. One advantage to this job is that he often finds himself driving down rural roads to out-of-the-way addresses, a perfect scenario for finding properties before they're on the market. Joe wanted to invest in real estate, so he started keeping his eye out for signs that a property was about to be for sale.

He first noticed a nice-looking but obviously vacant house on a corner lot. He checked the name on the mailbox and looked in the phone book for a phone number. Of course, the address in the phone book was the same as the vacant house, but when he called the number, he got a recording with a new listing in the 303 area code. Apparently the occupants had moved to Colorado.

He called the new number and got a voice mail message. He introduced himself as a neighbor back in Ohio, stated his interest in the house, and asked for a callback. Later that evening a nice young couple returned his call. They explained they had moved temporarily to Denver so that the husband could work on a six-month contract, and they planned to return to the house after it was done. "But thank you for calling," the wife said. "When we start a family, we'll need a bigger place, so when we're ready to sell, we'll be sure to let you know."

Joe wasn't disappointed—he knew better than to set his hopes on any one property. A few days later, he noticed a large portable storage unit on the lawn of an older home. He pulled over, hopped out of his truck, and knocked on the door. When a man answered, Joe explained that he'd noticed the storage unit and wondered if the house was for sale. "That's funny," the man said. "My mother is moving into a retirement community, and she does need to sell this house. I was planning to wait till she was all moved out to start showing it. But if you're interested in seeing it now, come on in!"

Joe wound up buying the house for $165,000, which he figured would be about half its market value if it had a new roof and other expensive repairs. He spent some time spiffing up the yard and trimming the trees, and had the exterior repainted. Then he put it on the market at $275,000, and sold it for $265,000.

Since then, he's been keeping an even keener eye out for pre-market properties. "I don't want to be cutting people's lawns forever," he says.

Investor: Laura Reese
Investment Goal: Start a real estate business
Buying Technique: Probate
Purchase Price (including repairs) $75,000
Sale Price: $105,000

Laura was part owner of a pet grooming shop in Vermont, but longed to find an easier and more lucrative line of work. She attended a free seminar on buying real estate at probate, decided the system made sense, and signed up for the course. Once she'd learned how to find probate properties, she began searching her local courthouses, and found several estates that sounded like good potential. She talked to several bereaved families before finding a good potential property, she says. "Some just needed an ear to talk to about their loved one."

Finally, she found a property whose owner had died months earlier. His son, the estate's executor, had been trying to sell the house, but no one was interested, as it was in very bad shape. "If I hadn't bought it, it probably would have been torn down," Laura says.

By the time she met him, the son was so sick of the property he refused to go there, but simply gave her the key and allowed her to visit alone.

After looking at the property, she made him an offer of $19,000. Why that number? "I knew he had already spent $8,000 on upkeep and insurance for the property," she explained. "This would cover that, allow $1,000 for his efforts, and $10,000 to distribute among his siblings—he wanted to make sure they got *something*." Best of all, the house would be out of his life. When he accepted the offer, it was as if a weight had lifted off him, he says.

Laura hired contractors and went to work. Soon, neighbors started dropping by to see what she was doing, clearly glad that the run-down house was getting a facelift. One of them mentioned that he'd looked at the house, but didn't want to take on the enormous repair job. Three months later, the repairs were completed at a cost of $56,000, and Laura was ready to put the house on the market. She started by hosting an open house for neighbors, local business owners, and her own friends. It turned out that one of her dog grooming employees was moving in with his girlfriend and needed a starter house, so he bought the property at the open house, for $105,000.

Investor: Carl Ruiz
Investment Goal: Rebuild assets after a setback
Buying Technique: Pre-foreclosure
Purchase Price (including repairs and profit sharing): $980,000
Sale Price: $1.1 million

Carl Ruiz is an advertising executive in Southern California. He had spent years building up a nice investment portfolio—part of which was wiped out when he and his wife divorced. Determined to build up his assets again, he decided to try investing in real estate, and took some courses to learn how.

Then he set about looking for homeowners in pre-foreclosure, putting the word out that he was interested in helping. He also printed up some business cards saying he would buy properties.

He soon received a phone call from a desperate family. They were going to be foreclosed the following week, they explained. They had a large home, right on a river, with its own dock and a spectacular view. It had been appraised at $1.4 million, they explained. But they'd been unable to sell it.

Carl visited the property and soon saw why. It was indeed a beautiful house, with a gorgeous view of the river. Unfortunately, weather patterns had changed, and heavy rains brought yearly flooding. The house had twice seen floods that completely washed out the basement and threatened the first floor. The house would need massive work to properly protect it from flooding.

"I had no idea how much something like that might cost," Carl says. "I thought maybe it would be as much as $200,000."

Carl told the homeowners that he thought their house represented a lot of risk. They said they'd heard the same thing by prospective buyers and real estate agents who refused to list the property. One investor had offered to buy the house for their outstanding debt plus only $5,000 for their equity. They'd refused...but they were running out of options.

"Look," Carl said, "This is a big investment and a lot of risk, so if I do this, I'm going to need some real profit. But past that amount I'd be willing to split the profits with you." He also said he would buy the house but allow them to stay in it until it was resold.

With less than a week till foreclosure, Carl went looking for an engineer who could explain exactly what was needed to protect the house from flooding and how much it would cost. Turned out the whole job could be done for less than $50,000. Carl didn't order the work, but he now had detailed estimates he could give potential buyers.

The couple had around $950,000 in debt, about $120,000 of it in arrears, Carl says. Once they had an agreement, he immediately paid off the arrearages (taking out an equity loan on his own house), and ordered some landscaping and other cosmetic work for about $5,000. He also took over the family's $8,000 monthly loan payments, and began aggressively marketing the house, including having the family's children put flyers out around the neighborhood, and organizing open houses. At the first open house a couple who'd been eyeing the neighborhood for years offered $30,000 over the asking price if he would cancel the subsequent open houses and commit to selling to them. He agreed. "They really wanted the house so the closing was very easy," he notes.

In the end, there was a total profit of about $145,000; Carl kept $120,000 and the family kept $25,000 to start over in a new place. Carl and his kids also helped the family move into a townhouse that, though much smaller, was only three miles away from their former home. Afterward, he says, "They wrote me a note and thanked me for sharing the profits, and helping them out."

Resources

Books

Buy Even Lower: The Regular People's Guide to Real Estate Riches by Andy Heller and Scott Frank (Kaplan, 2006)

A detailed overview of buying real estate below market value by pros who've spent decades doing just that, covering pre-foreclosure, foreclosure, and REO opportunities, as well as tax liens and deeds.

The Complete Idiot's Guide to Buying Foreclosures by Ted Beitler and Bobbi Dempsey (Alpha, 2005)

Thoroughly covers foreclosures, pre-foreclosures, and REO sales, and also gives details on how to find and buy properties from government agencies.

Web Sites/Courses

Robert Allen Institute: www.robertallenworkshop.com

Robert Allen's institute and instructors offer detailed information on every aspect of buying real estate below market value. It also offers enormous detail on how to structure a deal and how to buy real estate with little or no money down. The investor I've called Carl Ruiz took Robert Allen's workshop to learn the ins and outs of real estate investing.

J. G. Banks Institute: www.jgbanksinstitute.com

Banks focuses on buying at probate, and this course is designed to teach you how to find and buy probate properties. This is the course the investor I called Laura Reese took before investing in probate.

National Real Estate Investors Association: www.nationalreia.com

This is an affiliation of real estate investor groups and clubs. You can go through this site to find a real estate investment group in your area to network with experienced investors and learn which below-market-value techniques work best in your area.

RealtyTrac: www.realtytrac.com

A comprehensive site for finding foreclosure and FSBO (For Sale by Owner) listings in your area.

REI Club: www.reiclub.com

A huge informational site, including more than 500 articles about every aspect of real estate investing, written by a wide range of experts, as well as online chat and message boards where you can connect with other real estate investors.

3

High Prices at the Pump? Cash In with Income Trusts and Master Limited Partnerships

Our first two chapters focused on ways to make fast profits in the lucrative but labor-intensive real estate market. These next few chapters will take a look at ways to make money with financial instruments, such as stocks, bonds, and options.

Let's begin with income trusts and master limited partnerships. Anyone who's pulled up to the pump in the last few years has witnessed the historic run-up in oil prices. And it's not just filling your gas tank, but heating your home and even your electric bill that are heading decidedly north. Even people who heat with wood stoves report the price of a cord of wood is substantially higher than it was a few years ago.

Ever wish that, as well as paying more for everything energy-related (which is to say, pretty much everything), you could also profit off the rise in energy prices? Well you can, and there are several methods to choose from. One obvious tactic is to purchase shares in energy-related companies. The only problem with this is that every other investor with a newspaper subscription or Internet connection is just as aware as you are of rising energy prices, and many of them are buying energy stocks as a result. That has led to a record run-up in this sector, with popular energy stocks and mutual fund prices more than doubling over the last few years.

But there's another, less well-known strategy: profit not from the rising fortunes of energy companies (as stocks would let you do) but from the oil, natural gas, or coal itself. Trusts, especially Canadian income trusts, and master limited partnerships (MLPs) allow you to do this by acting as holding companies that distribute nearly all the company's profits directly to investors. I'll explain how all this works in a moment, but let's start with snapshots of these investment choices:

SNAPSHOT: Canadian Income Trusts

How They Work:

Trusts make money extracting energy—in the form of oil, gas, coal, or timber—from the earth and pass those earnings directly to investors through monthly dividends.

THE UPSIDE:

- Dividend yields of 10 percent or more
- Tax breaks possible for U.S. investors
- Will increase in value if natural resource prices continue to rise

THE DOWNSIDE:

- Changing Canadian legislation may reduce future yields
- Prices are volatile—you could lose if you sell at the wrong time
- Somewhat cyclical: If a slowing economy lowers natural resource prices, royalty shares may lose value

Who Should Invest:

Want a risk-free investment where you can withdraw your money anytime? Then don't invest in income trusts. On the other hand, if you have money to invest longer-term, consider income trusts, which can offer yields of 10 percent or more.

SNAPSHOT: Master Limited Partnerships

How They Work:

These are entities similar to the trusts described above. Though they are traded similarly to the trusts, legally speaking, you become a partner in the corporation, and receive a K-1 form, rather than a 1099 for tax purposes. Most master limited partnerships invest in pipelines for oil and gas, rather than the actual extraction of oil and gas.

THE UPSIDE:

- More stable prices than trusts
- Not affected by Canadian legislative changes
- You can invest in funds rather than specific companies

THE DOWNSIDE:

- Yields are generally lower than trusts, though still much higher than bonds or Treasury bills
- Tax reporting is more complex than for trusts
- Must not be used in nontaxable accounts (such as IRAs)

Who Should Invest:

If the volatility of income trusts seems daunting, master limited partnerships provide a less-exciting alternative. They also are not affected by changes in Canadian law. However, you may not see the spectacular returns available with trusts. Also, if you're investing a nontaxable account (such as an IRA) DO NOT invest directly in MLP shares. Believe it or not, this can actually cause the account to lose its tax-free status!

Trusts Offer Double-Digit Dividends

In the traditional investment model, a company sells shares to raise capital for its projects. Though it may occasionally issue dividends, investors buy with the hope that the price of the shares will go up. Traditional stocks are thus mostly considered growth, not income, investments.

Trusts take the exact opposite approach. Profits are channeled directly to investors and dividends are paid monthly. These dividends can be high—10 percent or much more on an annual basis. On the other hand, investors should assume the share price itself won't necessarily rise that much.

One of the most appealing things about trusts is that they get something of a break when it comes to taxes. Because a trust is not meant to be a real company, but merely a holding company that passes profits along to investors, trusts are not taxed at the corporate level. (At least, not yet. More about that in a minute.) They can pass those savings on to the investor in the form of bigger dividends—one reason trusts consistently pay higher yields than corporate bonds and other instruments. This is why they make such a great investment. (For more on taxes, see pages 78–79.)

Most, though not all, income trusts focus on a depleting natural resource, usually oil, gas, coal, or timber. U.S. trusts, called *royalty trusts,* are structured to simply pass along profits in the form of yields until the resource itself (a well, or a mine, for instance) is depleted. The drawback is, as the resource production peaks and then begins to decline, yields decline right along with production, until there may be little or nothing left.

Canadian *income trusts* are structured differently. They operate more like traditional companies, and can borrow money or sell shares in order to raise capital to acquire new resources. Thus, a Canadian trust with a well nearing depletion can begin exploring for new oil reserves, rather than face liquidation. This makes the Canadian trusts a more appealing and stable investment than American ones. What's more, U.S. investors can get a tax break (see below).

Most Canadian trusts, including my top recommendations, are in the oil and natural gas sector, conducting either exploration or production, or both. However, many different types of companies can operate effectively as trusts, and some of Canada's biggest trusts are in the telephone or yellow pages sectors.

The big disadvantage to Canadian trusts is that their share prices can be volatile. This proved particularly true on November 1, 2006, after an event dubbed the "Halloween Massacre" by many in the investment community. On October 31, knowing many members of the investment community would be trick-or-treating with their kids, rather than watching the news, the Canadian government announced a plan to tax trusts at the corporate level, the same as any other company. For trusts existing before the announcement, the changes would not take effect until 2011. Reports at the time said the move was intended to prevent some of Canada's largest companies from converting to an income trust structure—which would save them from paying taxes and dramatically lower the government's income.

Whatever the cause of the announcement, the effect was immediate.

On November 1, share prices for Canadian trusts tumbled, some by as much as 20 percent. Despite loud protests from income trust unit holders in Canada and elsewhere, the prime minister and finance minister say they will stand firm on what they term a necessary change, and, as of this writing, the proposal seems likely to become law.

Even if they are taxed at the corporate level, it's still worthwhile investing in Canadian income trusts. Here's why:

1. The yields beat anything else out there. Do you know any other investments that consistently offer double-digit yields? Historically, many of these trusts have offered yields in the 10 to 14 percent range, higher than bonds, Treasury bills, or blue chip stock dividends. Better yet, they pay dividends every month. That means, if you've made the wise choice to have your dividends reinvest automatically, monthly compounding makes your investment grow even faster. That's what I do, and I've had the pleasure of watching my income trust investments grow exponentially.

Now, what will happen to these phenomenal yields once the Canadian government begins taxing royalty income like any other corporation? At that point, they may begin to pay yields more in line with other corporations. In the energy sector, that will still mean better-than-market yields. And, since the law won't take effect before 2011, expect to earn exceptionally high yields till then.

2. U.S. citizens can get a tax break. U.S. royalty trust dividends are taxed as income, but there's a tax advantage to investing in Canadian income trusts. "The Canadian government withholds 15 percent on these dividends, but you can recover that on your U.S taxes," explains Richard Lehmann, president of Income Securities Advisors, and a columnist at *Forbes*. To get the tax advantage, he notes, they must be held in a taxable account, not a tax-deferred one such as an IRA. However, as he points out, "right now, returns are so extraordinary there's no attractive alternative." I agree—which is why I even have some income trust investments in my medical savings account (which compounds tax-free, so long as I spend the funds on medical expenses).

3. They benefit from a long-term trend. Remember when oil seemed expensive at $30 a barrel? I do too, but those days are gone forever. OPEC nations can't always agree on a strategy, and new oilfields turn up now and then, so oil prices may rise and fall many times over the next few years. And, tough economic times can lead to lower oil prices, simply because there's less commerce and less activity, and thus less need to burn oil for transportation or production.

But overall trends point to rising oil prices over the long term. However little we may want to admit it to ourselves, oil is a finite resource, and some geologists believe our planet is at or near "peak oil"—a point where oil resources will have reached their peak of production and, like a giant well slowly running dry, will begin to decline.

Whether or not this is true, ongoing turmoil in the Middle East, instability in Africa, and the unpredictable politics of Latin America all suggest that, in the long run, oil supplies will be uncertain at best. Meanwhile, drivers in the developed world show little signs of giving up their cars, or even trading them in for hybrids in significant numbers, while drivers in rapidly developing nations like China and India want gas for their own newly acquired vehicles. Match uncertain supply with hugely expanding demand, and you can pretty much count on both dividends and prices increasing over time.

This certainly is what has happened so far. Indeed, investors who held Canadian income trust shares for a year or two before November 2006 have seen prices rise high enough to more than compensate for the effects of the Halloween Massacre. My own Canadian trust investments have seen their share prices rise between 50 and 70 percent over the past few years. This is in addition to the very attractive yields I earned over those years. All in all, a very good deal.

4. The price is right. The prospect of corporate taxes on these trusts has driven down prices at a time when yields are still fabulously high, and likely to remain so until 2011, even if the new taxes become law. That means there's never been a better time to buy Canadian income trusts. In addition, several trusts have been taken over because their share prices were depressed to bargain levels, and more takeovers are likely in this sector.

Which trust or trusts should you buy? Not all of them are created equal. And the new laws for trusts mean smart investors must choose among them very carefully. The transition to a regular taxation is already putting a strain on some of the smaller and less-well-funded trusts. So, while now is certainly a great time to buy, it's more important than ever to pick the right trusts to invest in. Those are the large, well-established trusts with a strong track record, plenty of resources, and good cash flow. You will also find a list of the trusts I recommend in the Resources section of this chapter. This information should help you pick the trust or trusts that will work best for you.

Now, let's take a look at another way to cash in on high energy prices: master limited partnerships.

Master Limited Partnerships: The Profits Are in the Pipeline

Like Canadian income trusts and U.S. royalty trusts, MLPs present an opportunity for individual investors to make money off the relentless rise of energy prices. But the similarities end there. Here are some important ways MLPs differ from trusts.

1. MLPs are structured as partnerships. What does this mean to the individual investor? Like trusts, they are structured to "flow through" nearly all of their profits to their investors. However, since MLPs are U.S., not Canadian entities, they are not affected by the changes in Canadian law.

In the past, investors had to buy partnership units directly from the partnerships themselves. In the last few years, though, master limited partnerships have begun offering their shares on the New York Stock Exchange. That makes investing as easy as buying any other kind of stock. And that's good news for everyday investors who want to make money off high-priced energy.

2. Most MLPs are in infrastructure industries, primarily pipelines. This means MLPs tend to be much more stable than oil-and-gas-based income trusts, since their ability to make a profit may be less tied to the price of oil. In effect, it depends on what kind of payment arrangements the pipelines have with their customers. "The best is a blanket contract," says Roger Conrad, editor of the newsletters *Utility Forecast* and *Canadian Edge,* and associate editor of *Personal Finance.* "It's based on throughput, so they make money on capacity, and it doesn't matter what the price of oil or gas is." Though some MLPs have their fees tied to oil and/or gas prices, he says, most work on a throughput basis, so rising or falling prices don't matter.

As a practical matter, this tends to mean that MLP yields are very solid and share prices tend to offer stable growth. On the other hand, yields tend to be in the 6 to 9 percent range—definitely less spectacular than the double-digit yields trusts can offer.

You should also be aware that MLPs, like all energy investments, can be affected by a serious economic downturn. "If the economy screeches to a halt, less energy is used, so they might be in bad shape," Conrad says.

3. More pipelines are needed. "There's a shortage of energy infrastructure in the United States," Conrad explains. That means pipeline MLPs are in a growth industry. U.S. energy demand has been steadily growing for twenty years, and is expected to keep growing for the next twenty. That means the future is fairly secure for pipeline MLPs—and pipeline MLP investors.

When it comes to MLPs, bigger tends to be better: The best MLP investments are those with the most pipeline, and the most new pipeline projects—the more pipe there is, the more opportunity for revenue.

4. MLPs are taxed differently. Calculating MLP payments for tax purposes can be more complicated than with other types of investments. You may receive regular payments, but these are typically broken down with some percentage being taxed as regular income, and some different—usually much larger—percentage defined as return of capital. You must pay taxes on the income portion in the year you received the money, but won't have to pay taxes on the return of capital until you sell shares of the partnership. At that point any money you received as return of capital will be used to lower your cost basis for tax purposes. For example, if you bought the shares at $30 each, but received $5 in return of capital, the difference between $25 and $30 will be taxed as a capital gain.

In other words, you pay less tax on the yields you receive from your MLP investment. On the other hand, when you sell your shares, you'll pay higher capital gains taxes. Put these two facts together, and the conclusion is clear: You're much better off buying MLPs as income-generating investments that you intend to hold for a long time than as short-term investments you intend to cash out in a year or two.

BUT—unlike many long-term investments—MLPs are wrong for retirement accounts such as IRAs. They generate something called "unrelated business taxable income," and if a tax-free account earns more than $1,000 of this type of income, it can become a taxable account. *Be certain to avoid buying MLPs for any kind of tax-free account!* This goes for health savings accounts as well.

Some investors circumvent this problem by buying shares in MLP funds, rather than the MLPs themselves. This solves the unrelated business taxable income problem, and it also means you can spread your risks over many different MLPs, or even a combination of MLPs and other investments, such as Canadian trusts. The downside, of course, is that funds pay management fees, which means you're likely to see lower—though still solid—yields.

Since MLPs are still a fairly new phenomenon, there are a lot fewer of them than there are income trusts. For information on my own picks, as well as info on some MLP mutual funds, see pages 88–95.

  Both income trusts and master limited partnerships deserve serious consideration from investors looking to make fast profits. And, if you buy some shares, next time you pull up to a pump with depressingly high gas prices, you'll at least know that those prices mean a little more money in your pocket

JORDAN'S INCOME TRUST INVESTMENTS

I first began investing in income trusts in 2003. In the five years I've owned them, the shares have shown excellent performance, spurred on, of course, by rising oil prices. The main objective in buying income trust instruments is supposed to be high dividends, not an increase in the underlying share price. But it's great when you get both dividends and price appreciation, and that's exactly what's happened to my income trust investments. In the five years I've owned them, the prices of my shares have more than doubled—even taking into account declining prices after the Halloween Massacre.

  At the same time, the trusts have gone right on paying high dividends—about 10 to 13 percent per year. I have my account set up to automatically reinvest those dividends in shares—and the share prices keep on climbing. The combined effect is that my investment in income trusts has gone up by more than 150 percent in the five years I've owned them—for annualized returns of more than 35 percent.

  Wondering which trusts I invest in? Here are five, all traded on the New York Stock Exchange, that have performed very well for me over several years:

continued

- Penn West Energy Trust (PWE)
- Enerplus Resources Fund (ERF)
- Provident Energy Trust (PVX)
- Pengrowth Energy Trust (PGH)
- Baytex Energy Trust (BTE)

For more information on these and fifteen other income trusts I recommend for investment, see the Resources section of this chapter.

How Are Income Trusts Taxed?

Wondering how to report payments from income trusts for tax purposes? I get asked about this all the time at speeches and radio appearances. And no wonder—the rules can be confusing. Here are some basics to help you figure it out. Remember to consult your own tax professional with any detailed questions.

1. Canadian income trust distributions are subject to a 15 percent withholding tax by the Candian government. This tax is automatically withheld by your brokerage firm before the money ever reaches you, though you are notified how much has been withheld. You should then take a foreign tax credit toward your U.S. taxes while you file your 1040—if your income trust units are held in a taxable account. To get the credit, either submit Form 116 with your return, or take the tax as an itemized deduction on your 1040. If you hold the trusts in a tax-deferred account such as an IRA, you cannot claim the foreign tax credit, so in effect you are receiving a yield 15 percent lower than the gross amount of the distributions paid.

2. You will still have to figure out how to report the dividends you receive. This is where things get complicated. Most—but not all—Canadian trusts qualify as foreign corporations for U.S. tax purposes. (Those that don't are considered partnerships, and are taxed similarly to master limited partnerships.)

3. For those trusts that do qualify as foreign corporations, distributions are divided between what the IRS defines as qualified dividends and return of capital. The trust you invest in should provide the information (on its Web site and/or elsewhere) as to how the dividends it pays break down between these two categories each year.

Qualified dividends are taxed at 15 percent for most U.S. investors. As to return of capital, you don't need to pay taxes until the return of capital you receive exceeds the amount you originally paid for the units, including commissions and transfer fees. When this happens, you will have to report that excess as a capital gain, and pay taxes on it, usually at 15 percent.

4. The rules may change. All of the above assumes tax laws in effect today. A bill has been introduced in Congress to no longer classify Canadian trust distributions as qualified dividends. At this writing, the law is still at a very early stage of discussion, and it's unclear what the likelihood of its passage will be. If it is passed, tax reporting for income trusts will change, and they will likely be taxed similarly to other forms of income. Even so, their strong returns will still make income trusts a worthwhile investment.

How to Pick an Income Trust or MLP

Roger Conrad has spent the last fifteen years studying the ins and outs of income investing, including income trusts and master limited partnerships for his newsletters, *Canadian Edge* and *Utility Forecasting*. I asked him recently which were the most important metrics to look at when picking an income trust or MLP. Here's his advice:

Income Trusts

Payout ratio. Payout ratio is the ratio of dividends to distributable cash flow, less maintenance capital expenditures. Many trusts do this calculation for you, and provide their payout ratio. I look for a payout ratio of 60 to 80 percent. Cash flow should account for most of the distribution amounts.

Debt as a ratio of yearly operating cash flow. In addition to healthy payouts, you want an entity that isn't saddled with too much debt. Look for a debt to cash flow ratio of no more than 1.5 to 1, ideally 1 to 1, or even less.

Price to book value. A classic valuation measure for all types of companies. Consider all assets, minus debt, making sure your numbers are up to date. Divide by the number of shares to determine equity per share. Compare this number with actual share price. As a very general rule, the lower the price to book ratio, the better off you are, as more of your investment is backed by the company's actual assets. I look for equities with price to book value of 2 to 1 or less. For comparison, the average price to book value for S&P 500 companies is about 3 to 1.

Recently issued shares. The main reason I advocate buying Canadian income trusts rather than U.S. royalty trusts is that the Canadian entities don't face a limited life span. Rather than just depleting their assets, as U.S. royalty trusts must do, the Canadian trusts can keep their business going, raising capital with debt or by issuing shares. They can then use this capital to acquire new assets or conduct new exploration that will keep revenues coming in after the original well or mine is depleted. On the other hand, if they issue too many shares they can severely dilute yields, so frequent or recent issuances of shares should be something of a red flag. If a trust has issued large numbers of shares recently, be doubly sure to check its price against its book value to confirm it's still a good buy. This will become especially important beginning in 2011, when the new taxation will also exert downward pressure on yields.

Master Limited Partnerships

Payout ratio. Look for a payout ratio of 1.2 or 1.1 to 1.

Focus on infrastructure. The more tightly the MLP is focused on providing infrastructure, such as pipelines, the more solid an investment it is. (The description of the MLP on its Web site or offering materials should tell you what its assets are and exactly what mix of products and services it provides.)

Debt in relation to infrastructure. Also, the more the MLP is focused on providing infrastructure, the more debt it can safely carry. For infrastructure-based MLPs, a debt to cash flow ratio of 2 to 1 or even 3 to 1 is acceptable.

Limited exposure to energy prices. Look for MLPs with capacity-based contracts that will make money whether energy prices are high or low.

And don't forget: If you don't want to do the math yourself, check out my suggestions for income trusts and MLPs in the Resources section of this chapter.

Lower Your Risk—Income Trusts

1. Buy well-established trusts with substantial assets.
2. Consider these long-term, not short-term, investments.
3. Buy trusts for taxable, not nontaxable accounts.
4. For U.S. investors, make sure you understand tax credit rules, and make sure to obtain detailed information, usually available on the trust's Web site, that you can attach to your tax return, if needed, showing what taxes were paid in Canada.

Lower Your Risk—Master Limited Partnerships

1. Buy partnerships that focus on infrastructure, especially pipelines.
2. Invest for the long term (but not for tax-free accounts).
3. Consider an MLP fund rather than investing directly in MLPs.

Income Trust/MLP Action Plan

1. Pick the right investment type for you. Do you want to ride the wave of huge profits that go with endlessly climbing energy prices? Then income trusts may be the right choice for you. Keep in mind that yield levels may change in 2011, when the new taxation goes into effect.

Would you rather give up some of the huge growth for more stable share prices and dependable yields? Then MLPs may be the better option. If you'd like to reduce risk even further—or if you want to buy for a tax-free account, such as an IRA, consider MLP funds.

2. Do a little homework. Once you've decided which type of investment is right for you, check the Resources section of this chapter. There you'll find a wide range of choices, with contact information and Web sites, so you can find out more about those that interest you. You'll also find information on newsletters and Web sites where you can learn even more about these investments.

3. Decide how much to invest. Remember, these should be regarded as long-term investments, so if you're planning to withdraw the money in six months or a year, you should probably choose a different investment option. (Don't worry! Upcoming chapters will teach you about other investment choices that are more appropriate for short-term investing.)

4. Set up dividend reinvestment plans. One of the great advantages of income trusts and MLPs is that they pay monthly or quarterly dividends, which can compound nicely if you set them up to reinvest in more shares. Dividend reinvestment can keep your investment growing, even when share prices are on the decline.

Resources

Newsletters/Web Sites

Carla Pasternak's & Paul Tracy's High-Yield Investing
Published by:
StreetAuthority, LLC
P.O. Box 83217
Gaithersburg, MD 20883-3217
301-762-3336
www.streetauthority.com
This newsletter focuses entirely on income-oriented investing, including both income trusts and MLPs. It's published monthly, and comes with mid-month updates, investment listings, and special reports. Full of good recommendations on which stocks or funds deserve your attention.

Roger Conrad's Canadian Edge
Utility Forecaster
Published by:
KCI Communications, Inc.
7600A Leesburg Pike
West Building, Suite 300
Falls Church, VA 22043
800-832-2330
www.kci-com.com
Canadian Edge covers Canadian income trusts, while *Utility Forecaster* is entirely devoted to the utility industry, including MLPs. Both can help you gain an education in energy investing, and both offer solid advice about what to buy now.

Association:
Canadian Association of Income Trust Investors (CAITI)
www.caiti.info
Several advocacy groups sprang up in the aftermath of Canada's move to tax income trusts. Needless to say, their main objective was to change or miti-

gate the new taxation law. CAITI is an association for investors and, though it was brand-new as this book went to press, it is planning to provide a wide variety of services for investors, beyond legislative advocacy. For instance, CAITI says it will provide access to a resource library for its members. It's inexpensive to join, and worth taking a look.

Top 20 Income Trusts

Here (in alphabetical order) are my top 20 selections for Canadian income trusts that have performed well over the years:

A&W Revenue Royalties Income Fund
(TSE symbol T.AW.UN)
300-171 West Esplanade
North Vancouver, BC V7M 3K9
Canada
604-988-2141
www.awincomefund.ca
A&W Revenue Royalties Income Fund is a limited-purpose trust. It invests solely in A&W Trade Marks Inc., which owns the A&W trademarks and licenses A&W Food Services of Canada Inc. to franchise and operate A&W restaurants.

Acadian Timber Income Trust
(TSE symbol T.ADN.UN)
Suite 2050
Royal Centre
1055 West Georgia Street
Vancouver, BC V6E 3R5
Canada
416-956-5154
www.acadiantimber.com
Acadian Timber Income Fund is an open-end, limited-purpose trust that is a supplier of primary forest products in eastern Canada and the northeastern United States.

Advantage Energy Income Fund
(NYSE symbol AAV)
Petro-Canada Centre
West Tower
3100 150-6 Avenue SW
Calgary, AB T2P 3Y7

Canada
403-261-8810
www.advantageincome.com
Advantage Energy Income Fund is an open-end oil and gas royalty trust whose principal business is to indirectly acquire and hold interests in petroleum and natural gas properties and related assets throughout Canada.

ARC Energy Trust
(TSE symbol T.AET.UN)
2100, 440-2nd Avenue SW
Calgary, AB T2P 5E9
Canada
www.arcenergytrust.com
ARC Energy Trust is an oil and gas royalty trust that invests in all types of energy-business-related assets, including petroleum and natural-gas-related assets, and gathering, processing, and transportation assets.

Baytex Energy Trust
(NYSE symbol BTE)
Suite 2200
205-5th Avenue SW
Calgary, AB T2P 2V7
Canada
403-269-4282
www.baytex.ab.ca
Baytex Energy Trust is an open-end investment trust with heavy and light crude oil and natural gas operations.

Canetic Resources Trust
(NYSE symbol CNE)
1900, 255-5th Avenue SW
Calgary, AB T2P 3G6
Canada
403-539-6300
www.canetictrust.com
Canetic Resources Trust is a royalty trust engaged in the development and acquisition of oil and natural gas reserves in Western Canada.

Canexus Income Fund
(TSE symbol T.CUS.UN)
801-7th Avenue SW
Calgary, AB T2P 3P7

Canada

403-571-7300

www.canexus.ca

Canexus Income Fund is an open-end trust that produces sodium chlorate and chlor-alkali products in several plants located in Canada and one in Brazil, largely for the pulp and paper and water treatment industries.

Cargojet Income Fund

(TSE symbol T.CJT.UN)

350 Britannia Road East

Units 5 & 6

Mississauga, ON L4Z 1X9

Canada

905-501-7373

www.cargojet.com

Cargojet Income Fund is a provider of time-sensitive overnight air cargo service with a co-load network that constitutes approximately 50 percent of Canada's domestic overnight air cargo capacity.

Cineplex Galaxy Income Fund

(TSE symbol: T.CGX.UN)

1303 Yonge Street

2nd Floor

Toronto, ON M4T 2Y9

Canada

416-323-6600

www.cineplex.com

Cineplex Galaxy Income Fund is an unincorporated, open-end, limited-purpose trust that operates movie theaters throughout Canada.

Enerplus Resources Fund

(NYSE symbol ERF)

The Dome Tower

Suite 3000

333-7th Avenue SW

Calgary, AB T2P 2Z1

Canada

403-298-2200

www.enerplus.com

Enerplus Resources Fund is an open-end investment trust producing oil and gas.

Fording Canadian Coal Trust
(NYSE symbol FDG)
205-9th Avenue SE
Suite 1000
Calgary, AB T2G 0R3
Canada
403-260-9800
www.fording.ca
Fording Canadian Coal Trust is an open-end mutual fund trust that mines and produces coal from its mines in Canada and the United States.

Harvest Energy Trust
(NYSE symbol HTE)
Suite 2100
330-5th Avenue SW
Calgary, AB T2P 0L4
Canada
403-265-1178
www.harvestenergy.ca
Harvest Energy Trust is an integrated energy trust with operations in the production, refining, and marketing of petroleum and natural gas.

The Keg Royalties Income Fund
(TSE symbol T.KEG.UN)
10100 Shellbridge Way
Richmond, BC V6X 2W7
Canada
604-821-6416
www.kegincomefund.com
The Keg Royalties Income Fund is an unincorporated open-end limited-purpose trust that owns the trademarks, trade names, operating procedures and systems, and other intellectual property (collectively, the Keg Rights) used in connection with the operation of Keg steakhouse restaurants and bars.

Pengrowth Energy Trust
(NYSE symbol PGH)
Petro-Canada Centre
East Tower
2900, 240-4th Avenue SW
Calgary, AB T2P 4H4
Canada

416-362-8191

www.pengrowth.com

Pengrowth Energy Trust is an energy trust producing oil coalbed methane and natural gas.

Penn West Energy Trust
(NYSE symbol PWE)
Suite 2200
425 First Street SW
Calgary, AB T2P 3L8
Canada
403-777-2500
www.pennwest.com

Penn West Energy Trust is an open-end investment trust that acquires and develops petroleum and natural gas properties in Canada.

Provident Energy Trust
(NYSE symbol PVX)
800 112-4th Avenue SW
Calgary, AB T2P 0H3
Canada
403-296-2233
www.providentenergy.com

Provident Energy Trust is an open-end investment trust created to hold all types of petroleum and natural-gas- and energy-related assets, including facilities of any kind, oil sands interests, electricity or power generating assets, and pipeline, gathering, processing, and transportation assets in Canada and the United States.

TimberWest Forest Corporation
(TSE symbol T.TWF.UN)
Suite 2300
1055 West Georgia
Vancouver, BC V6E 3P3
Canada
604-654-4600
www.timberwest.com

TimberWest Forest Corporation operates in the solid wood segment of the forest industry, engaged primarily in the harvesting and sale of logs.

Total Energy Services Fund
(TSE symbol T.TOT.UN)
520-5th Avenue SW

Suite 2410
Calgary, AB T2P 3R7
Canada
403-216-3939
www.totalenergy.ca
Total Energy Services Fund is an income trust that provides drilling and production services for oil and gas wells in Canada.

Vermillion Energy Trust
(TSE symbol T.VET.UN)
2800, 24th Avenue SW
Calgary, AB T2P 0J4
Canada
403-269-4884
www.vermilionresources.com
Vermilion Energy Trust is actively engaged in the business of oil and natural gas development, acquisition, and production in Canada, France, the Netherlands, and Australia.

Yellow Pages Income Fund
(TSE symbol T.YLO.UN)
16 Place du Commerce
Iles des Soeurs
Verdun, QC H3E 2A5
Canada
514-934-2611
www.ypg.com
Yellow Pages Income Fund is a telephone directories publisher and the owner of the Yellow Pages, Pages Jaunes, and Walking Fingers & Design trademarks and is the official publisher of Bell Canada's directories.

Master Limited Partnerships
Interested in investing in MLPs? Here are some that have performed well over time:

AmeriGas Partners LP (APU)
460 North Gulph Road
King of Prussia, PA 19406
610-337-7000
www.amerigas.com

The nation's largest propane company, serving over 1.3 million residential, commercial, industrial, agricultural, and motor fuel propane customers in nearly fifty states.

Atlas Pipeline Partners, L.P. (APL)
311 Rouser Road
Moon Township, PA 15108
412-262-2830
www.atlaspipelinepartners.com
Owns and operates natural gas pipeline gathering systems in eastern Ohio, western New York, and western Pennsylvania.

Boardwalk Pipeline Partners, LP (BWP)
3800 Frederica Street
Owensboro, KY 42301
270-926-8686
www.boardwalkpipelines.com
Engages in interstate transportation and storage of natural gas in the United States. Owns and operates two interstate pipeline systems with approximately 13,400 miles of pipeline.

Buckeye Partners LP (BPL)
9999 Hamilton Boulevard
Breinigsville, PA 18031
610-904-4000
www.buckeye.com
One of the largest independent refined petroleum products pipeline systems in the United States by volume, with approximately 5,400 miles of pipeline. Also owns and operates forty-nine refined petroleum products terminals in Illinois, Indiana, Massachusetts, Michigan, Missouri, New York, Ohio, Pennsylvania, and Wisconsin. Operates and maintains approximately 2,500 miles of pipeline under agreements with major oil and chemical companies.

Copano Energy LLC (CPNO)
2727 Allen Parkway
Suite 1200
Houston, TX 77019
713-621-9547
www.copanoenergy.com
Provides midstream natural gas services in the United States, including natural gas gathering and related compression and dehydration services, and natural gas processing in central and eastern Oklahoma and Texas' Gulf Coast.

Operates approximately 5,000 miles of natural gas gathering and transmission pipelines, as well as five natural gas processing plants.

Enbridge Energy Partners LP (EEP)
1100 Louisiana Street
Houston, TX 77002
713-821-2000
www.enbridgepartners.com
Provides crude oil and liquid petroleum gathering, transportation, and storage services in the United States. It also offers natural gas gathering, treating, marketing, transportation, and processing services.

Energy Transfer Partners LP (ETP)
2838 Woodside Street
Dallas, TX 75204
214-981-0700
www.energytransfer.com
Operates natural gas midstream, and transportation and storage businesses. The company owns and operates natural gas pipeline systems, and processing and treating plants through which it gathers, compresses, treats, blends, processes, and markets natural gas. It also transports natural gas from various natural gas producing areas through connections with other pipeline systems. In addition, the company operates natural gas storage facilities; and engages in the wholesale and retail of propane.

Enterprise Products Partners LP (EPD)
1100 Louisiana Street
10th Floor
Houston, TX 77002
713-381-6500
www.epplp.com
Provides services to producers and consumers of natural gas, natural gas liquids (NGL), crude oil, and petrochemicals in North America.

Ferrellgas Partners LP (FGP)
7500 College Boulevard
Suite 1000
Overland Park, KS 66210
913-661-1500
www.ferrellgas.com
Distributes propane and related equipment and supplies primarily in the United States. The company's propane is used in residential and commercial buildings, space heating, water heating, cooking agricultural applications, irri-

gation, weed control, among other uses. The company also operates common carrier services, wholesale marketing of propane appliances and propane, and sells refined fuels and carbon dioxide.

Inergy LP (NRGP)
2 Brush Creek Boulevard
Suite 200
Kansas City, MO 64112
816-842-8181
www.inergypropane.com
Provides retail and wholesale propane supply, marketing, and distribution in the United States. It markets propane products under various regional brand names, including, among others: Arrow Gas, Blue Flame, Bradley Propane, Burnwell Gas, Country Gas, Dowdle Gas, Gaylord Gas, Hancock Gas, Highland Propane, Hoosier Propane, Independent Propane, Maingas, McCracken, Modern Gas, Moulton Gas Service, Northwest Energy, Ohio Gas, Pearl Gas, Pro Gas, Pulver Gas, United Propane, and Tru-Gas.

Linn Energy, LLC (LINE)
JPMorgan Chase Tower
600 Travis
Houston, TX 77002
United States
713-223-0880
www.linnenergy.com
Engages in the development and acquisition of gas and oil properties in the United States. The company has oil and gas reserves in West Virginia, Pennsylvania, New York, Virginia, California, Oklahoma, and Texas.

Magellan Midstream Partners LP (MMP)
One Williams Center
Tulsa, OK 74172
918-574-7000
www.magellanlp.com
Engages in transportation, storage, and distribution of refined petroleum products in the United States. Pipeline system transports petroleum products and liquefied petroleum gases from the Gulf Coast refining region of Texas through the Midwest to Colorado, North Dakota, Minnesota, and Illinois. The company owns and operates marine terminals, which are storage and distribution facilities that handle refined petroleum products, blendstocks, ethanol, heavy oils, feedstocks, crude oils, and condensates, as well as inland terminals that deliver refined petroleum products transported on common

carrier interstate pipelines. The company's ammonia pipeline system transports ammonia from production facilities in Texas and Oklahoma to terminals in the Midwest.

NuStar Energy LP (NS)
(Formerly Valero LP)
One Valero Way
San Antonio, TX 78249
United States
210-345-2000
www.valerolp.com

Engages in crude oil and refined product transportation, terminaling, and storage in the United States, the Netherland Antilles, Canada, Mexico, the Netherlands, and the United Kingdom.

Oneok Partners LP (OKS)
100 West Fifth Street
Tulsa, OK 74103-4298
918-588-7000
www.oneokpartners.com

Engages in the ownership and management of natural gas gathering, processing, storage, and interstate and intrastate pipeline assets, as well as natural gas liquids (NGLs) gathering and distribution pipelines, and storage and fractionators in the United States.

Rio Vista Energy Partners LP (RVEP)
820 Gessner Road
Suite 1285
Houston, TX 77024
713-467-8235
www.riovistaenergy.com

Engages in the purchase, transportation, and sale of liquefied petroleum gas (LPG). It owns and operates LPG terminal facilities in Brownsville, Texas, and in Matamoros, Tamaulipas, Mexico, as well as approximately twenty-three miles of pipelines, which connect the Brownsville Terminal Facility to the Matamoros Terminal Facility. The company primarily markets its LPG in the northeastern region of Mexico.

Suburban Propane Partners LP (SPH)
240 Route 10 West
Whippany, NJ 07981
973-887-5300
www.suburbanpropane.com

Engages in distribution and marketing of propane, fuel oil, and refined fuels, as well as the marketing of natural gas and electricity in deregulated markets. The partnership serves approximately 1 million residential, commercial, industrial, and agricultural customers through approximately 300 locations in thirty states located primarily in the East and West Coast regions of the United States.

Teekay LNG Partners LP (TGP)
Bayside Executive Park
West Bay Street & Blake Road
P.O. Box AP-59212
Nassau, The Bahamas
242-502-8820
www.teekaylng.com
Provides marine transportation services for liquefied natural gas (LNG), liquefied petroleum gas (LPG), and crude oil worldwide. It transports various LPGs, including propane, butane, and ethane; petrochemical gases, such as ethylene, propylene, and butadiene; and ammonia. Owns and operates seven LNG carriers, one LPG carrier, and eight Suezmax-class crude oil tankers.

Terra Nitrogen Co. LP (TNH)
Terra Centre
P.O. Box 6000
600 Fourth Street
Sioux City, IA 51102-6000
712-277-1340
www.terranitrogen.com
Engages in the production and distribution of nitrogen fertilizer products for use in agricultural and industrial markets. Its nitrogen products include anhydrous ammonia, a form of nitrogen fertilizer and the feedstock for the production of other nitrogen fertilizers, such as urea ammonium nitrate solutions (UAN). Terra also produces UAN by combining urea solution and ammonium nitrate solution. It sells its products primarily in the Central and Southern Plains and Corn Belt regions of the United States.

US Shipping Partners LP (USS)
399 Thornall Street
8th Floor
Edison, NJ 08837
732-635-1500
www.usslp.com
Provides long-haul marine transportation services to oil and gas companies, primarily for refined petroleum products in the United States. It also engages in

the coastwise transportation of petrochemical and commodity chemical products. Fleet consists of ten tank vessels, including six integrated tug barge units, one product tanker, and three chemical parcel tankers.

Master Limited Partnership Mutual Funds

Want to minimize risk with your MLP investment? Then check out MLP mutual funds. These closed-end funds trade stability and diversification for slightly lower yields than single MLPs sometimes offer—but with baseline yields so high, they're still an attractive investment. Here are four funds to consider:

Energy Income And Growth Fund (FEN)
First Trust Portfolios L.P.
1001 Warrenville Road
Suite 300
Lisle, Il 60532
800-621-1675
www.ftportfolios.com (search ticker FEN)
One of several First Trust funds, this fund's investment objective is to seek a high level of after-tax total return with an emphasis on current distributions paid to shareholders, generally on a quarterly basis.

Fiduciary/Claymore MLP Opportunity Fund (FMO)
Claymore Advisors, LLC
2455 Corporate West Drive
Lisle, IL 60532
888-991-0091
www.fiduciaryclaymore.com
Under normal market conditions, this fund invests at least 80 percent of its managed assets in MLPs, and at least 65 percent in equity securities of MLP entities, primarily in the energy, natural resources, and real estate sectors.

Kayne Anderson MLP Investment Company (KYN)
1800 Avenue of the Stars
2nd Floor
Los Angeles, CA 90067
877-MLP-FUND
www.kaynemlp.com
Invests at least 85 percent of total assets (including borrowings) in energy-related master limited partnerships and their affiliates.

Tortoise Energy Infrastructure Corp. (TYG)
Tortoise Capital Advisors, L.L.C.
10801 Mastin Boulevard, Suite 222
Overland Park, KS 66210
866-362-9331
www.tortoiseadvisors.com/tyg.cfm
One of several investment companies managed by Tortoise Capital Advisors, Tortoise Energy Infrastructure is designed to provide an efficient vehicle to invest in a portfolio of publicly traded master limited partnerships and their affiliates in the energy infrastructure sector.

CHAPTER

4

Many Happy Returns—Earn Fast Profits with High-Yield Equities

It's investing 101: You buy stocks for long-term growth, hoping their price per share will increase with time. Yes they pay dividends—sometimes—but in amounts that are usually inconsequential. If what you want is income, you buy something else—bonds, probably, or perhaps Treasury bills.

This is what many small investors are taught—*and it's completely wrong!* Buying high-yielding stocks in order to earn income from their dividends is a great way to make fast profits and lower your risk. In fact, no matter what your investing goal, there are many reasons why buying stocks for their dividends might be the smartest way to make money in the market.

In this chapter, I'll show you why picking stocks for their dividends is better than picking them for their potential growth. I'll highlight my favorite categories of high-yield stocks, the benefits of each, and some good examples of equities you might want to consider for your portfolio. And I'll tell you about some funds designed to take full advantage of the high-yield market. But first, a snapshot:

SNAPSHOT: Investing in High-Yield Stock

How It Works:

Rather than comparing stock prices and trying to anticipate which ones have potential for growth, investing in high-yield stocks means looking to dividends, rather than price increases to make your money grow.

THE UPSIDE:

- Cash in Hand: With a growth stock, you can't cash in until you sell—and pay capital gains tax. But when your payoff comes from dividends, that's money you can use right away to pay your bills, invest in other instruments, or increase your holding of stock by reinvesting.
- Greater Stability: High-yield stocks generally are more stable than low-yield ones.
- Protection in Bad Times: If the price of your stock falls, the fact that your earnings are paid in cash will preserve at least some of your profits.

THE DOWNSIDE:

- Earlier Taxes: Dividends are income, which is taxed in the year it is earned. If you buy and hold a stock that pays little or no dividends but increases in value, you won't have to pay taxes until the stock is sold.
- Less Growth: High-yield stock may see less appreciation in underlying share value than pure growth stock. However, if you want to grow your investment, you can do so by automatically investing your dividends in more stock.
- Some Study Required: You will have to spend at least a little time learning what category of stock (or mutual fund) makes most sense to you, and keeping an eye on the stock and/or its industry.

Who Should Invest:

Some high-yield companies probably belong in most stock portfolios—keeping in mind that risks tend to be higher than with the most established growth stocks. Receiving dividend income should be particularly appealing to those contemplating retirement—or anyone else who needs ongoing income.

The Case for Yield Over Growth

Imagine you buy 100 shares of stock at $10, giving you a portfolio worth $1,000. The company has a good year and the share price rises by 25 percent. You're very pleased: Your portfolio is now worth $1,250. But then, disaster strikes. The company treasurer is indicted for embezzling. Overnight, the share price loses 25 percent of its value, dropping to $937.50. All of a sudden, you're not so happy.

Now, imagine a different scenario. Your 100 shares of stock pay *dividends* of 25 percent, or $250. Again, you're happy with a $1,250 portfolio. This time, when the treasurer is caught embezzling and the stock value tumbles 25 percent, you wind up back at $1,000—you haven't profited, but you haven't lost either. Because, while the company's share price may have tumbled, *the value of the cash it paid you did not change.*

This is one of the biggest benefits of investing in high-yield stock: You get to take your profits in today's cash, not in a rising share price that could sink again tomorrow. But there are many other advantages to buying for dividends rather than growth. Here are some more:

1. You can cash in without cashing out. Let's say you need some cash for an unexpected expense or investment opportunity. You're holding a growth stock that has appreciated, and you want to use some of that money. Your only option is to sell some of your shares. This will mean paying capital gains tax, and those shares will no longer be earning money for you. With dividends, you regularly receive cash that you can use for other expenses—and you can leave your shares in place, to continue earning for you.

2. Taxes may not be as bad as you thought. The top tax rate on dividends for most investors is now 15 percent, a rate that is in effect at least until 2010. (The tax rate for most capital gains is also 15 percent.) In lower tax brackets, the dividend tax rate is 10 percent. Keep in mind, however, that you'll have to pay the taxes in the year the dividend is earned, rather than wait to pay them when you sell your stock, as you would with capital gains tax.

3. Paying dividends often indicates a company is financially healthy. Companies or their accountants can make profits appear better than they are, depending on how they choose to present financial information. But paying dividends to shareholders requires producing real cash earnings, plain and simple, and only a company with sufficient cash on hand, or a substantial line of credit, can afford to do it.

4. Companies paying dividends tend to have more stable share prices. This makes perfect sense if you think about it. An investor buys a growth stock in the hopes that the price will rise. If it doesn't, he or she will eventually sell the shares and go looking for something more profitable. And if prices do rise, he or she might sell the stock anyhow to do some profit taking.

People who buy shares in order to collect dividends are less likely to react immediately to share price fluctuations, because they never really expected to make as much money from share price increases, but from regularly paid dividends.

How High Is "High"?

Before we get into the specific types of high-yield stocks, let's take a quick look at the field as a whole. First let's start with the question— how high is "high-yield"? Different experts have different criteria for calling something a high-yielding investment, but for the purposes of this chapter I'm defining "high-yield" as paying dividends over the course of a year that are equal to or greater than 5 percent of the share price. To be clear, I'm counting dividends only—price appreciation, while most welcome of course—does not count toward the 5 percent.

Five percent annual dividends may not seem like much—indeed, you can get nearly that return from a risk-free investment such as a Treasury bill. However, it's a lot higher dividend than most large companies currently pay. At this writing, the companies of the S&P 500 paid an average annual dividend of less than 2 percent of their share price. It's interesting to note that over the past eighty years, more companies paid higher dividends than do now, and that in that period, two-thirds of the money made by investors in S&P 500 companies came from dividends. Dividends fell out of favor during the 1990s, but since the turn of the twenty-first century, more large companies are offering meaningful dividend amounts. This is good news for the high-yield investors.

Okay, so if 5 percent is considered a minimum return for our high-yield stocks, what's the maximum—how high can returns go?

Depending on the stock in question, they can reach into the double dig-its, but as always, there's higher risk to go with the higher payoffs. "Higher yield equals higher risk, generally," says Carla Pasternak, edi-tor, with Paul Tracy, of the newsletter *High-Yield Investing*, which examines every aspect of the high-yield marketplace. "I'm constantly trying to find the highest yield with the lowest risk." The best way to lower your risk, she adds, is to do your homework—carefully study a company or mutual fund before you invest.

One question you should ask yourself is why the fund or company is paying high yields. There are many different possible answers. In some cases, such as income trusts discussed in Chapter 3, or real estate invest-ment trusts (REITS), the company is structured to "pass through" most of the profits it makes directly to investors. In other cases, high divi-dends can be a way of deliberately stabilizing the stock price by discour-aging people from selling. In effect, they are paying shareholders not to sell their shares.

Which brings me to another point: When evaluating a company's yield over time, be aware of how changes in share price can artificially affect yield. Let's say you own one share of X company that you bought for $20. Dividend payment time comes, and the company issues you $1—for a 5 percent yield.

Then a year goes by and the company's industry suffers a setback. Your $20 share is now trading at $10. Dividend time rolls around, and you are once again paid $1. However, with the new, lower share price, that $1 now represents a 10 percent yield on your investment. Nothing got better—in fact, things got much worse—but dividend as a percent-age of share price—known as the payout ratio—has doubled. You want to be aware of these kinds of factors when evaluating a company's divi-dend performance over time.

Getting in the High-Yield Game

Now that I've given you a quick look at some of the principles behind high-yield investing, let's take a look at the specifics. There are several different approaches to investing in high-yield stocks, and some indus-tries that tend to deliver those high dividend numbers. Income trusts and master limited partnerships are two categories of companies that routinely offer very high yields, which we explored in the previous chapter. In this chapter, I'll take a close look at some of them, along with some specific companies that might be worth buying:

High-Yield Industries

Oil Tankers

"Shipping companies tend to have assets that churn out cash flow, which they use to pay shareholders," according to Pasternak. The idea, she says, is to try to stabilize share price in an extremely volatile industry.

Like oil itself, she explains, oil shipping is a commodity and subject to rapid ups and downs as market conditions change. "If OPEC reduces oil production output to buoy prices, then tanker rates go down because of the oversupply of tankers on the market." In this kind of situation—and despite paying high dividends—share prices can drop 50 percent in a couple of days. In short, this is not an investment for the faint of heart.

If you do decide to invest in tankers, Pasternak advises thoroughly studying a company before buying its stock. "You really have to look into the company itself—and into its order book, to judge what the demand is," she says. How do you do this research? Oil shipping companies sometimes publish a list of their current charter contracts and rates as part of their quarterly financial presentations for investors, and you can often find this type of information in the investor pages of their Web sites.

Recommended Investments:

Frontline Ltd.
(NYSE symbol FRO)
Par-la-Ville Place
14 Par-la-Ville Road
Hamilton, HM 08
Bermuda
441-295-6935
www.frontline.com

Frontline is engaged primarily in the ownership and operation of oil tankers, including oil/bulk/ore (OBO) carriers.

Knightsbridge Tankers
(NASDAQ symbol VLCCF)
Par-la-Ville Place
14 Par-la-Ville Road
Hamilton HM 08
Bermuda
468-613-3030
www.knightsbridgetankers.com
Knightsbridge Tankers is an international tanker company whose primary business activity is the international seaborne transportation of crude oil.

Double Hull Tankers
(NYSE symbol DHT)
26 New Street
St. Helier, Jersey
UK
(44)1534-639759
www.dhtankers.com
Double Hull Tankers operates a fleet of double hull tankers.

Utilities

As this book was going to press, there were few utilities paying in the 5 percent and above dividend range. However, utilities traditionally have been a good source of high dividends. I asked Roger Conrad, editor of the newsletters *Utility Forecast* and *Canadian Edge,* and associate editor of *Personal Finance.* He is a top expert in the area of utility investing.

"Traditional utilities historically offered yields of 5 percent and up," he says. "A number still do, but many of the companies are now plowing a lot of the money back into the business for debt reduction, new assets, and capital investment." Eventually, he adds, this reinvestment in the business will slow. At that point, utilities will begin offering higher dividends again. "Utilities are still a prime business for generating a lot of cash flow, which is where dividends come from," he says. "So even if yields are low at the moment, this is a dividend-friendly business."

Recommended Investments:

Consolidated Edison Inc.
(NYSE symbol ED)
4 Irving Place
New York, NY 10003
212-460-4600
www.conedison.com
Con Edison is the holding company of Con Edison of New York and Orange and Rockland Utilities, both of which are regulated electric, gas, and steam utilities.

FairPoint Communications
(NYSE symbol FRP)
521 East Morehead Street
Suite 250
Charlotte, NC 28202
704-344-8150
www.fairpoint.com
FairPoint Communications is a provider of communications services in rural and small urban communities, offering an array of services, including local and long-distance voice, data, Internet, and broadband product offerings.

KeySpan Corporation
(NYSE symbol KSE)
One MetroTech Center
Brooklyn, NY 11201
718-403-1000
www.keyspanenergy.com
KeySpan Corporation operates in the gas distribution, electric services, energy services, and energy investments segments.

Business Development Corporations

This is a special class of company, created by an act of Congress in 1980, whose purpose, as its name suggests, is to invest in small companies and help them grow their businesses. At least 90 percent of their taxable income is returned to shareholders in the form of dividends.

BDCs have always been a good source for high dividends. At this writing, however, some are experiencing lower yields than usual. In part, Pasternak says, this is because of competition from large private equity firms with deep reserves of cash, engaging in leveraged buyouts of some of the companies the BDCs might otherwise invest in. The result, Pasternak says, is a bidding war, in which BDCs can't invest as profitably as in the past. As economic circumstances change, however, this may change too, and BDC yields may increase.

Recommended Investments:

Capital Source
(NYSE symbol CSE)
4445 Willard Avenue
12th Floor
Chevy Chase, MD 20815
800-370-9431
www.capitalsource.com
Capital Source is a commercial lending, investment, and asset management company focused on the middle market. The company operates as a real estate investment trust (REIT) and provides senior and subordinated commercial loans, invests in real estate, engages in asset management and servicing activities, and invests in residential mortgage assets.

Gramercy Capital Corporation
(NYSE symbol GKK)
420 Lexington Avenue
New York, NY 10170
212-297-1000
www.gramercycapitalcorp.com
Gramercy Capital is a commercial real estate specialty finance company that specializes in the direct origination and acquisition of real estate loans and securities, including whole loans, bridge loans, subordinate interests in whole loans, distressed debt, mortgage-backed securities, mezzanine loans, preferred equity, and net lease investments involving commercial properties throughout the United States.

Allied Capital Corporation
(NYSE symbol ALD)

1919 Pennsylvania Avenue, NW
Washington, DC 20006
202-721-6100
www.alliedcapital.com

Allied Capital Corporation is engaged in the private equity business. The company provides long-term debt and equity capital primarily to private middle market companies in a variety of industries.

High-Yield Instruments

Convertible Bonds

Convertible bonds are a hybrid of corporate bonds and stock. They start out life as bonds, paying a specified yield with a specified maturity. And they can end life that way too, if the price of the underlying stock goes down. However, if it goes up, convertible bonds can be converted to shares of stock, at a price determined when the bond is issued. The issuing company also has the right to convert bonds into shares, and this usually happens if the price of the stock rises above its preset conversion price. Since there are a lot of variables, you should know the specific rules for your convertible bond before you buy.

In essence, convertible bonds offer some measure of downside protection while allowing their owners to still play the market. They can offer the best of both worlds. If the stock price tanks, you simply hold the bond until maturity and earn interest from it. If the price rises, you can convert it into a stock that's gaining value.

Having the safety net of the bond in place may allow some investors to take a chance on companies that are less financially solid than they normally would. This can be a big opportunity to earn higher yields because, as we know, the higher the risk, the higher the return is likely to be. But the bond offers protection only to a point, because if the company does *really* badly—is forced out of business or files for bankruptcy protection—you wind up with nothing. So, once again, it's important to do your homework and carefully check out the company behind any less-than-investment-grade (BBB or less) convertible bonds before you buy them.

Recommended Investments:

Schlumberger 2.125% convertible
Schlumberger
5599 San Felipe
17th Floor
Houston, TX 77056
713-375-3535
www.slb.com
Schlumberger is one of the largest oil services firms in the world.

Walt Disney 2.125% convertible
The Walt Disney Company
500 South Buena Vista Street
Burbank, CA 91521-9722
818-560-1000
http://corporate.disney.go.com
Disney is one of the largest media and entertainment companies in the world.

Electronic Data Systems (EDS) 3.875% convertible
EDS
5400 Legacy Drive
Plano, TX 75024
972 604 6000
www.eds.com
EDS is one of the largest information management companies in the world.

In addition to these companies, there are about eighty open-end mutual funds that specialize in convertibles. Here are six of my favorites:

Calamos Convertible Fund
800-823-7386
www.calamos.com

Columbia Convertible Securities
800-345-6611
www.columbiafunds.com

Fidelity Convertible Securities
800-544-8544
www.fidelity.com

Franklin Convertible Securities
800-632-2301
www.franklintempleton.com

Putnam Convertible Income Fund
800-225-1581
www.putnaminvestments.com

Vanguard Convertible Securities Fund
800-662-6273
www.vanguard.com

Preferred Stock

These instruments are equities, but bear some similarities to corporate bonds. Like bonds, they pay a set amount on a set date, although since these are equities, the payments are defined as dividends rather than interest. This can be an important distinction if the company finds itself in a cash crunch, because it has a legal obligation to pay bond interest on schedule, but can suspend dividend payments to preferred stock owners. However, these payments take precedence over dividends to common shareholders and must be paid first.

Unlike bonds, preferreds have no maturity date and could theoretically go on forever. However, many preferreds can be converted to shares of common stock at the investor's option, and they may all be "called"—converted into common stock—at the discretion of the issuer, after a specific date. Unlike common stock, by the way, preferreds usually carry no voting rights.

The big advantage of preferreds is that they offer a predetermined income, which often compares favorably to interest rates on bonds, as well as the flexibility to trade them in for common stock if it stock prices are on the rise.

Recommended Investments:

General Motors 7.5% Preferred
(NYSE symbol GMS)
300 Renaissance Center
Detroit, MI 48265
313-556-5000
www.gm.com
General Motors Corporation is primarily engaged in the worldwide development, production, and marketing of cars, trucks, and parts.

Flaherty & Crumrine Preferred Income Fund
(NYSE symbol PFD)
301 East Colorado Boulevard
Suite 720
Pasadena, CA 91101
626-795-7300
www.flaherty-crumrine.com
Flaherty & Crumrine Preferred Income Fund is a diversified closed-end management investment company whose investment objective is to provide high current income consistent with the preservation of capital. The fund invests in a diversified portfolio of preferred securities.

Pacific Gas & Electric 6% Preferred
(AMEX Symbol PCG-A)
One Market
Spear Tower
San Francisco, CA 94105
415-267-7000
www.pgecorp.com
PG&E Corporation is an energy-based holding company that engages primarily in the businesses of electricity and natural gas distribution, electricity generation, procurement and transmission, and natural gas procurement, transportation, and storage.

Real Estate Investment Trusts (REITs)

REITs are similar to income trusts in that they own and operate money-making real estate and are obliged by law to distribute the bulk of their earnings directly to investors (and avoid being taxed on them at the corporate level). As with income trusts, the nature of REITs is to pay dividends, and when the real estate markets are strong, REITs can easily produce very high yields indeed.

There are two types of REITs: those that own actual property (buying and selling or renting it), and those that deal specifically with mortgages, either buying mortgages on the secondary markets or issuing them themselves. Mortgage REITs tend to do badly in an environment where interest rates are going up, because they have to borrow large sums in order to fund the mortgages. Nevertheless, both equity REITs and mortgage REITs can offer a good opportunity to invest at higher than 5 percent returns.

Recommended Investments:

Cedar Shopping Centers
(NYSE symbol CDR)
44 South Bayles Avenue
Suite 304
Port Washington, NY 11050
516-767-6492
www.cedarshoppingcenters.com
Cedar Shopping Centers is a real estate company that focuses primarily on ownership, operation, development, and redevelopment of supermarket-anchored community shopping centers and drugstore-anchored convenience centers.

NorthStar Realty Finance
(NYSE Symbol NRF)
399 Park Avenue
18th Floor
New York, New York 10022
212-547-2600
www.nrfc.com
NorthStar Realty Finance is a real estate finance company that focuses primarily on originating and acquiring real estate debt, real estate securities, and net lease properties.

Medical Properties Trust
(NYSE symbol MPW)
100 Urban Center Drive
Suite 501

Birmingham, AL 35242

205-969-3755

www.medicalpropertiestrust.com

Medical Properties Trust is a real estate investment trust that acquires, develops, leases, and makes other investments in health care facilities providing health care services.

Mutual Funds

Mutual funds can be a great way to get into the high-yield market and mitigate some of the risk. Mutual funds offer a more diversified portfolio, and the expertise of a trained manager choosing which companies to invest in, all of which may make them a safer way to try out some of the high-yield markets.

As always, with mutual funds, one drawback is the need to pay managers annual management fees of 1 to 2 percent of assets, which can have the effect of lowering yields. Still, this is a great way for small investors, especially those who want to reduce risk, to try out high-yield investing.

Closed-end or open-end? Open-end, or traditional, mutual funds are a way for many investors to pool their resources and have a pro manage a large portfolio on their behalf. The fund manager invests the money in the fund, or sells investments when fund participants wish to withdraw money. This can mean that fund managers are forced to sell assets when prices are down, instead of being able to wait for an upturn.

This is not an issue in closed-end funds, where assets are already owned, and new investors don't invest by directly adding their money to the pool—or withdrawing it when they want to cash out. Instead, they buy and sell shares of the fund, which are traded on the exchanges, like any other stock.

Like any other stock, the share price of closed-end funds is determined not by its underlying assets or some other set formula, but simply by what investors are willing to pay for it. This means the fund might be trading at a *premium* over its net asset value, or a *discount* off its net asset value. Knowing the net asset value is important when deciding whether to invest in a high-yield closed-end fund.

Buying a fund at a discount to what the asset shares actually represent is likely to be a good deal, but even buying at a premium can make sense; it depends on how dividends are paid, whether dividend payments are in part return of capital (which would erode net assets), and what the trend in value is. Pasternak says: "If you're at a premium, but the net asset value is growing, that may not be a danger sign."

Recommended Investments:

Zweig Total Return Fund
(NYSE symbol ZTR)
900 Third Avenue
31st Floor
New York, NY 10022
212-451-1100
www.phoenixinvestments.com

The Zweig Total Return Fund is a closed-end diversified management investment company that invests in various sectors, including U.S. government securities, financials, information technology, agency non-mortgage backed securities, health care, consumer staples, industrials, and others.

BlackRock Enhanced Government Fund
(NYSE symbol EGF)
800 Scudders Mill Road
Plainsboro, NJ 08536
609-282-1212
www.blackrock.com

BlackRock Enhanced Government Fund is a diversified closed-end management investment company that seeks to provide current income and gains by investing primarily in a portfolio of U.S. government securities and U.S. government agency securities, including mortgage-backed securities. The fund writes call options (see Chapter 7 for an explanation of call options) on individual or baskets of U.S. government or agency securities, or other debt securities held by the fund, in an attempt to generate gains from option premiums.

ING Global Equity Dividend and Premium Opportunity Fund
(NYSE symbol IGD)
7337 E. Doubletree Ranch Road
Scottsdale, AZ 85258

800-992-0180

www.ing.com

ING Global Equity Dividend and Premium Opportunity Fund is a nondiversified, closed-end management investment company whose primary investment objective is to provide a high level of income. The fund invests in a portfolio of global common stocks that have a history of dividend yields. It writes covered call options on a substantial portion of the portfolio of common stocks held in its portfolio.

Is the world of high-yield investing for you? Some high-yield investments may carry somewhat higher risk than blue chip stocks or government bonds, but there are opportunities for really impressive returns. And remember—once a dividend has been paid, it's yours! No matter how much share prices fall, nothing can take that money back again.

CAPTURE IT IF YOU CAN!

The purpose of buying high-yield stock is to earn dividends, and most companies pay dividends once a quarter. Since they don't all pay on the same day, wouldn't it make sense to buy stock in these companies shortly before the dividend was paid, hold the stock long enough to qualify for the dividend, then sell it again shortly thereafter, and find another about-to-pay company to buy?

Indeed it would, and this strategy, termed "dividend capture," has been adopted by many high-yield investors and even some new mutual funds. Dividend capture can dramatically increase your dividend revenues by giving you more opportunities to collect dividends each year. By law, in order to pay the new 15 percent tax rate on dividend income, you need to hold the stock in question for a minimum of sixty-one days, but even so, there are six sixty-one-day periods in a year, allowing you to collect dividends six times (if you time it correctly), rather than the four times you would collect if you were simply holding one stock. All things being equal, this strategy would increase your dividends by 50 percent (before trading fees).

To take advantage of dividend capture strategy, it helps to understand the schedule used when companies make dividend payments. Usually, the dividend is announced a few weeks before the payment date, along with an "of record" date, as in dividends will be paid to owners "of record" on X

continued

date. Shortly before the record date is the "ex-dividend" date—the date on which it becomes too late to qualify for the dividend. Those seeking dividend capture try to buy shortly before the ex-dividend date and (for tax purposes) usually hold the stock for sixty-one days before they sell it and go looking for the next dividend capture. The *High-Yield Investing* newsletter includes a listing of companies that have announced plans to pay substantial dividends in the coming weeks.

One caveat with a dividend capture strategy: Taking a short-term position in any stock can leave you selling at a loss, especially since share prices tend to fall on the ex-dividend date, and don't always bounce back. You can mitigate this risk (and, of course, spare yourself the work of frequent buying and selling) by investing in a dividend capture mutual fund instead. Though this approach has obvious advantages, one disadvantage is fees, which can be higher than with other types of funds because of the frequent trades. You should also find out whether the fund holds equities for sixty-one days in order to maintain its dividend income at the 15 percent tax level.

Recommended Investments:

John Hancock Patriot Premium Dividend Fund
(NYSE symbol PDF)
601 Congress Street
Boston, MA 02210
617-663-3000
www.johnhancockfunds.com

John Hancock Patriot Premium Dividend Fund is a diversified closed-end management investment company whose investment objective is to provide a high current income together with capital growth. It invests in a portfolio of dividend-paying preferred and common stocks.

Nuveen Equity Premium Advantage Fund
(NYSE symbol JLA)
333 West Wacker Drive
Chicago, IL 60606
800-257-8787
www.nuveen.com

Nuveen Equity Premium Advantage Fund is a diversified closed-end management investment company whose investment objective is to provide a high current income together with capital growth. It invests in a portfolio of dividend-paying preferred and common stocks.

BlackRock Enhanced Dividend Achievers Trust
(NYSE symbol BDJ)
100 Bellevue Parkway
Mutual Fund Department
Wilmington, DE 19809
888-825-2257
www.blackrock.com

BlackRock Enhanced Dividend Achievers Trust is a diversified closed-end management investment company that seeks to provide long-term total return through a combination of current income and capital appreciation by investing in common stocks that pay above-average dividends and have the potential for capital appreciation.

Lower Your Risk—High-Yield Stock

1. Do your homework! Investigate the fundamentals of any company offering high dividends before you invest.
2. Spread your risk over many investments by choosing a mutual fund rather than a single company to invest in.
3. Hedge your bets even more by choosing a closed-end mutual fund whose shares are trading at a discount to its net asset value. If the portion of assets a share represents is actually worth more than what you paid for the share, you likely have made a solid investment.
4. Choose convertible bonds or preferred stock. These instruments offer a fixed rate of return (interest for bonds, dividends for stock), which means your investment should earn at least some money, no matter what happens to share prices.

High-Yield Investing Action Plan

1. Choose the right type of high-yield investment for you. Do you want preferred stock? Convertible bonds? A mutual fund where you can let someone else do the research for you? Pick an option that fits well with your overall investment goals and risk preferences.

2. Pick an industry that makes sense for you, from the dramatic ups and downs of oil tankers to the relative stability of utilities.

3. Research, research, research! If you're investing in a company, check into several years' worth of dividend performance, as well as fundamentals like earnings per share and cash flow.

4. If investing in a fund, review its past performance carefully.

5. Once you've invested, begin looking for your next high-yield choice. This is especially important if you are looking to try dividend capture investing, where you will need to pick a new investment every two months or more.

Resources

Book

The 25% Cash Machine: Double Digit Income Investing by Bryan Perry (Wiley, 2007).

Bryan Perry is an expert with many years' experience in income investing. In this comprehensive book he lays out a plan for building fast profits with double-digit income investing, as well as an approach to building a very strong portfolio using a combination of income and growth.

Newsletter

High-Yield Investing
Published by: StreetAuthority.com
P.O. Box 323
Williamsport, PA 17703-9966
(800) 796-8025
support@streetauthority.com

Carla Pasternak and Paul Tracy's *High-Yield Investing* is the single best source for information on every type of high-yield investment. Pasternak's thorough research brings not only useful information on the principles behind high-yield investing, but also specific stocks, mutual funds, trusts, and so on that deserve serious consideration. For those interested in a dividend capture strategy, Pasternak also publishes a monthly list of companies that have announced plans to pay substantial dividends.

Web Sites/Newsletters

The 25% Cash Machine

In addition to the book, Bryan Perry provides a monthly newsletter with information about high-yield investing, as well as a blog, an online archive of past articles, and special reports. These are all a service of the ChangeWave investing information site.

ChangeWave
2420A Gehman Lane
Lancaster, PA 17602
888-225-9373
www.changewave.com/cashmachine

For closed-end fund investing:

Closed-End Fund Association: www.closed-endfunds.com

If you're interested in buying into closed-end funds as a way to earn high yields, this site is a great place to start. It offers a listing of hundreds of high-yield funds along with their return rates, net asset values, and other useful information. The site is not just limited to high-yield funds—this is a great place to start your research into any type of closed-end fund.

The Investor's Guide to Closed-End Funds

This newsletter from closed-end experts Thomas J. Herzfeld Advisors is available both as a print publication and online.

Thomas J. Herzfeld Advisors, Inc.
PO Box 161465
Miami, FL 33116
305-271-1900
www.herzfeldresearch.com

For utilities:

Roger Conrad's Utility Forecaster
7600A Leesburg Pike
West Building
Suite 300
Falls Church, VA 22043
(703) 394-4931
www.utilityforecaster.com

If you're interested in investing in utilities, then this newsletter is a worthwhile investment, full of information about every type of utility investment, in the United States and abroad. Roger Conrad knows this traditionally high-yield industry like no one else.

For REIT investing:

National Association of Real Estate Investment Trusts (NAREIT): www.nareit.com.

Similar to the Closed-End Fund Association site, only for REITs, this Web site offers listings of REITs, their ticker symbols, and basic information, as well as general information and topical articles on REIT investing.

For Business Development Corporation (BDC) investing:

National Association of Development Companies: www.nadco.org

This Web site is for the benefit of the association, and also to allow small business owners seeking funding an easy way to find an appropriate company. It offers a list of BDCs by state, though little or no investment information.

CHAPTER

5

DRIPing Your Way to Wealth

Investing in the stock market can be a frustrating prospect for the small investor. You know that equities have historically provided much larger profits than safer investments such as bonds. But getting into the market can be tricky if you don't have a substantial sum to invest. Sure, you can get an online brokerage account and build a small portfolio of carefully selected shares, but since you pay a fee for every trade, it's tough to make money on small transactions, or to protect yourself by building in diversification.

One solution to this problem—the only one many small investors know—is to invest in mutual funds, which have some diversification built into them. But while mutual funds have their advantages, they can have disadvantages too, such as management fees that eat into earnings. There's another alternative—and one all small investors should know: DRIPs.

DRIPs are a fantastic way to build up your portfolio with very little effort. DRIP, sometimes written as DRiP, stands for *dividend reinvestment plan*. As the name suggests, many companies offer DRIPs as a way to allow investors to plow their dividends back into more stock, thus allowing their investments to grow on automatic pilot. Acronyms aside, DRIP investing sounds exactly like what it is: growing your money by drips and drops—small amounts that over time add up to big assets.

There are several different types of DRIPs, and different ways you can use them to meet your investment goals. Before I get into the details, let's start with a snapshot:

SNAPSHOT: DRIP Investing

How It Works:

Companies offer DRIPs, allowing individual investors to purchase shares directly from their transfer agent, thus bypassing brokerage houses—and brokerage fees. Most require a small minimum investment, and some charge a low fee for transactions, but many charge no transaction fee at all. Most allow dividends to be automatically channeled into further stock purchases, thus compounding your portfolio's assets. Some offer their shares at a discount, making DRIP investing even more attractive.

THE UPSIDE:

- Low Cost of Entry: Sure, you can buy a single stock with a brokerage account, but even a discount broker will charge you at least $7 for the trade, and then another $7 when you sell, meaning your single share must make $14 of profit just to break even. But it's easy to buy a single share with a DRIP, and there are no brokerage fees to eat into profits.
- Greater Safety: Because you can buy shares in very small amounts, you can more easily diversify even a modest portfolio. You also reduce your risk by buying shares gradually over time, rather than all at once, a strategy called *dollar cost averaging*.
- Instant Profits: If you choose discount DRIPs, you'll be in the money from the moment you buy your shares.

THE DOWNSIDE:

- Long-term strategy: You can get out of a plan at any time. However, it doesn't make sense to get into a DRIP unless you plan to leave your investment in place for a fairly long time. You won't get the benefits of DRIP investing, and it may even cost you, depending on the setup fee.
- Some study required: You invest in a DRIP based on its long-term prospects, not today's stock price. Before you make this kind of commitment to a company, you should spend a little time checking it out.
- Less excitement: You're allowing the stock market to work for you, not "playing" the market. So, while you're protected from wild price fluctuations, you also cannot take advantage of those fluctuations, as day

traders try to do. (Many day traders lose money, but they do get more entertainment out of watching their portfolios than DRIP investors do.)

Who Should Invest:

DRIPs are a good idea for nearly every investor. They're a perfect investment if you'd like to use small sums to build a strong portfolio over time, especially if you're willing to do a little initial research. Once you get started, they're a classic set-it-and-forget-it investment whose value will grow while you're busy doing other things. They also allow you to continue adding to your investment in small increments, and some of them let you do this automatically. DRIPs are a great choice for a long-term investment.

The Benefits of DRIP

A wide variety of companies—at least 1,300 as of this writing—offer various forms of DRIPs for individual investors. What's in it for them? All companies issue shares for one reason—to raise capital—and selling shares directly to investors makes a lot of sense. They eliminate the middleman and can get an ongoing supply of share purchases (instead of having to do a large public offering). Best of all, from the company's point of view, is the type of investors they get—those with a view to building a portfolio over the long term, rather than those who will want to sell the stock after making a quick buck. Long-term shareholders are better for the company's financial stability and its price per share.

What's in it for the investor? There are many advantages of DRIPs, depending on how you use them:

1. Your portfolio grows by itself. Most people assume that the whole point of buying a stock is to watch its price grow. But over time many stocks build value both by increasing share price and by paying dividends to shareholders. These dividends are often small amounts that may be left to accumulate in a typical brokerage account. But, with a DRIP, you can use those dividends to grow your holdings by automatically folding them right back into buying more stock. In effect, every time the company pays a dividend, you'll wind up owning more of its stock. With more stock you will, of course, earn higher dividend amounts, which will plow right back into yet more stock. With a company paying good yields, you can see your position grow dramatically over time. Most DRIPs allow you to set this up automatically, so that once the plan is in place, dividends reinvest automatically while you're busy doing other things.

The only possible drawback to this strategy is if things go badly and the share price falls over the long term, then the dividends you've reinvested will lose value as well. This is why it's important to choose companies wisely for DRIP investment. *You should go into DRIP investing with the mind-set that you're making a long-term commitment to a solid company.* It's also why it's wise to diversify your DRIP holdings—and fortunately, it's easier to diversify with DRIP investing than any other kind. (Read on to learn why.)

2. You eliminate the middleman. The most common way individual investors buy stock is through a brokerage, either a full-service financial company or a discount brokerage that doesn't provide financial advice but charges reduced fees. Even a discount brokerage limits your options for investing small sums, because you must normally pay a fee for every trade. Let's say you can save $50 a month, and you want to invest it in the stock market. Chances are you won't buy shares every week, thus cutting your investment down to $43 right from the start. You would probably have to leave the money sitting in some sort of cash account till you could build up enough to make a trade worthwhile.

Fees also make it harder for you to diversify. If you have only $200 to invest, you will likely put it all in one stock (leaving yourself an investment of, say, $193 after paying a $7 fee for the trade), rather than spread it among five different investments, and winding up with only $165.

Many DRIPs, on the other hand, don't charge any per-transaction fee, and if they do, the fees are much lower than even a discount brokerage fee. This makes it easy to buy as many shares as you like, even if it's just one at a time.

"This is what I consider the biggest advantage of DRIPs—they allow you to be diversified," says Vita Nelson, editor and publisher of *The Moneypaper,* a newspaper considered by many to be the premier source of information on DRIP investing. "Instead of having to take a position in one company, you can buy a single share of stock in ten companies."

3. You can invest small sums over time. No per-transaction fee means there's nothing to prevent you from buying very small amounts of shares whenever you want or are able. In fact, you may not even have to buy a whole share. Many DRIPs offer "fractional" shares so that, for instance, if the shares are trading at $50 but you only invest $25, you'll get half a share—and be entitled to a half share's worth of dividends.

This creates a whole new set of options for small investors who want to set aside small sums on a monthly or weekly basis to put into the stock market. While this type of investing would be awkward in a traditional brokerage arrangement, it's perfect in the DRIP world. In fact, many companies that offer DRIPs also offer automatic investment plans that deduct a set amount from your bank account every month to invest in the DRIP, so your investment keeps building even when you're too busy to pay attention to it.

4. You can do dollar cost averaging. What is dollar cost averaging? It's the simple act of buying small quantities of shares over time, rather than buying them all at once for one lump sum. Sounds like no big deal, but it's such a powerful advantage that many investment experts think this alone is a good enough reason to invest in DRIPs.

To understand why, let's begin by taking a look at what happens to most individual investors when they play the stock market. We all know the mantra of the market: "Buy low, sell high." Sounds logical enough, but many individual investors wind up doing the exact opposite. This is because the overwhelming majority of small investor stock purchases are made for emotional, not rational, reasons. This often involves jumping on a stock that's already had a nice run-up, just as earlier investors are getting ready to sell and will thus drive the price down.

Dollar cost averaging works on the assumption that though share prices may fluctuate wildly in the short run, they are likely to rise in the long run—assuming you've done your homework and chosen solid companies to invest in. Since you're generally investing a set amount each time, rather than buying a specific number of shares, you'll automatically buy more shares when prices are lower—because your money will buy more of them—than when prices are higher and the same amount buys fewer shares. Thus, though you'll be investing the same amount each month, DRIP-style investing will tend to push your average share price down over time.

The downside is that if you had the option to invest your money all at once, and then the share price doubled overnight, with dollar cost averaging you couldn't take advantage of it. On the other hand, if the share price fell by half overnight, you'd be much more protected.

"The good thing is you're not trying to speculate on the direction of the market," Nelson says. "Over the long term, the market is going to go up, so that's what you plan for. And if you're nervous about investing in stocks, this can be a good way to get into it."

Instant Profits: Investing in Discount DRIPs

Would you like to be able to buy stock and have a guarantee that its price would go up immediately? You can—if you invest in a DRIP from one of the many companies that offer discount pricing to plan participants.

In most cases, discounts apply to dividends you earn that are reinvested in stock, and many plans also offer a discount on cash purchases. Typical discounts range from 2 to 5 percent. (That is, if a share was trading on the market for $100, plan participants might get it for $95 or $98.) Discounts are a great way to make your DRIP investment grow faster and build up a bigger portfolio over time.

Okay, you ask—but what's in it for the company? Why would they sell their own shares for less than they're actually worth? There must be a catch in it somewhere—right?

Basically, they do it for the same reason companies offer DRIPs in the first place: It's a cheaper, easier, and more consistent way for them to raise capital than taking out bank loans or organizing public offerings. The problem is that there are at least 1,300 companies offering DRIPs, and many of them are household names. Offering discounts is a quick, easy, and relatively inexpensive way for less-high-profile companies to lure investors to lesser-known DRIPs.

Even so, on the principle that there's no such thing as a free lunch, some investors and investment experts are wary of discount DRIPs. "I'm always suspicious of companies that offer discounts," Nelson says. "Why is their need for money so great?"

She adds this note of caution: "It's all well and good if you picked a company you liked and it happens to have a discount. But the discount shouldn't be the reason that you picked it."

I disagree: I think discounts can indeed be a good reason for selecting a DRIP. But Nelson poses a wise question about the company's need for cash. The answer is to do your due diligence, as you should with any stock purchase, but especially with any DRIP, since you are investing for the long term. When reviewing a discount DRIP's financials, pay special attention to issues of cash flow and debt. You want to be as sure as you can that the reason they're offering the discount is to draw long-term investors, and not that they're desperate to shore up dwindling cash reserves.

Getting Started in DRIPs

Starting out as a DRIP investor is easy, and you can do it with small amounts of money most stockbrokers would never touch. But it's not quite as simple as traditional methods of buying shares. Most companies with DRIPs have a minimum ownership requirement, often as little as one share, *before* you can join the plan.

I realize this is completely paradoxical—the whole reason most people invest in DRIPs in the first place is because they want to try equity investing with a small initial outlay. Why should you have to buy stock in order to buy stock?

This requirement may have come about because of the way DRIPs were first conceived, as an extension of employee stock ownership programs and a way for investors who already have an interest in a company to make a long-term investment. Whatever the reason, you have three choices for fulfilling it:

1. Use a service. This is the quickest and easiest way to invest in DRIPs. Rather than charging a fee per trade, they will charge a flat initial fee to set you up with a DRIP account, including purchasing the shares you're required to own before joining and registering them in your name.

One of the oldest and best of the DRIP services is Temper Enrollment Service, which is affiliated with *The Moneypaper*. Temper offers access to about 1,300 DRIPs, and will set you up in any of them for an initial fee of $50, or $25 if you're a *Moneypaper* subscriber. (Once you're in the plan, subsequent transactions go directly between you and the company, and Temper collects no further fees.)

There are many good reasons for using a service, but the most important is that this is the quickest and easiest way to get into DRIP investing. One big advantage to DRIPs is they allow you to diversify with a small amount of money. But that advantage can quickly be lost if every time you invest in a new company, you have to buy a single share elsewhere first. This could get to be a problem fast if, like many DRIP investors, your goal is to wind up in many different DRIPs.

Services like Temper also allow for quick comparison of different plans, and you can even create a list of DRIPs based on specific search criteria, such as which industry the company is in, whether it's traditionally paid high dividends, or whether it charges fees for investing. In fact, I used just such a search to create the list of discount DRIPs in the Resources section of this chapter.

ShareBuilder is an example of another type of service that in essence creates its own reinvestment plan. ShareBuilder offers a choice of 6,000 companies and exchange-traded funds (ETFs), and investors can have their dividends automatically reinvested, as well as have a regular investment automatically deducted from their bank accounts either weekly or monthly. The difference is that the companies and funds in question aren't all offering reinvestment plans—instead ShareBuilder itself handles the automatic deductions, reinvesting, and purchasing of partial shares.

2. Buy the required share or shares through a broker. If you'd rather not use a DRIP service, another option is to buy the required share or shares through a traditional broker. Obviously, brokerage commissions make buying a single share of most stock seem like an unwise proposition, but your goal is not to make money on this initial purchase, but rather to qualify for the DRIP, where you will make money over the long term.

Making the purchase, though, is only the first step. Though you own the stock, and receive dividends and the proceeds when you eventually sell, shares you buy through a brokerage are usually purchased in the brokerage's name, sometimes called a "street name." To qualify for most DRIPs, you need the stock certificate actually to be registered in your name. Most brokerages will do this, if you request it, though some charge an extra fee. Also, it may take a few weeks for you to receive your certificate, which will delay your joining the DRIP. But since you're investing for the long term in any case—and since you'll be dollar cost averaging your purchases—the delay should not make that much of a difference.

3. Choose a plan with no prior ownership requirement. This is a variant on the traditional DRIP where investors can buy shares directly from a company, which may sometimes act as its own transfer agent. These types of plans are sometimes called DIPs (direct investment plans), DSPs (direct stock purchase plans), or DPPs (direct purchase plans). This will certainly limit your selection, as there are at most a few hundred DIP programs, compared to at least 1,300 offering traditional DRIPs. But there seems to be a trend toward more companies offering DIPs.

These plans offer many advantages, but they may also come with disadvantages; for instance, there may be limits on when you can sell your shares. Make sure you understand all the rules before joining the plan.

Choosing the Right DRIP

Which DRIPs are best to invest in? I look at a variety of factors. First and foremost, remember you are investing for the very long term, so you want to pick a company that you're certain will still be going strong a decade or two from now. As I explained earlier, discount DRIPs that survive such scrutiny can be excellent investments, because the value of your investment increases right on the day that you buy it.

In addition, I recommend stocks with high yields—particularly companies that have historically paid 3 percent per year or more in dividends. Not all companies with DRIPs pay high dividends, and some pay very small dividends. But if your DRIP stock earns a decent dividend, you are guaranteed to have your stake in the company increase over time. This is why I think DRIPs offered by utility companies, banks, and REITs—real estate investment trusts (see Chapter 4)—often provide the kinds of yields that can help your investment keep growing.

Picking the right stock is important, and you should choose carefully. But the important thing is that you do pick a DRIP—or, ideally, several DRIPs—and get started. There's a list of twenty-six discount DRIPs in the Resources section of this chapter, along with information on where you can find detailed information on thousands of other DRIPs as well.

Remember, you're in this for the long term, and in the long term, more stocks gain value than lose. And, the sooner you start, the more DRIP value you'll be able to build over time.

DRIPS VS. MUTUAL FUNDS

Is DRIP investing the only way for an investor to make a small outlay of cash and take advantage of the equities market with enough diversification to lower risk? No, there's another way: investing in mutual funds. Unlike DRIPs, mutual funds are typically sold through brokerage houses and directly to the public, and perhaps for this reason, they are a much more familiar option for many investors.

Which is better? Mutual funds certainly provide several advantages. One is ease of use: Instead of analyzing a variety of companies to determine which are the best investment prospects, you can let a trained professional do it for you. And, since the mutual fund itself is spreading your money over many different companies, your onetime investment will provide diversification that may lower your risk.

But DRIPs provide some significant advantages over mutual funds. For one thing, the fact that someone is managing the fund means that someone must be paid, and so ongoing management fees will detract from the mutual funds' gains when it's doing well, and increase losses when it isn't. With DRIPs, you manage your own portfolio, and may not pay any fee at all for purchases or sales, so once you've paid for enrollment, your profits won't ever be reduced by fees. All other things being equal, a portfolio of DRIPs in a profitable industry will provide better returns than a mutual fund covering the same industry.

If DRIPs are likely to outpace mutual funds in good times, they can provide a real advantage in bad times, when a given industry, or the market at large, experiences falling share prices. When this happens, many small investors think the time is right to sell their shares, either to lock in the profits they've received up till then, or to cut their losses while they still can. This is often a terrible time to sell, but mutual fund managers have no choice: If large numbers of their investors want to cash out then, the fund must sell some shares to obtain that cash. The whole value of the fund goes down, and there's nothing you can do about it, except exacerbate the problem by cashing out yourself.

DRIP investors have the option to wait and give the shares they own time to regain their lost value. And experienced DRIP investors tend to weather stock market storms without panicking—because they know they're investing for the long haul.

Lower Your Risk—DRIP Investing

1. DRIP investing gives you the opportunity to diversify, even with a small amount of money. So take advantage of the opportunity by dividing your investment among several DRIPs. Or, if you're starting with a small amount, add a new DRIP every time you have a small sum to invest until you have a diversified group.

2. Buy high-yielding DRIPs. If you receive regular dividends that are automatically converted into more stock, the value of your DRIP account will grow, even if the actual stock price stays flat.

3. Think in decades. A company can have a down quarter or a down year, but it's rare for a solid, well-run company to have a down decade. Seasoned DRIP investors tend to think in terms of decades, and this allows them to take both the extreme highs and lows of the market a little less seriously.

DRIP Investing Action Plan

1. Start by exploring lists of possible DRIPs to invest in. Since I believe discount DRIPs provide a special opportunity, I've supplied a list of them in the Resources section of this chapter. But there are many more DRIPs and types of DRIP plans, and you should check out as many of them as you can. Use the Web sites listed in the Resources section to find lists of DRIPs that might be right for you.

2. Match your DRIP to your investing goals. Deciding precisely what you want from your DRIP investment will help you decide what type of DRIP you need. Do you want to make sure your investment will grow, even if you're not adding much to it? Then look for DRIPs with high yields and set up automatic dividend reinvestment—at a discounted price, if possible. Do you want to add a little to your DRIP on a monthly or weekly basis to help it grow? Then select a plan that offers automatic deductions and avoid those with transaction fees.

3. Decide how you'll buy into your DRIPs. If you want to get going quickly and you don't mind a startup fee for each DRIP you buy into, consider using an enrollment service to buy the required shares, register them in your name, and set you up in a DRIP program. If you enjoy doing things yourself, you can buy the required initial shares and get stock certificates registered in your name instead. Or, you might want to try out some of the companies that allow direct purchase without a pre-

vious ownership requirement. ShareBuilder—www.sharebuilder.com—
is one source for information on which companies offer these plans,
sometimes called direct investment plans (DIPs), direct purchase plans
(DPPs), or direct stock purchase plans (DSPs).

4. Make a short list of likely DRIPs. Pick plans that have the reinvestment and automatic deduction features you prefer, along with no fees, if
this is important to you. In some cases, the transfer agent that actually
sells the stock charges a fee, but the company pays the fee for you; Temper (the service affiliated with *The Moneypaper*) lists these in a separate
category from no-fee DRIPs. Pick discount DRIPs, if the benefit of
instant profits appeals to you, or DRIPs in industries you believe are
ready to soar. Whatever criteria you use, keep in mind you should be
ready to commit to these companies for years to come.

5. Do your due diligence. Because these are long-term investments,
you want companies that have a solid future in front of them. So once
you've picked some likely candidates, narrow the list by taking a good
long look at their financials to make sure they'll stay strong for years to
come. Pay special attention to issues of debt and cash flow.

6. Sign up for a plan. If you've chosen to go the broker route, once
you pick a DRIP you'd like to join, contact the brokerage house to find
out about purchasing your minimum required shares and having the
stock certificate registered in your name. If you don't have a brokerage
house (or its fees are too high) consider trying a discount brokerage
instead.

If you prefer, you can take the easier way and use an enrollment service such as Temper to sign up for the DRIP, or stick to DIPs, which
require no previous ownership.

7. Set your investment to grow. To reap the benefit of the DRIP concept, make sure dividends will be automatically reinvested in stock. To
help your investment grow even faster, you can also set up an automatic
monthly or weekly deduction from your bank account.

8. Do it all over again. One major benefit of DRIP investing is the
opportunity to diversify, so the more different DRIPs you have, the better off you are. Plan to keep building: Some of the most successful DRIP
investors have portfolios of 100 DRIPs or more.

IT'S NEVER TOO EARLY: PROGRAM
TEACHES DRIP INVESTING TO DETROIT KIDS

Robert L. Walker picked up his first *Wall Street Journal* and made his first stock purchase around the age of fourteen, and he's been doing it ever since. "I love investing. I love everything about it," he says. Over the years, he came to feel he had something to teach young people about investing, and the value of starting a lifelong program of building wealth. So, in 1999, he and his wife, Kyleen, co-founded Wise Steward Ministries in Detroit. Despite its name, Wise Steward is not a faith-based organization, though it works with several churches as well as schools in Detroit. Its purpose is to teach high school and middle school children financial literacy, and get them started investing, even with very small sums. So far, he says, the program has helped about 200 youthful investors start building financial independence.

Detroit is a mostly lower- and middle-income community, largely African-American and Latino, Walker says. Which means that many of the parents of children in Wise Steward's programs know little more about the financial world than the children do. "A couple of years ago, we started getting phone calls from these parents, saying they wanted to learn financial literacy themselves," Walker says. "So we began allowing the parents to come in and observe what the children were learning. Because of that, there's greater dialogue about it, and the parents wind up reinforcing what we're teaching when they go home."

DRIPs are tailor-made for the investing approaches Walker teaches. Not only can the kids get going with very small sums, the long-term focus of DRIPs dovetails with the philosophy Walker teaches.

"We're always telling young people, if you're only interested in how much money you can make in the next year or two, this isn't really for you," he says. Instead, he tells them to think in terms of earnings in ten or twenty years, and that investing should be part of what they do for the rest of their lives. "With a DRIP account, you buy one share. I tell them, you're consistently going to buy one share all the time. Eventually, you'll have 100 or 200 shares. And you do this with a number of companies over a long period. Remember, the Great Wall of China was built one brick at a time."

continued

The other big advantage DRIPs offer, he adds, is that they help motivate the kids to become committed investors. "To say you own this mutual fund would be a lot different from saying you own a part of this company," he says. "The kids love receiving stock certificates. It helps encourage them to continue investing for a long time."

Case Studies

To help show you how these strategies actually work, I've provided two real case studies. The names and locations have been changed.

Jane Morris first started DRIP investing on behalf of her daughter, Andrea. When Andrea got her degree in education, she found herself recruited by a chain of international high schools, with locations all over the world. The job appealed to Andrea's spirit of adventure, and she accepted a teaching position in Singapore. Over the years, Andrea moved from job to job and country to country. One day, Jane received a sum of money in the mail. "Andrea said, 'Do something with this,'" Jane recalls.

But what? Jane had little experience as an investor. One of Andrea's high school classmates had become a stockbroker, so Jane called him and opened an account with his firm. But the broker kept buying and selling in rapid succession—"churning" the account—and earning a fee on each transaction. "It didn't seem right to me," Jane says.

Around this time, Jane saw an ad for *The Moneypaper,* and decided to try it out. "I didn't know what I needed to learn," she says. In the newsletter, she learned about DRIPs, and decided the concept made sense for Andrea's money. "We didn't start with one chunk of money," Jane says. "She would send money home, and I'd invest $100 here and another $100 there."

That was about fifteen years ago. Today, Andrea has climbed the administrative ranks at her school, and is sending more investment money home. Jane says the contributions are now around $1,000 a month. Meanwhile the DRIPs have kept growing, so that Andrea is invested in about eighty different plans, and her portfolio is worth more than $1.6 million. "If I died tomorrow, she wouldn't have to do a thing," Jane says. "The portfolio would keep rolling along by itself. It's almost foolproof."

*   *   *

George Grayson, now retired, was a small-town lawyer whose clients had limited funds, and he rarely earned more than $50,000 a year, he says. He wanted to invest, but couldn't get enough money together. "My brother-in-law was a stockbroker, and even he wouldn't invest less than $500," George recalls. "I never had that kind of money all at once."

DRIP investing turned out to be the solution. "I had to start $25 at a time," he says. He began by investing in utilities, choosing those that offered a discount on dividend reinvestment. He would use a notebook to keep track of the investments, and record every dividend that came in, something he says he still does. Now his notebooks fill an entire bookshelf.

George started investing in his mid-forties. Now in his mid-seventies, he has a portfolio of more than eighty stocks, worth more than $400,000. "All from penny-ante contributions," he says. "It's been phenomenal. Kids should start this when they're young."

Resources

Books

All About DRIPs and DSPs by George C. Fisher (McGraw-Hill, 2001)
One of the very few books to focus on DRIPs and direct investing, this book offers a good grounding in the topic, explains in detail how DRIPs work, and provides a list of sixteen DRIPs that (at the time it was written) had shown a ten-year annual return rate of 20 percent and increasing dividends.

Buying Stocks Without a Broker and *No-Load Stocks* by Charles B. Carlson (McGraw-Hill, 1996)
These are classic books about DRIPs and DIPs by the editor of *The DRIP Investor* newsletter. Carlson provides a directory of DRIP plans and model portfolios of DRIPs, and he explains how to buy stocks directly from issuing companies without fees.

Newsletters

The Moneypaper
www.moneypaper.com
(800) 388-9993
The Moneypaper covers more than just DRIPs, but it is considered the premier source for learning about DRIP investing. *The Moneypaper* is affiliated

with Temper of the Times, which, through Temper Enrollment Service, helps people enroll in DRIPs and provides an online database of DRIP offerings.

Drip Investor
7412 Calumet Avenue
Hammond, IN 46324
219-852-3200
www.dripinvestor.com

This newsletter, edited by investment expert Chuck Carlson, offers information on a wide variety of DRIPs, and also offers an online archive of past issues, commentary on many DRIPs and industries, and online message boards where subscribers can trade information.

Web Sites/Services:

DirectInvesting.com (www.directinvesting.com).

This site is affiliated with *The Moneypaper* and provides basic information about DRIPs. The real draw, though, is the database of DRIP companies, searchable by many different criteria, ranging from industry, to the rate of dividends paid, to what kind of fees they charge. You can also use this site to access Temper Enrollment Service, which will enroll you in any of 1,300 DRIPs, for a $50 fee ($25 for *Moneypaper* subscribers).

Temper also offers its own mutual fund, named MP63, which invests in Temper's index of DRIP stocks, taking advantage of dividend reinvestment and offering diversification at the same time. (The name MP63 came about because there are 63 companies in the index.)

DividendInvestor.com (www.dividendinvestor.com) Complete Web site to search for top dividend-paying companies.

King Investors (www.kinginvestors.citymax.com) (P.O. Box 619, 104 Evans Street, La Crosse, Virginia 23950) 866-831-5817;

Offers a direct stock purchase plan enrollment service to facilitate direct investing, dividend reinvestment, and optional stock purchases.

ShareBuilder (www.sharebuilder.com)

This is another site for DRIP investing. It also provides what some call a "pseudo-DRIP"—dividend reinvestment plan created by brokerages and other financial companies to mimic a traditional DRIP, providing dividend reinvestment and automatic purchases for companies that don't offer DRIPs themselves.

The DriP Investing Resource Center (www.dripinvesting.org)

This is a great place to learn a lot about DRIP investing. The site is a clearinghouse for DRIP expertise, with links to dozens of articles as well as message boards for discussing DRIP investing and strategies for figuring out how much to invest in each.

Discount DRIP List

This list of twenty-six companies with discount dividend reinvestment plans was compiled courtesy of *The Moneypaper*'s DRIP site, www.directinvesting. com. I've listed DRIPs that offer discounts on direct purchases, dividend reinvestments, or both, because I believe these discounts make particularly attractive investments. But subscribers to the site can search a number of different ways—for DRIPs with historic yield rates of 3 percent or more, for instance, or by industry.

In addition to providing the address, ticker symbol, phone number, and Web site for these companies, I've also included some basic information on each company's reinvestment plan. For instance, most plans (all except one in this list) require you to own only one share, registered in your own name, before you can join the plan, but some also allow investors who aren't shareholders to join the plan with a minimum direct investment. Some provide an automatic investment option, allowing for automatic deductions (usually once a month) from your bank account.

All plans have a minimum investment requirement, and all in this list offer discounts on direct purchases or reinvestments, usually both. At least, some of the time. You will note that a few plans show discount amounts in a range whose low end is zero, such as 0–5 percent. This means the company *may* offer a discount on purchases or reinvestments at certain times or under certain circumstances. Please review the company's DRIP prospectus (usually available through its Web site) for details on these types of discounts.

Access National Corp.
(NASDAQ Symbol: ANCX)
1800 Robert Fulton Drive
Suite 300
Reston, VA 20191
703-871-2100
www.accessnationalbank.com
Industry: Banking

Shares to Qualify for DRIP: 1
Minimum Investment: $150
Auto Investment Available
Discount on Cash: 0–5 percent
Discount on Dividend: 0–5 percent

Anthracite Capital
(NYSE Symbol: AHR)
345 Park Avenue
New York, NY 10154
212-810-3333
www.ahr.blackrock.com
Industry: REIT (Real Estate Investment Trust)

Shares to Qualify for DRIP: 1 (or $250 direct investment)
Minimum Investment: $100
Auto Investment Available
Discount on Cash: 2 percent
Discount on Dividend: 2 percent

Anworth Mortgage Asset Corp.
(NYSE Symbol: ANH)
1299 Ocean Avenue
Suite 250
Santa Monica, CA 90401
310-255-4493
www.anworth.com
Industry: REIT

Shares to Qualify for DRIP: 1 (or $1,000 direct investment)
Minimum Investment: $50
Auto Investment Available
Discount on Cash: 0–5 percent
Discount on Dividend: 5 percent

Archstone-Smith
(NYSE Symbol: ASN)
7670 South Chester Street
Suite 100
Englewood, CO 80112
800-982-9293
www.archstonecommunities.com
Industry: REIT

Shares to Qualify for DRIP: 1
Minimum Investment: $200
Auto Investment Available
Discount on Cash: 2 percent
Discount on Dividend: none

BRT Realty Trust
(NYSE Symbol: BRT)
60 Cutter Mill Road
Great Neck, NY 11021
516-466-3100
www.brtrealty.com
Industry: REIT

Shares to Qualify for DRIP: 1
Minimum Investment: $100
No Auto Investment Available
Discount on Cash: 2 percent
Discount on Dividend: 2 percent

CapitalSource, Inc.
(NYSE Symbol: CSE)
4445 Willard Avenue
12th Floor
Chevy Chase, MD 20815
800-370-9431
www.capitalsource.com
Industry: Financial Services

Shares to Qualify for DRIP: 1 (or $100 direct investment)
Minimum Investment: $100
Auto Investment Available
Discount on Cash: 2 percent
Discount on Dividend: 2 percent

Colonial Properties Trust
(NYSE Symbol: CLP)
2101 6th Avenue North
Suite 750
Birmingham, AL 35203
800-645-3917
www.colonialprop.com
Industry: REIT

Shares to Qualify for Drip: 1 (or $200 direct investment)
Minimum Investment: $25
Auto Investment Available
Discount on Cash: 3 percent
Discount on Dividend: 3 percent

Education Realty Trust Inc.
(NYSE Symbol: EDR)
530 Oak Court Drive
Suite 300
Memphis, TN 38117
www.educationrealty.com
Industry: Student Housing REIT

Shares to Qualify for DRIP: 1 (or $300 direct investment)
Minimum Investment: $300
Auto Investment Available
Discount on Cash: 1.5 percent
Discount on Dividend: 1.5 percent

Equity Lifestyle Properties, Inc.
(NYSE Symbol: ELS)
2 North Riverside Plaza
Suite 800
Chicago, IL 60606
800-247-5279
www.mhchomes.com
Industry: REIT

Shares to Qualify for DRIP: 1 (or $100 direct investment)
Minimum Investment: $250
No Auto Investment Available
Discount on Cash: 0–5 percent
Discount on Dividend: none

First National Community Bancorp Inc.
(OTC Symbol: FNCB)
102 East Drinker Street
Dunmore, PA 18512-2491
570-348-6438
www.fncb.com
Industry: Bank Holding Company

Shares to Qualify for DRIP: 1
Minimum Investment: $100
No Auto Investment Available
Discount on Cash: 5 percent
Discount on Dividend: 5 percent

Health Care Property Investors, Inc.
(NYSE Symbol: HCP)
3760 Kilroy Airport Way
Suite 300
Long Beach, CA 90806
888-604-1990
www.hcpi.com
Industry: REIT

Shares to Qualify for DRIP: 1 (or $750 direct investment)
Minimum Investment: $100
Auto Investment Available
Discount on Cash: 0–5 percent
Discount on Dividend: 0–5 percent

Health Care REIT
(NYSE Symbol: HCN)
1 SeaGate
Suite 1500
Box 1475
Toledo, OH 43603-1475
419-247-2800
Industry: REIT

Shares to Qualify for DRIP: 1 (or $1,000 direct investment)
Minimum Investment: $50
No Auto Investment Available
Discount on Cash: 4 percent
Discount on Dividend: 4 percent

Marathon Oil Corporation
(NYSE Symbol: MRO)
5555 San Felipe Road
Houston, TX 77253
713-296-1996
www.marathon.com
Industry: Oil & Gas

Shares to Qualify for DRIP: 1 (or $500 direct investment)
Minimum Investment: $50
Auto Investment Available
Discount on Cash: 0–3 percent
Discount on Dividend: 0–3 percent

Monmouth REIT
(NASDAQ Symbol: MNRTA)
3499 Rt. 9 North
Suite 3-C
Freehold, NJ 07728
732-577-9996
www.mreic.com
Industry: REIT

Shares to Qualify for DRIP: 1
Minimum Investment: $500
No Auto Investment Available
Discount on Cash: 5 percent
Discount on Dividend: 5 percent

Nationwide Health Properties Inc.
(NYSE Symbol: NHP)
610 Newport Center Drive
Suite 1150
Newport Beach, CA 92660
949-718-4407
www.nhp-reit.com

Shares to Qualify for DRIP: 1 (or $750 direct investment)
Minimum Investment: $100
Auto Investment Available
Discount on Cash: 2 percent
Discount on Dividend: 2 percent

OceanFirst Financial Corp.
(NASDAQ Symbol: OCFC)
975 Hooper Avenue
Toms River, NJ 08754-2009
732-240-4500
www.oceanfirst.com
Industry: Bank Holding Company

Shares to Qualify for DRIP: 1
Minimum Investment: $100
No Auto Investment Available
Discount on Cash: 3 percent
Discount on Dividend: 3 percent

Parkway Properties Inc.
(NYSE Symbol: PKY)
1 Jackson Place
Suite 1000
188 East Capitol Street
Jackson, MS 39225
601-948-4091
www.pky.com
Industry: REIT

Shares to Qualify for DRIP: 1 (or $100 direct investment)
Minimum Investment: $100
Auto Investment Available: Yes
Discount on Cash: 3 percent
Discount on Dividend: 3 percent

Pennsylvania Commerce Bancorp, Inc.
(NASDAQ Symbol: COBH)
100 Senate Avenue
Box 8599
Camp Hill, PA 17011-8599
717-975-5630
www.commercepc.com
Industry: Bank Holding Company

Shares to Qualify for DRIP: 1
Minimum Investment: $100
No Auto Investment Available
Discount on Cash: 3 percent
Discount on Dividend: 3 percent

Pulaski Financial Corp.
(NASDAQ Symbol: PULB)
12300 Olive Boulevard
St. Louis, MO 63141-6434
314-878-2210
www.pulaskibankstl.com
Industry: Banking

Shares to Qualify for DRIP: 5
Minimum Investment: $250
Auto Investment Available

Discount on Cash: 2 percent
Discount on Dividend: 2 percent

Redwood Trust, Inc.
(NASDAQ Symbol: RWT)
One Belvedere Place
Suite 300
Mill Valley, CA 94941
415-389-7373
www.redwoodtrust.com
Industry: REIT

Shares to Qualify for DRIP: 1 (or $100 direct investment)
Auto Investment Available
Discount on Cash: 0–2 percent
Discount on Dividend: no

SL Green Realty Corp.
(NYSE Symbol: SLG)
420 Lexington Avenue
New York, NY 10170
212-216-1601
www.slgreen.com
Industry: REIT

Shares to Qualify for DRIP: 1
Minimum Investment: $250
No Auto Investment Available
Discount on Cash: 3 percent
Discount on Dividend: 3 percent

South Jersey Industries, Inc.
(NYSE Symbol: SJI)
One South Jersey Plaza
Folsom, NJ 08037
609-561-9000 x 4321
www.sjindustries.com
Industry: Utility-Gas

Shares to Qualify for DRIP: 1 (or $100 direct investment)
Minimum Investment: $25
No Auto Investment Available

Discount on Cash: 2 percent
Discount on Dividend: 2 percent

Sovran Self Storage, Inc.
(NYSE Symbol: SSS)
6467 Main Street
Buffalo, NY 14221
716-633-1850
www.sovranss.com
Industry: REIT

Shares to Qualify for DRIP: 1 (or $100 direct investment)
Minimum Investment: $100
No Auto Investment Available
Discount on Cash: 2 percent
Discount on Dividend: 2 percent

State Bancorp, Inc.
(NASDAQ Symbol: STBC)
699 Hillside Avenue
New Hyde Park, NY 11040
516-437-1000
www.statebankofli.com
Industry: Bank Holding Company

Shares to Qualify for DRIP: 1
Minimum Investment: $100
No Auto Investment Available
Discount on Cash: 5 percent
Discount on Dividend: 5 percent

Thornburg Mortgage, Inc.
(NYSE Symbol: TMA)
150 Washington Avenue
Suite 302
Santa Fe, NM 87501
505-989-1900
www.thornburg.com
Industry: REIT

Shares to Qualify for DRIP: 1 (or $500 direct investment)
Minimum Investment: $100

Auto Investment Available
Discount on Cash: 0–5 percent
Discount on Dividend: 0–5 percent

Ventas Inc.
(NYSE Symbol: VTR)
10350 Ormsby Park Place
Suite 300
Louisville, KY 40223
502-357-9000
www.ventasreit.com
Industry: Health Care REIT

Shares to Qualify for DRIP: 1 (or $250 direct investment)
Minimum Investment: $250
No Auto Investment Available
Discount on Cash: 2 percent
Discount on Dividend: 2 percent

Source: www.directinvesting.com

CHAPTER

6

Bonds and More Bonds

When we think of bonds, we think safety—even stodgy—but to dismiss the asset class for lack of excitement would be to throw some very spunky babies out with the bathwater.

Bonds have been around forever and represent substantially more invested money than stocks. Yet I'm always surprised at the number of people who don't understand basic things about bonds, such as how the same bond can be both very safe and very risky, why the yields and prices of outstanding bonds rise and fall in opposite directions, and why some bonds are more volatile than others.

Today you can choose from many varieties of bonds and bond funds. While there is surprisingly little difference ("spread") in the yields of traditional, interest-bearing, "risk-free" Treasury bonds and "investment-grade" corporate issues having the same maturities, the good news is that significantly higher yields are available on quality bonds that are less widely publicized. These "under the radar" bonds include foreign issues, tax-exempt municipals, zero coupon bonds, mortgage-backed pass-through securities, and a selection of bond-related structured products, newly invented hybrid securities that offer a winning combination of attractive yields, upside potential, and guaranteed return of principal.

Such "unusual bonds," as I like to call them, come with their own risks, but I believe represent special opportunities for profit and I plan to focus on them in this chapter. But first I think you should have a clear understanding of the more common, plain vanilla bond, so here's a snapshot that will serve as a good frame of reference for the more interesting variations to come.

SNAPSHOT: Traditional Coupon Bond and Its Pros and Cons

How It Works:

Traditional bonds are contractual debt obligations having original maturity of ten years or longer. When you hold or own a bond, you hold the debt of a company, a municipality, or a government. You are the lender and in return for making the loan, you are paid interest. The principal and final interest rate are due upon maturity—that's the date at which a debt instrument is due and payable. Traditional bonds have a fixed interest rate (still called a "coupon" although electronic bookkeeping has made physical coupons obsolete) determined by market conditions at the time of issue, the issuer's credit quality, and the term to maturity.

Bonds will almost always pay more than the rate bank CDs and money market funds are paying at the time you buy them. Bonds typically have a face ("par") value of $1,000 at which they are redeemable at maturity, and pay interest semiannually.

You can purchase bonds individually or invest in them via bond funds.

THE UPSIDE:

- Relative Safety: You can be fairly certain that interest will be paid as scheduled and the face value of principal will be repaid at maturity. Bond contracts, called bond agreements or indentures, have provisions aimed at keeping the financial condition of issuers strong enough to make the payments required.
- Higher Yield: Bonds offer better yields than certificates of deposit or money market funds.
- First in Line: As creditors, bondholders have a claim on assets that puts them ahead of stockholders in the unlikely event of default.

THE DOWNSIDE:

- Interest Rate Risk. Fixed-rate bonds have the risk that their market value will be lower than face value if they are sold prior to maturity when interest rates are rising.

- Call Risk: If the issuer redeems the bond before maturity, exercising a call provision in the bond contract, you get your principal back, but lose the opportunity for future interest income.
- Reinvestment Risk: This is the possibility that rates will be lower when you reinvest interest payments or the proceeds from redemption. Bond portfolios with staggered or laddered maturities mitigate this risk. Zero coupon bonds lock in the rate at which interest is compounded.

Who Should Invest:

Individuals seeking safety of income and yields higher than bank CDs or money market funds, and who are able to accept interest rate risk.

Bond Basics

Basically, the issuers of bonds held by individuals fall into three categories: government bonds, which include (1) "risk-free" United States Treasury issues and indirect obligations of government agencies; (2) municipal bonds, which are exempt from federal income taxes and the income taxes of their states of issue and sometimes of their localities as well; and (3) corporate bonds issued to raise capital or created by a process called *securitization,* whereby income-producing corporate assets are transferred to legally separate special purpose entities, where they are pooled, packaged, and reissued as asset-backed securities standing on their own credit strength.

There is another type of bond—securitized, asset-backed bonds that are largely marketed to institutional investors having specialized portfolio requirements, such as pension plans, insurance companies, and banks. Why are these important to individual investors? Even though you can't invest in them as an individual, for corporations raising capital, they are a cheaper source of financing than direct bond offerings, which are accounting for less of the financing done. At the capital market level, they redistribute risk and make risk management more efficient. This, in turn, makes possible the structured products increasingly available to retail investors as bond alternatives. Structured products are just one of the group of "unusual bonds" I will discuss throughout this chapter.

Why Bond Prices and Yields Move Inversely

It is baffling to many people that the market prices of bonds and other fixed income securities go up when prevailing interest rates go down and vice versa. The following example should help you understand the reason for this inverse relationship.

Say I hold a $1,000 bond with a coupon (interest rate) of 5 percent, the prevailing rate at the time I bought it. Now I need cash and want to sell my bond to you, but economic conditions have changed and similar newly issued bonds are paying 10 percent. You'd logically say "Why should I buy your 5 percent bond when I can get a identical bond paying 10 percent?" My response would be, "Obviously you wouldn't want a 5 percent bond when you could have a 10 percent bond and I can't change the fact that my bond has a 5 percent coupon and will never pay more than $50 annually. But what I can do is sell you my bond for $500, so that the $50 you receive each year will give you a yield of 10 percent. Deal?" Deal. As happens every day in the bond market, prices change to bring yields in line with prevailing rates. When rates go up, prices go down and vice versa.

The Meaning of Bond Duration

The example I just provided is simplified to illustrate its point. In reality, market prices of bonds react to rate change to the extent of a bond's *duration*. Duration is a mathematical concept that you really don't have to understand fully. Basically, it refers to the amount of time remaining until the bond matures and all the remaining cash flows (principal and unpaid interest) are in the hands of the investor. The longer the duration, which, generally speaking, is the term to maturity, the more sensitive the bond's price is to an incremental change in prevailing rates. Funds for example, will boast that their bond portfolios have an average duration of (only) three years, making the point that the fund's volatility is minimal. With zero coupon bonds, an innovation whereby bonds are bought at a deep discount, no periodic interest payments are made, and the face value paid at maturity is a lump sum representing both principal and accumulated compound interest, volatility is maximized because duration equals maturity. More about zeros later.

The Essential Difference Between Stocks and Bonds

The most defining point about bonds, in the final analysis, is that they are contractual debt obligations, with all that implies in contrast to stocks. Everything else about bonds can be changed to attract investors, but bondholders are lenders not owners. In the ultimate event of default and liquidation, bondholders get in ahead of stockholders to rake the rubble for what assets might still exist.

So bonds are safer than stocks and since it's a time-honored verity that risk equals return, bonds should yield less and you should pay more to own them. That's not necessarily the way investors look at it, however, unless a recent stock market crash has stunned them in remembering the relative risks of stocks and bonds. When bonds are cheaper than stocks, it's generally advantageous to buy them. Their yields are better and when the relationship normalizes, though it may take time, bond prices will rise as rates decline.

How to Tell When Bonds Are a Better Buy Than Stocks

Whether you are considering a traditional bond or an unusual bond, it's important to understand when bonds are a smart choice overall. Bond and stock prices are comparable to each other when the *current yield* on bonds (the coupon divided by the market price) is related not to dividend yields of stocks, but rather to stocks' *earnings yields*. Earnings yield, sometimes called intrinsic yield, is the ratio of earnings to price, the price/earnings ratio in reverse. For example, if the P/E of a stock or an index is 20/1 or 20, the earnings yield would be 1/20 or 5. It tells us what a company earns for its owners in relation to the price of a share, which is a more complete and realistic measure of the value of a share than the dividend yield. The latter tells us only what portion of those earnings the owners chose to pay out as dividends rather than retain as business capital.

To make stocks more expensive than bonds, which the marketplace has done for extended periods in recent history, is to assume that because stocks *can* rise in value, they *will* rise in value. It's like the old "irrational exuberance" former fed chairman Alan Greenspan once bemoaned. When one of the broad indexes, like the Standard & Poor's

500 stock index, has an overall earnings yield less than the yield of comparable corporate bonds, it signifies a stock market inflated by speculation, one that is overvalued and due for a correction.

When that relationship exists and bonds are cheaper than stocks, it is an opportune time to own bonds. Not only are they yielding more than stocks, but when the relationship corrects, bond prices will rise, creating capital gains.

A dramatic example of this occurred in the year 2000. Bonds were cheaper than stocks, which were at the peak of the dot-com bubble. Then the tech-heavy Nasdaq stock index dropped nearly 40 percent, interest rates dropped by 15 percent, and holders of volatile thirty-year zero coupon Treasury bonds (Separate Trading of Registered Interest and Principal of Securities, or STRIPS) had a positive return, from price appreciation, of 30 percent. Speculating on interest rates using the most volatile bonds is not something to try casually, but the example shows the kind of difference a professional trader can make in the portfolio of a managed bond fund.

Unusual Bonds: Where to Look for Better Deals

You probably didn't buy this book to learn about how basic bonds can help you build wealth. I've spent some time explaining what they are and how they work so you can decide if these other bondlike investment products are for you. So here are some areas of the current bond market where I believe special opportunities exist:

Foreign Bonds

SNAPSHOT: Investing in Foreign Bonds

How It Works:

Here I am talking about bonds issued by the governments of developed foreign countries and investment-quality bonds issued by corporations in those countries and that are denominated in the currency of those countries. Foreign bonds are traded by domestic broker-dealers specializing in foreign investments and able to process orders through local exchanges abroad.

THE UPSIDE:

- Higher Yields: Knowledgeable broker-dealers who specialize in foreign stocks and bonds can usually find bonds paying moderately better yields than their domestic counterparts.
- Currency Profits: With the United States dollar in a secular decline against major foreign currencies, profits on currency translation can be reasonably expected.
- International Diversification: Money managers generally recommend that portfolios be diversified with investments in securities denominated in several foreign currencies.

THE DOWNSIDE:

- Higher Costs: Steep transaction fees can eat away at returns.
- Currency Loss: Despite a clearly downward United States dollar trend there is the risk that the dollar might be in a bear market rally at the time of conversion.
- Interest Risk: As is the case in traditional bonds, risk surrounding interest rates, inflation, downgrading, and reinvestment apply. Floating or adjustable-rate issues would have less interest rate and inflation risk.

Who Should Invest:

Investors seeking dependable income, somewhat higher yields than comparable domestic bonds, currency diversification, and an excellent chance that returns will be augmented by currency profits.

Commentary:

Globalization has been happening for a number of years. Business-friendly, developed countries in Europe and Asia, with faster-growing economies and less onerous regulation, are now a source of government and corporate bonds that pay somewhat higher yields than domestic issues and, with the United States dollar weakening against major foreign currencies, hold the additional prospect of gains on currency exchange. Foreign bonds can be bought these days with relative ease and traditional problems having to do with financial disclosure, now that the large multinational auditing firms are applying similar standards of transparency worldwide, are largely a thing of the past.

You can also open accounts abroad, but to achieve country diversification you would need multiple accounts. Multinational banks and brokers may or may not handle foreign bond trades and those that do may have high minimum order requirements. Good values in foreign bonds can be identified and bought directly with the help of specialized broker-dealers or, often more efficiently, through a growing selection of open- and closed-end mutual funds, which are discussed later.

My Recommendations:

PIMCO International StocksPLUS Total Return Strategy is an open-end fund traded under the symbol PIPDX that has been paying an annual dividend yield of about 14 percent since its inception in 2003. The fund is managed by PIMCO, one of the world's largest and most respected fixed-income managers. The fund focuses on bonds issued by governments and companies in Europe, Southeast Asia, and the rest of Asia. The minimum investment is $5,000 and you can find out more about the fund by calling 800-426-0107 or going to the fund company's Web site at www.pimco.com.

Henderson Income Advantage Fund is an open-end fund sold to investors through financial advisors under the ticker symbol HFAAX. It pays a yield of about 6 percent and has been in existence since 2005. It holds a widely diversified portfolio of bonds issued by governments and companies around the world. The minimum initial investment in the fund is $500 and you can find out more about it by calling the fund at 866-343-6337 or going to the fund company's Web site at www.henderson globalinvestors.com.

Payden Global Fixed Income Fund is an open-end fund sold directly to investors under the ticker symbol PYGFX. It pays a yield of about 5 to 6 percent and has been in existence since 1998. It holds a widely diversified portfolio of bonds issued by governments and companies around the world. The minimum initial investment in the fund is $5,000 and you can find out more about it by calling the fund at 800-572-9336 or going to the fund company's Web site at www.payden.com.

Templeton Global Bond Fund is an open-end fund sold to investors through financial advisors under the ticker symbol TPINX. It pays a yield of about 5 to 6 percent and has been in existence since 2001. It holds a widely diversified portfolio of bonds issued by governments and companies around the world. The minimum initial investment in the fund is $1,000 and you can find out more about it by calling the fund at 800-632-2301 or going to the fund company's Web site at www.franklin templeton.com.

Emerging Market Bonds

SNAPSHOT: Investing in Government and Corporate Bonds of Emerging (Developing) Economies

How It Works:

Country and corporate bonds of developing economies of Eastern Europe, Africa, the Pacific Rim, and South America are riskier and produce commensurately higher returns. Sovereign risk, also called country or political risk, exists to a significant degree. For example, a developing economy might default if the country has borrowed heavily to cover a trade deficit, or a new political regime might trigger the default by failing to honor guarantees by the previous administration.

Eurobonds, issued in foreign countries and denominated in United States dollars, are popular with individuals because they have low minimums and are very liquid.

Brady bonds, created by Treasury Secretary Nicholas Brady during the presidency of George H. W Bush, are also a popular option. Most Brady bonds are denominated in United States dollars, and the principal, but not the interest, of most Brady bonds is collateralized by United States Treasury zero coupon bonds having corresponding maturities and held in escrow at the Federal Reserve. Other types are collateralized with cash and several types are not collateralized. Brady bonds are accessible to individual investors via bond funds.

THE UPSIDE:

- Potential High Yield: Reward is commensurate with high risk.
- Some U.S. Protection: Brady bond principal is collateralized by United States Treasury zero coupon bonds held in escrow. Brady par and discount bonds have cash collateral protection for six to eighteen months.
- Diversification: Like foreign bonds, emerging market bonds allow you to expand your investment options outside of the U.S. market.

THE DOWNSIDE:

- Traditional Bond Risks: Like traditional bonds, risks surrounding interest rates, inflation, credit, and reinvestment are present—even to a higher degree.
- Sovereign Risk: Political or economic instability is more likely to be a factor in a developing country. This may trigger volatility.
- Currency-Convertibility Risk: Related to sovereign risk, this is the risk that a non–United States country may not be able to convert its currency into dollars. Lack of disclosure surrounding this sort of risk is also a potential downside for emerging market debt.

Who Should Invest:

Only investors with a high tolerance for risk. You'll need access to high-quality advice on where to place your investment. And then you'll need to monitor its activity.

Commentary:

Emerging economies often have faster growth rates than developed economies and are attractive to speculators. Many open-end, closed-end, and exchange-traded funds offer managed emerging market portfolios, and if you are tempted by investments having such myriad risks I think it's wisest to consider investing in these markets via funds. I discuss the pros and cons of using funds later on and have some recommendations.

My Recommendations:

AllianceBernstein Emerging Market Debt Fund is an open-end fund sold directly to investors by AllianceBernstein under the ticker symbol AGDAX. It pays a yield of about 6 to 7 percent and has been in existence since 2002. It holds a widely diversified portfolio of medium-quality bonds issued by governments and companies throughout the developing world. The minimum initial investment in the fund is $2,500 and you can find out more about it by calling the fund at 800-221-5672 or going to the fund company's Web site at www.alliancecapital.com.

Fidelity New Markets Income Fund is an open-end fund sold directly to investors by Fidelity under the ticker symbol FNMIX. It pays a yield of about 6 percent and has been in existence since 1995. It holds a widely diversified portfolio of bonds issued by governments and companies throughout the developing world. The minimum initial investment in the fund is $2,500 and you can find out more about it by calling the fund at 877-208-0098 or going to the fund company's Web site at www.fidelity.com.

Morgan Stanley Emerging Markets Debt Fund is a closed-end fund traded on the New York Stock Exchange under the symbol MSD that has been paying an annual dividend of about 8 percent since its inception in 1993. The fund invests in the bonds of government or quasi-governmental organizations in the world's fastest-growing and highest-yielding markets, including Mexico, Russia, and Brazil. You can find out more about the fund at Morgan Stanley's Web site at www.morganstanley.com.

T. Rowe Price Emerging Markets Bond Fund is an open-end fund sold directly to investors by T. Rowe Price under the ticker symbol PREMX. It pays a yield of about 7 percent and has been in existence since 1994. It holds a widely diversified portfolio of bonds issued by governments and companies throughout the developing world. The minimum initial investment in the fund is $2,500 and you can find out more about it by calling the fund at 800-225-5132 or going to the fund company's Web site at www.troweprice.com.

Zero Coupon Bonds

SNAPSHOT: Investing In Zero Coupon Bonds

How It Works:

Zero coupon bonds, which are bought at deep discounts and pay interest at maturity in a lump sum, take the guesswork out of bond investing. The attraction of zeros is not that they offer higher yields than comparable interest-bearing bonds, but that they can be initially bought for a discounted price. Zeros are issued as taxable and tax-exempt bonds or are created by brokerage firms that "strip" the coupon from the principal and issue each as separate bonds. They are also issued as securities that are convertible either into common stock by way of a put option (see Chapter 7) giving them growth potential or into interest-bearing bonds, usually as tax-exempt municipals giving their high-bracket holders tax-free income at retirement.

THE UPSIDE:

- Low Original Purchase Price: Zero coupon bonds are sold at a substantial discount from the face amount. When a zero coupon bond matures, the investor receives the full face amount of the bond. The difference represents the interest.
- Locked-in Reinvestment Rate: You can lock in a particular rate of return, without having to worry about reinvestment risk or interest rates in the future.
- Low Risk: Most zero coupon municipal bonds are rated A or better by the three major rating services.

THE DOWNSIDE:

- Taxes Due: Holders of taxable zeros must pay annual taxes on imputed interest.
- Secondary Market Volatility: If you have to sell before the bond reaches maturity and interest rates have gone up, you could suffer a loss.
- Call Risk: Some municipal issues are callable. If the issuer redeems the bond before maturity, exercising a call provision in the bond contract, you get your principal back, but lose the opportunity for future interest income.

Who Should Invest:

Investors with long-term objectives who value predictability more than yield. Convertible issues may appeal to investors willing to trade off some yield for the growth potential of common stocks or, in the case of municipals, to high-bracket individuals seeking tax-free retirement income.

Commentary:

Although corporations issue zeros, their yield spreads do not offset the greater exposure investors have in the event of default because no periodic income is received while taxes have to be paid annually. For this reason, corporate zeros are not a good bet for most individual investors and I do not recommend them.

For individual investors, I especially like United States government issues, which are state and local tax-free. Government zeros are issued by the Treasury as STRIPS (acronym for Separate Trading of Registered Interest and Principal of Securities) or are created by brokers who separate interest and principal (also called strips because they are, in effect, stripped apart). Zeros created that way by brokers are technically the broker's obligations, but the underlying Treasury bond is normally held in escrow as collateral backing.

Some say municipal STRIPS, a product created by brokers, such as M-CATS, have indirect government backing.

My Recommendation:

American Century Target Maturity mutual funds are a series of zero coupon bond funds that mature every five years. The fund is invested completely in U.S. Treasury zero coupon bonds. Currently, the company offers funds maturing in 2015 (symbol ACTTX), in 2020 (symbol ACTEX), and in 2025 (symbol ACTVX). The minimum initial investment in each fund is $2,500 and you can find out more about them by calling the fund at 800-345-2021 or going to the fund company's Web site at www.americancentury.com.

Mortgage-Backed Bonds

SNAPSHOT: Investing in Mortgage-Backed Securities

How It Works:

Mortgage-backed (pass-through) bonds are issued by government-sponsored entities and provide yields often a full percentage point higher than other bonds of comparable credit standing. The trade-off, however, is that monthly income payments fluctuate, and prepayments, especially where underlying mortgages have relatively high rates, can shorten maturities. They are the only form of asset-backed securities available to individuals, who can buy them directly on the market in minimum amounts of $25,000 or own them indirectly through mutual funds.

THE UPSIDE:

- Higher Yields: Mortgage-backed bonds often offer higher coupon rates than similarly rated bonds.

- Low Risk of Defaults: The mortgage originator has prequalified the mortgage taker as credit-worthy. Some issuers of mortgage-based securities, such as Fannie Mae, Freddie Mac, and Ginnie Mae, guarantee against homeowner default risk.
- Tax Advantages: This occurs to the extent monthly payments represent underlying principal as opposed to interest. The principal portion is a nontaxable return of capital.

THE DOWNSIDE:

- Payments Fluctuate: Monthly income is subject to the experience of the underlying mortgages.
- Prepayment Risk: Should interest rates fall, investors may have their principal returned to them sooner than they expect.
- High minimum purchase requirement if bought directly.

Who Should Invest:

Investors seeking better-than-average yields with a high degree of safety but willing to live with fluctuating monthly income and the risk that prepayments on underlying mortgages will shorten term of bonds, reducing the interest potential.

Commentary:

I recommend mortgage-backed pass-throughs. They are probably the best risk/return deal out there. Prepayment risk is greatest when yields on underlying mortgages are highest, so a pool of low-interest mortgages can be bought at a discount resulting in high bond yields and minimal prepayment risk.

My Recommendations:

American Century Government Bond Investors Fund is an open-end fund sold directly to investors by American Century under the ticker symbol CPTNX. It pays a yield of about 5 percent and has been in existence since 1998. It holds a widely diversified portfolio of mortgage-backed securities. The minimum initial investment in the fund is $2,500 and you can find out more about it by calling the fund at 800-345-2021 or going to the fund company's Web site at www.americancentury.com.

BlackRock Enhanced Government Fund is a closed-end fund traded on the New York Stock Exchange under the symbol EGF that invests in risk-free U.S. Treasuries and mortgage-backed securities, as well as other government-backed agencies of the U.S. government. To boost its payout to shareholders, the fund also writes options on its portfolio of bonds, which helps to cushion any capital losses when interest rates rise. It has been paying an annual yield of between 7 and 8 percent since it was launched in 2005, and it pays dividends monthly. You can find out more by calling the fund at 800-882-0052 or going to the fund company's Web site at www.blackrock.com.

Morgan Stanley Mortgage Securities Trust is an open-end fund sold to investors directly and through financial advisors under the ticker symbol MTGAX. It pays a yield of about 5 to 6 percent and has been in existence since 2003. It holds a widely diversified portfolio of mortgage-backed securities. The minimum initial investment in the fund is $1,000 and you can find out more about it by calling the fund at 800-869-6937 or going to the fund company's Web site at www.morganstanley individual.com.

Schwab GNMA Fund Investor Shares is an open-end fund sold directly to investors by Schwab under the ticker symbol SWGIX. It pays a yield of about 5 percent and has been in existence since 2003. It holds a widely diversified portfolio of GNMA (Government National Mortgage Association, or Ginnie Mae) mortgage-backed securities. The minimum initial investment in the fund is $2,500 and you can find out more about it by calling the fund at 800-407-0256 or going to the fund company's Web site at www.schwab.com.

Vanguard GNMA Fund is an open-end fund sold directly to investors by Vanguard under the ticker symbol VFIIX. It pays a yield of about 5 to 6 percent and has been in existence since 1994 and is one of the largest GNMA funds in the industry. It holds a widely diversified portfolio of GNMA mortgage-backed securities. The minimum initial investment in the fund is $3,000 and you can find out more about it by calling the fund at 800-662-2739 or going to the fund company's Web site at www.vanguard.com.

Tax-Exempt Municipal Bonds

SNAPSHOT: Investing in Tax-Exempt Municipal Bonds

How it works: Tax-exempt municipal bonds, or munis, are qualifying public-purpose bonds of states and their political subdivisions and authorities. They are widely available as both fixed-income and zero coupon issues directly and through funds. They frequently have higher adjusted yields than taxable bonds of comparable quality.

THE UPSIDE:

- Triple-Tax-Free: They are exempt from federal income taxes, state income taxes of state where issued, and often local income taxes.
- Bonus for the Wealthy: Taxable equivalent yield—the yield that a taxable bond would have to pay to equal the tax-free yield of a municipal bond—makes municipal bonds advantageous to investors in higher tax brackets.
- Safety: Issuers of municipal bonds have a strong track record of meeting interest and principal payments.

THE DOWNSIDE:

- Less-Affluent Miss Out: Bonds have lower yields, making them disadvantageous to investors in tax brackets too low to benefit.
- Inflation Risk: Lower yields make munis more vulnerable to inflation impact.
- Economic Risk: Prolonged economic downturns can increase the risk of default.

Who should invest:

Only investors in high tax brackets who benefit from tax exemption.

Commentary:

Most high-bracket investors would benefit by owning munis through professionally managed funds. Broker-dealers normally have high minimum order requirements. Muni quotes, not published in daily newspapers, must be obtained by calling brokers or subscribing to *The Bond Buyer* or to Standard & Poor's Blue List of Current Municipal Offerings.

My Recommendations:

Alliance National Municipal Income Fund is a closed-end fund traded on the New York Stock Exchange under the symbol AFB that pays a tax-free yield of about 6 to 7 percent. The fund manager holds a widely diversified portfolio of high-quality municipal bonds from many states, representing many economic sectors. The fund tends to hold bonds with a duration of five years or less, which makes the fund's share price less volatile. You can find out more about the fund by calling the fund at 800-221-5672 or going to the fund company's Web site at www.alliance bernstein.com.

BlackRock Munivest Fund II is a closed-end fund traded on the New York Stock Exchange under the symbol MVT that pays a tax-free yield of about 6 to 7 percent. The fund manager holds a widely diversified portfolio of high-quality municipal bonds from many states, representing many economic sectors. The fund tends to hold bonds with a duration of five years or less, which makes the fund's share price less volatile. You can find out more about the fund by calling the fund at 800-882-0052 or going to the fund company's Web site at www.blackrock.com.

BlackRock Strategic Municipal Income Fund is a closed-end fund traded on the New York Stock Exchange under the symbol BSD that pays a tax-free yield of about 6 to 7 percent. The fund manager holds a widely diversified portfolio of high-quality municipal bonds from many states, representing many economic sectors. The fund tends to hold bonds with a duration of five years or less, which makes the fund's share price less volatile. You can find out more about the fund by calling the fund at 800-882-0052 or going to the fund company's Web site at www.black rock.com.

Fidelity Advisor Municipal Income Fund is an open-end fund sold directly to investors by Fidelity under the ticker symbol FMPIX. It pays a tax-free yield of about 4 percent and has been in existence since 1998. It holds a widely diversified portfolio of high-quality municipal bonds from many states and sectors of the economy. The minimum initial investment in the fund is $2,500 and you can find out more about it by calling the fund at 800-544-4774 or going to the fund company's Web site at www.fidelity.com.

Nuveen Municipal High Income Opportunity Fund is a closed-end fund traded on the New York Stock Exchange under the symbol NMZ that pays a tax-free yield of about 6 to 7 percent. The fund holds a widely diversified portfolio of medium-investment-grade bonds from many states and representing many economic sectors. The fund borrows some money to invest in more bonds, which increases the fund's yield but also adds a bit to volatility if interest rates rise. You can find out more about it by calling the fund at 800-257-8787 or going to the fund company's Web site at www.nuveen.com.

Structured (Hybrid) Bond-Based Products

SNAPSHOT: Seeking Yield, Growth, and Safety Through Bond-Related Hybrid Structured Securities

How It Works:

Structured products comprise hybrid securities usually invented by investment banks and sold under catchy acronyms such as ELKS, HITS, MITTS, SEQUINS, and STRIDES. These products combine, in various ways, features of fixed- or floating-rate debt, stocks, and derivative instruments such as options. They typically offer guaranteed return of principal along with good yields and potential bonuses based on how underlying instruments or indexes perform.

THE UPSIDE:

- Being customized products in a sense, the variety, novelty, and complexity of these hybrid investments make it hard to generalize, but generally they aim to combine the best of several worlds: safety, yield, and growth potential.

THE DOWNSIDE:

- However ingeniously structured, they will have risks generally equal to their returns and you must take pains to understand them completely.

Who Should Invest:

These products are designed to meet a variety of needs and probably have a place in every portfolio. It's up to you to find the wrench that fits the bolt.

Commentary:

My favorite source for this kind of investment is Carla Pasternak's monthly newsletter, *High-Yield Investing,* published by Street Authority (www.street authority.com).

Carla Pasternak's Recommendations:

In a special report issued recently, Carla discussed three representative examples of structured products, whose features and risks are summarized below:

Citigroup Funding ELKS (Equity Linked Securities) 12% Celgene Corporation notes due March 6, 2008, traded under the ticker symbol EZC on the American Stock Exchange

These notes pay a total of $1.23 per note over their one-year maturity, giving you an annual yield of 12 percent. The notes are linked to the stock of Celgene Corporation, traded on Nasdaq under the symbol CELG, which is a leading biotechnology company that has developed drugs to treat cancer and other diseases. When the notes mature, you will get either $10 a share in cash or 18.2 percent of a share of Celgene for each note you hold. You will receive stock only if Celgene shares trade at or below $39.78 at any time between the issue and expiration date of the notes.

Morgan Stanley HITS (High Income Trigger Securities) 10.5% Apple Inc. notes due February 20, 2008, traded under the ticker symbol APK on the American Stock Exchange

These notes pay $1.05 per note over their one-year maturity, giving you an annual yield of 10.5 percent. The notes are linked to the stock of Apple Inc., traded on Nasdaq under the symbol AAPL which is the leading maker of computers, iPods, and iPhones, and other high-tech gear. When the notes mature, you will get either $10 a share in cash or 11.5 percent of a share of Apple for each note you hold. You will receive stock only if Apple shares trade at or below $65.03 at any time between the issue and expiration date of the notes.

10% ELKS (Equity Linked Securities) notes due January 8, 2008, linked to Best Buy Corporation stock traded under the ticker symbol EBC on the American Stock Exchange

These notes pay a total of $1.05 per note over their one-year maturity, giving you an annual yield of 10 percent. The notes are linked to the stock of Best Buy Corporation, traded on Nasdaq under the symbol BBY, which is the leading retailer of consumer electronics. When the notes mature, you will get either $10 a share in cash or 0.19845 shares of Best Buy for each note you hold. You will receive stock only if Best Buy shares trade at or below $37.79 at any time between the issue and expiration date of the notes.

My Recommendations:

Centerplate IDS (Income Deposit Securities) yielding 10%, traded under the ticker symbol CVP on the American Stock Exchange.

Income deposit securities comprise one share of stock and one high-yield bond. Therefore half of the yield comes from common share dividends and the rest comes from the high-yield bond. Centerplate is one of the largest catering and concession stand operators in America, operating in major stadiums and convention centers. The phone number for investor relations is 864-598-8600.

B&G Foods IDS (Income Deposit Securities) yielding 8%, traded under the ticker symbol BGF on the American Stock Exchange.

Income deposit securities comprise one share of stock and one high-yield bond. Therefore half of the yield comes from common share dividends and the rest comes from the high-yield bond. B&G Foods is one of the largest makers of specialty foods, such as salsa and pickles, in America. The phone number for investor relations is 866-211-8151.

Direct Ownership vs. Ownership Through Funds or Unit Trusts

What's the best way for you to participate in these investment opportunities? My general preference is for managed funds. I'm frequently asked why I think most investors are better advised to own bonds through managed bond funds rather than own them directly. Here are my thoughts on that question:

Everything considered, investors lacking skill, wealth, and time are probably better advised to go the fund route. Of course, bond funds offer a selection of portfolios with different objectives, risk levels, and average maturities (meaning more or less volatility). Most funds pay dividends monthly in amounts that vary and many offer automatic reinvestment of dividend and capital gains distributions, although taxes are due whether distributions are reinvested or not.

A common complaint about mutual funds in general is that because they compete on a quarterly return basis, management is forced into a short-term focus at the expense of rewards famously associated with patience and discipline. While there is undoubtedly something to this argument, it is probably more applicable to stock funds than to bond funds.

For some, direct ownership is a viable option. Essentially direct ownership of bonds frees holders from management fees and other fund-related charges, puts cash flow timing under the investor's control, and gives the investor control over capital gains tax exposure. If the direct investor is able to structure a portfolio when rates are at a high point, he or she has advantages over funds that should result in outperforming returns. Direct investors are free to choose between holding securities paying high yields or, when rates decline, enjoying capital gains. Fund managers, who are buying and selling constantly to put new money to work and to meet redemptions, do not enjoy the same freedoms and will probably see lower returns.

For these benefits, though, the direct buyer makes a good many trade-offs to avoid the downside risks associated with bonds.

For starters, whereas an open-end mutual fund can be purchased for whatever relatively small amount represents its minimum, the direct buyer needs $1,000 per bond plus transaction costs multiplied by the number of bonds he or she feels is needed for a comfortable level of diversification. A large portfolio is desirable not only because it reduces the risk of loss from default (while making it possible to safely own some higher-risk, higher-yielding bonds), but also because it permits the arrangement of maturities in a way that evens out cash flow and minimizes reinvestment risk.

So, while the direct investor buying in a favorable environment is able to retain greater freedom of choice and can get better returns than a fund manager, a substantial investment is necessary to get the diversification, liquidity, and other benefits provided by a large portfolio. Nor will the same access to market intelligence and professional research usually be available to nonprofessionals.

Closed-End Bond Funds: A Different Breed Offering Unique Advantages

You should also consider investing in closed-end bond funds. I like closed-end funds because of the opportunity they offer to augment portfolio returns, which makes them an ideal way to own unusual bonds. An example: AllianceBernstein's Income Fund (ACG) buys global fixed-income securities in developed economies and, as this is written, is yielding 7.2 percent.

So unique are the characteristics and opportunities of closed-end funds that some investors view them as a separate asset class. Their structure provides opportunities to profit, whatever they hold as assets. I compare the closed-end fund to a water bed on a boat. Both bounce around, but each is responding to separate dynamics.

The fund's portfolio fluctuates with values the market puts on the stocks or bonds comprising it, while the shares representing ownership of the fund trade at premiums or discounts to the portfolio's net asset value. The discrepancies reflect a number of factors, such as investor expectations regarding the portfolio's future value and performance, supply and demand for the asset class held by the fund, and higher interest rates that cause bond holdings to drop in price thus reducing net asset value and prompting stockholders to sell.

But net asset values and stock prices eventually converge, and the narrowed discount or widened premium produces additional returns in the form of gains for stockholders. Investors have enjoyed excellent yields enhanced by appreciation with bond funds bought both at premiums and at discounts. But the attraction is mainly to funds trading at significant discounts, which have gains when the discount disappears due to rising share prices or are monetized by other corporate actions such as conversion to open-end funds.

Closed-end bond funds of every description are available, including funds holding foreign bonds, tax-exempt bonds, and floating-rate bonds along with traditional fixed-income bonds with a range of credit qualities and average maturities.

Many CEFs use leverage to boost yields on their shares, adding additional risk and increasing the volatility both of the portfolio and the stock price, so risk-averse investors should investigate carefully before they invest.

But CEFs have advantages over open-end funds. Not having to deal with unpredictable cash inflows and redemptions, closed-end funds save on trading expenses, are free to buy less-liquid bonds providing higher returns, and are spared the dilution caused by sudden cash inflows that either sit idle or have to be invested under unfavorable conditions. On the negative side, discounts and premiums, however temporary, create market risk for stockholders needing to sell shares. Closed-end funds holding corporate and municipal bonds are subject to call risk and those holding mortgage-backed securities to prepayment risk.

Exchange-Traded Funds

Specialized bond portfolios are also available through a vehicle quite new to the scene and rapidly proliferating, called the exchange-traded fund (ETF). These are managed portfolios that trade as stocks but differ from closed-end funds in that differences between their market prices and portfolio values are largely eliminated on an intraday basis by arbitrage operators who trade in *creation units,* typically 50,000-share blocks, that are bought and sold "in kind" and are the only way shares can be bought at net asset values unless share values and NAVs happen to be the same.

My problem with ETFs arises directly from how they operate. Since ETFs always trade at their net asset value, you never have a chance to buy them at a discount to their NAV and sell them when they rise to a premium as you do with closed-end funds. About anything you'd want to know about CEFs and ETFs, you'll find at www.ETFconnect.com, operated by Nuveen Investments.

Unusual Bonds Action Plan

1. Decide what your objectives are. Are you looking to reduce your tax bill? Or in search of a predictable income stream? It can be assumed you read this chapter because you want a combination of yield and safety not available elsewhere. Any investment-grade bond will probably pay you a higher yield than a money market investment, but be prepared to hold it to maturity or risk taking a loss in the secondary market if rates rise and you need to sell it to raise cash.

2. Research Your Options. There is no one-size-fits-all strategy. Are you in a high tax bracket? If not, forget tax-exempt municipals because their advantage will be lost on you. Do you need predictable monthly income? If so, you won't be comfortable with mortgage-backed securities, whose monthly income, although probably better than straight bonds on average, fluctuates, or with zero coupon bonds, which pay no income at all.

3. Evaluate Your Risk Tolerance. Do you have a block of money you can afford to put at greater risk? Emerging market bonds might be your cup of tea, but realize the risk you'll be taking. One of the new structured products might just be ideal for your particular set of requirements, but make sure you understand the product thoroughly and know its particular upsides and downsides.

4. Choose a Managed Fund. I especially recommend a closed-end fund trading at a discount. If a managed portfolio is available through a fund, as an alternative to buying a suitable investment directly, I would recommend buying the fund, especially if it is a closed-end fund trading at a discount.

5. Be Educated. I strongly recommend, whether you use professional management or not, that you take the trouble to stay informed about an investment class that is dynamic and coming up with innovations almost daily. I'm going to suggest some readings in the form of books and newsletters, and give you names of Web sites, trade associations, and other sources I have found valuable.

Resources

Thomas J. Herzfeld Advisors (PO Box 161465, Miami, Florida 33116, 305-271-1900, www.herzfeld.com) is a leading source of comprehensive information about closed-end funds. The firm publishes the monthly *Investor's Guide to Closed-End Funds,* which has complete details on all closed-end bond funds.

Web Sites

www.bondtrac.com
www.emuni.com (information about municipal bonds)

CHAPTER

7

Hedging Your Bets with Options

For years, options were considered an investment playground reserved for professionals—too complicated and risky for the rest of us. But the advent of online trading has helped to demystify the process. Now options are becoming more accessible—and more popular—with the average investor.

Options can create huge gains on small amounts invested whether markets are going up, down, or sideways. They can also be very risky, although with software now available, you can start in a basic way and gradually develop sophistication while keeping risk within acceptable limits.

And here's a little known fact: You can also use options in conservative ways. You can sell covered calls, which I'll explain shortly. You can earn extra income from stocks you already hold, without taking any downside risk at all. And you can use options to protect profits you have already made.

I'm going to show you how these conservative strategies work. I will also introduce you to some more advanced strategies that have the potential to pay off handsomely. In the end, the returns you can get using options are not so much a function of what you know or don't know about the technical aspects of using options. That part looks more complicated than it is. The hard part has to do with predicting the direction, extent, and timing of the movements of the stocks that underlie them. Of course, that's really knowledge required for successful stock investing anyway. But when it comes to options, the time frame in which you have to work is much tighter, meaning your prediction must be precise and accurate in order to earn a profit.

SNAPSHOT: Strategies Using Put and Call Options

How It Works:

Rather than buying and selling actual stocks, you can, for a fraction of the cost, trade rights, which have their own market value. You can contract to buy and sell those stocks at specified prices until the arrangement "expires" at specified future times, usually within a year.

THE UPSIDE:

- Market-Neutral: Options work in all kinds of markets.
- Leverage: Using options, you can control a large amount of money with a much smaller investment. Since a small percentage change in the value of the underlying financial asset can result in a much larger change in the value of an option, large gains are possible.
- Limited risk: As long as you own the underlying stock, your losses as an option buyer are never more than the premium plus transaction expense.

THE DOWNSIDE:

- Time Is Short: Unlike other investments, you cannot simply take the long view. The cost of an option (the premium) is lost money if the underlying stock fails to move favorably and the contract expires.
- Tax Bites: Profits on option positions that are sold rather than exercised are short-term capital gains taxable at ordinary rates when the holding period is one year or less, as it usually is. This differs from gains on stocks you own, which are more often long-term holdings and taxed at lower rates.
- Volatility: Unforeseen events (e.g., a takeover rumor) may cause trading halts or a major price movement in the underlying stock and related options. If the rumored event actually occurs, the stock and option may reopen at a significantly higher or lower price, resulting in a loss that cannot be offset because the cost might be prohibitive, time has run out, or your option has been automatically exercised.

Who Should Invest:

Any investor seeking a conservative way of earning additional income on stocks already owned; any investor wanting to hedge downside risk; or any investor seeking capital gains who is willing to make use of available resources (listed later) and become knowledgeable enough to try the strategies I describe.

Options are typically priced in single digits but traded in round lots representing 100 shares of stock. A typical transaction might be XYZ at 4, meaning an option on 100 shares would cost you $400 plus commission.

The Language of Options

I've long suspected that somebody with a diabolical sense of humor must have invented the vocabulary of options. There is only one term that doesn't need explanation: "buyer." In what must have been a lapse of imagination, buyers of options are actually called buyers.

The rest require a glossary. Here are the basics of the language of options:

- Call: A call is an option to buy. A call gives you the right to buy a stock at a prearranged price, known as a strike price (or exercise price). It's a bet that the stock will rise.
- Put: A put is an option to sell. A put is the mirror image of a call. It gives you the right to sell shares, rather than buy them, at the strike price. It's a bet that the stock will fall.
- Premium: The price you pay to buy a put or call is not called a price, it's called a premium.
- Writers: Sellers of options are not called sellers, they are called writers. If they own the stock, they are called covered writers. If they don't own the underlying stock and are selling short, they are termed naked writers.

Here's how these terms come together:

An *option* is a contract that gives its holder the right, at a cost called the *premium,* to sell or buy a related stock, called the *underlying,* at a specified price, synonymously called the *strike price* or the *exercise price,* before a specified date, called the *expiration.* An option buyer owns a right, but not an obligation. An option seller has an obligation. If you own a stock and want to sell a call or a put, you are called the *writer* or, because you own the underlying, a *covered writer*. *Naked writers* are sellers of options on stock that is borrowed, not owned, but such short selling of options gets complicated and is beyond the scope of this discussion. (Which is not to say it's unimportant or irrelevant; it's for advanced investors and is fully covered in the Resources section at the end of this chapter.)

Options are also available on financial assets other than stocks, such as on stock indexes, debt instruments, foreign currencies, and futures of different types. But I will be talking in this chapter about options on stocks. The same principles apply to the other types, but options on stocks are the most popular.

Within the world of stock options, there is some variety. *Listed options* are different from *conventional options*. A listed option is traded on national stock and commodities exchanges and generally has both high visibility and liquidity, the latter being traded over-the-counter and tending to be individually negotiated and therefore less liquid and more expensive.

Options Have a Life of Their Own: A Plain Language Explanation

Most options are bought and sold for their premium values and are never exercised and settled. Investors will buy an options contract and sell it, hopefully at a higher price. The option to convert the contract into actual shares of stock is typically not exercised.

In other words, you are making money by buying and selling the options contracts without ever converting the options into actual shares of stock.

Option values are mainly determined by three factors:

- The relationship between the exercise price and the market price of the underlying stock.
- The volatility (the propensity to fluctuate) of the underlying stock.
- The amount of time remaining before the option expires.

The relationship between the exercise price and market price creates three basic categories that affect the option's premium value:

1. In-the-money (ITM): When exercising the option would be profitable (exclusive of the cost of the option and related commissions), the option has *intrinsic value* and is said to be *in-the-money (ITM)*. Examples of ITM options would be where the market value of the stock underlying a call is higher than the strike price, or where the market price of a stock underlying a put is lower than the strike price. An option will normally trade for a premium at least equal to its intrinsic value, where intrinsic value exists.

2. At-the-money (ATM): When the market value and the strike price are equal, the option is said to be *at-the-money (ATM)*.

3. Out-of-the-money (OTM): When exercising the option would cause a loss, the option is said to be *out-of-the-money (OTM)*. Examples would be the opposite of those illustrating an ITM option, namely a call where the strike price is less than the market price or a put where the strike price is higher than the market price.

Volatility, the extent to which market prices can be expected to be variable within a short-term period, is a key element in option pricing. It is what gives options trading both its opportunity and its danger. Since both parties to a transaction, buyers and sellers, are presumed to be rational, volatility can be measured historically but never predicted with certainty. Options on highly volatile stocks command higher premiums because they are more likely to produce profits when and if they move up and down.

Time is an important factor in options investing. Because they have a specified expiration date, the time in which the investment can pay off is constantly shrinking. The time remaining before expiration represents opportunity for movements in the prices of stock to occur and thus adds the element of time value to the investment. Options are thus called "wasting assets," meaning their value decreases as they get closer to expiration. When an option is out-of-the-money, its value is all time-related, whereas an in-the-money option has a value that is part intrinsic and part time-related. In the final analysis, the closer an option is to being in-the-money, the further it is from expiration: and the greater is its volatility, the higher the premium it will command.

Weighing all these factors is a complex mathematical process. Robert C. Merton, Fischer Black, and Myron Scholes were awarded the Nobel Prize in 1997 for expanding our mathematical understanding of the options pricing model. Their work coined the term "Black-Scholes" options pricing model.

Derivative pricing has been made easier by computer programs and

Internet services, and its meaning to you and me is that the premium assigned by the market can be judged as over-, under- or fairly valued. This ultimately contributes to a consistent price structure.

A Sampling of How Options Strategies Work

Using Covered Calls to Generate Income

This is the conservative strategy I mentioned at the start of this chapter. If you are an owner of stocks, you can add significantly to the income you receive from dividends by becoming a writer of covered calls. I know we've covered the special language of options, but no one learns a new language in one sitting so I'll try to explain it again in context. A call is an option to buy and a covered call is when an investor writes a call option contract while at the same time owning an equivalent number of shares of the underlying stock.

Here's an example: Let's say your stock, XYZ, is currently trading at $60. You might decide to write a call exercisable at $70, having assured yourself that with the market going sideways and nothing of great significance brewing at XYZ, the chances are the option will not be exercised and you will be richer by the amount of the premium. You are betting that the stock price will not go above $70. If it did, that would be a bad thing for you because you have essentially sold away your rights to profits above the $70 strike price.

The only risk you take here is the risk that, in the argot of options trading, your stock will be "called away"—which means the price of the stock rises above the strike price and the owner of the option has the right to buy your shares at the strike price.

You don't think XYZ will move that much, but the fact that a buyer, who is presumed to be rational, thinks it will, gives you your premium income. In the light of the above discussion of how premium value is determined, it should be obvious that the amount of premium you receive for your covered call varies with the probability of your stock being called away.

In a sense, you have entered into a win-win transaction. If the option expires worthless, you have the premium income. If the option is exercised, you have made a $10 profit above the original value of the stock.

The catch, of course, is that XYZ might go from $60 to $100, leaving you deprived of a $30 additional profit. So the trick here is to know enough about XYZ to be assured the odds are in your favor. You can enhance those odds by trading off some premium for a higher strike price or a longer expiration. It's your call, no pun intended.

The fact is that writing covered calls is a widely used strategy for earning income, meaning that investors who pursue it knowledgeably generally come out ahead. Internet services exist that help identify stocks that command good premiums and minimize the risk of lost opportunity.

Using Options as Insurance Against Downside Risk

Again you are an owner of stocks, but here you are afraid the market is headed for a prolonged down cycle and you want to protect the value of your portfolio as best you can.

The strategy in this case is to buy puts—options to sell—on the stocks you hold (or on a stock index representative of the broad market or a sub-index representative of your specialized portfolio) exercisable at a price close enough to market value to protect the bulk of your downside exposure, yet with enough room to make sure you are not paying a high premium to protect against what might be just a temporary market dip.

For example, let's say you are again the holder of XYZ, which has a market value of $60, but now you think the stock is going to $70 and want to be protected if it goes the other way. So this time you might buy, for a premium (price) of $125, a put with a strike price of $55 expiring in three months.

If, as you expected, XYZ went up, you would have paid $125 for downside insurance and would subtract that much from your capital gain. No big deal.

If XYZ declined, however, you would exercise the put at $55 limiting your loss to $625, representing $60 less $55 (multiplied by 100 shares) plus the premium of $125. Your savings: $2,000.

The Straddle: A Basic Multi-Option Strategy
to Profit from Expected Volatility

This is a strategy used when you expect a big price movement on a stock, but don't know in which direction the price will go. Barron's *Dictionary* of *Finance and Investment Terms,* which I coauthored, has this definition of straddle: "[A] strategy consisting of an equal number of put options and call options on the same underlying stock at the same strike price and expiration date."

To implement the straddle strategy you buy at-the-money strike puts as step one. At step two, you buy at-the-money strike calls with the same expiration date. Since you are paying for equal numbers of puts and calls, transaction costs are on the high side for this strategy. Your maximum risk is again the net debit—that's the premium paid plus commissions. The maximum reward, however, is unlimited.

The Butterfly Spread: A Multi-Option Strategy to Profit from Sideways Movement

This rather complex strategy pays off if, in contrast to the straddle discussed above, the underlying stock makes no dramatic movements.

To implement the butterfly spread you would either use three calls or three puts, but not mix the two. Using calls, the strategy would have you buy one ITM—in-the-money—call with a strike price lower than the market price; sell two ATM—at-the-money—calls (strike price equal to market price); and buy one OTM—out-of-the-money—call at a strike price higher than the market price.

Using puts instead of calls, you would buy one OTM put with a strike lower than market; sell two ATM puts; and buy one ITM put with a strike price higher than the market price.

Without getting into a lot of detail, which would involve diagrams and can be found in any of the recommended books on options, the maximum risk here is the *net debit* of the trade, meaning the total of premiums plus transaction costs. The maximum payoff would be the difference between the adjacent strike prices less the net debit paid.

My own personal approach to option strategies is to use trailing stop-loss orders to protect my profits by allowing them to run. The stops (called trailing because they rise as the option value rises) are kept far enough below market to avoid being triggered by mild fluctuations but not so far that they would permit significant losses should the trend reverse.

Put and Call Option Action Plan

My purpose in this chapter has been to introduce you to conservative uses of puts and calls and to the exciting possibilities that multi-option strategies offer for capital gains. It was not intended as a tutorial. The subject is vast and complex and whole books have been written on single aspects of it. The complexity should not, however, discourage you if you are a beginner from getting involved with options at basic levels and later getting into more advanced strategies as you gain knowledge, experience, and comfort. The most successful options traders are people who have made a life hobby of it and they all began as novices. Remember, covered calls are the least risky, most conservative, and easiest to implement strategy.

1. Decide what you want from options. If it is extra income from the stocks you own, consider covered call writing. Read one of the books I recommend, and then talk to a broker you trust or subscribe to an online service, and through one or the other try it on a small scale. But above all, make sure you understand the risks involved. In the case of covered calls, it's the risk of having your stock called away (bought by the owner of the option), so make sure you're ready to part with XYZ if that happens.

2. Start slow. If you are looking for downside protection, consider buying puts. Like covered calls, it is a simple strategy with little risk that can be done with a phone call, but make sure you understand fully what risk you are taking—in this case, the risk of selling out in overreaction to what may turn out to be a temporary market downturn.

3. Do your research. If you are looking for capital gains and want to try out multi-stock strategies, you'll need to know a lot more about it than you learned here. Make full use of the resources—there are plenty available—and look into one of the investment services available online. They can be expensive and require a commitment of time, so get details, talk to people who have used them, and when you are ready to start, start slowly!

4. Apply your knowledge of stocks. Remember that your choice of option strategies is one thing; your selection of underlying stocks another. Ultimately, the ability to read and understand stock analysis will determine whether you make or lose money using option strategies.

Resources

Books

Options as a Strategic Investment, 4th edition, by Lawrence G. McMillan, (FT Prentice Hall, 2001). A well-regarded advanced discussion of option strategies.

Options Made Easy, 2nd edition, by Guy Cohen (FT Prentice Hall, 2005). A clear and easy-to-understand guide to profitable trading enhanced by effective diagrams.

The New Options Market, 4th edition, by Max Ansbacher (Wiley, 2000). The "bible of options books," includes illustrations and Web site suggestions.

Getting Started in Options, 6th edition, by Michael C. Thomsett (Wiley 2005). An excellent primer.

Options Trading for the Conservative Investor, by Michael C. Thomsett, (FT Prentice Hall, 2005). Focuses on conservative options strategies. Highly recommended.

Magazine/Newsletter

Futures & Options Trader Magazine (www.futuresandoptionstrader.com)

Investor Web Sites Offering Educational, Stock Screening, and Other Options-Related Tools and Services

InvesTools (www.investools.com)
GainsKeeper (www.gainskeeper.com)
Investors Edge (www.investorsedge.com)

Other Resource

Options Industry Council
1 North Wacker Drive
Suite 500
Chicago, IL 60606
(312) 463-6193
www.888options.com
Educates the investing public and brokers about exchange-traded options.

CHAPTER

8

Money Makes the World Go Round: Earning Fast Profits from Foreign Exchange

Stocks and bonds and mutual funds are boring, you say? You'd like some excitement in your investment life? You're willing to take on a little risk for the possibility of huge returns?

If this sounds like you, it's probably time to take a serious look at investing in the foreign exchange market. The foreign exchange market (also called "forex" and "FX") is, by a wide margin, the biggest market in the world, accounting for nearly $2 *trillion*. Few investors talk about their investments with quite the same passion as do forex traders, and I can see why. In a market where wild ups and downs are the norm and many investors are intensely leveraged—trading up to 400 times as much in forex currency as the actual cash in their accounts—well, it's easy to understand why this market is so exciting. Add the fact that the market literally never sleeps—it's always business hours somewhere in the world—which means you can trade in real time, any time of the day or night.

If you're a small investor, you've probably taken note of the huge expansion of options for investing in equities that has taken place in the last decade, thanks to the Internet. In the past few years, technology has allowed investors who are interested to have stock prices in near–real time show up all day long on their computer screens, or even their cell phones. Most of us can barely remember the days when only financial professionals had this information, scrolling on the screens of Quotron boxes at great expense. With the rise of the Internet came discount online trading, allowing investors to analyze numbers and follow stock prices on their own, then enter orders directly online without having to use a human intermediary. This opened up stock trading to many small investors without the funds to make investing worthwhile through a traditional brokerage account.

The last few years have seen a similar transformation in the world of forex, and a wide array of companies have sprung up, offering software for monitoring the foreign exchange market and making trades online. They make it possible for investors to get in the game, sometimes with as little as a few hundred dollars. In this chapter, I'll tell you how to get involved, and explain some of the terminology and basic strategies traders use to make money in this exciting worldwide arena. First, a snapshot:

SNAPSHOT: Investing in Foreign Exchange

How It Works:

You trade one currency against another currency, on the expectation that their values will shift so that the currency you're holding gains in value relative to the one you traded away.

THE UPSIDE:

- Huge profits are possible, even with a very small investment.
- It's Independent of the U.S. Economy: Hard times here may be boom times in other countries, and forex trading lets you make money on those differences.
- No Set Schedule: If you have a nine-to-five job, it can be tough to trade during the New York Stock Exchange's hours of operation. Forex trading lets you take advantage of active markets in other countries when it's early morning or late at night in the United States.

THE DOWNSIDE:

- High Risk: You can lose big if currency trends don't go as you predicted.
- Little Regulation: Forex is an international market with only some policing by some countries. If you get ripped off, there's a good chance you'll be on your own.

- Study Required: Trading in forex is fairly complex, so you'll have to devote some time to learning how to do it. Fortunately, most Internet trading companies allow you to practice with "paper" trades that have no actual value.

Who Should Invest:

If you want the excitement and potential fast gains of foreign exchange, if you have money that you don't mind risking on a volatile investment, and you're willing to spend some time learning how the market works (plus some more time reading international news, watching the market, and investing), forex trading might well be for you.

It also makes a lot of sense if you're concerned about the future health of the U.S. economy, or if you want some part of your investment portfolio in an international market as a hedge against economic problems here at home.

Foreign Exchange

Have you ever traveled to another country and exchanged your U.S. dollars for the local currency? If so, guess what? You've traded foreign exchange. Of course, there are some significant differences between trading currency on vacation and investing in the foreign exchange market—beyond the obvious fact that the purpose of the exchange is to make money, not spend money. But since foreign exchange can be daunting to understand, let's start with the similarities between buying local currency on vacation and investing in the foreign exchange markets before we focus on the differences.

Similarity #1: Buying = Selling

Let's say you want to make money on collectible baseball cards. You find a collector with a card you believe will appreciate in value. You give him $100 and he gives you the card. He's sold it, you've bought it; you now own it. You can sell it if you want to. He can't sell it again.

If you're accustomed to traditional investment venues, this is a logical way of looking at things, but the world of foreign exchange throws this perception out of whack. Why? Because, the definition of buying something is to exchange money for it. In this instance, what you're exchanging money for is...just a different kind of money.

So, as you stand there at the currency exchange booth, you hand the man behind the counter $100, and he hands back 72 euros and some change. You've just bought 72 euros—and you've also sold 100 dollars. You are both a buyer and a seller in this transaction, and so is he.

Same goes for trading foreign exchange. If you think the euro will gain value against the yen, then you want to buy euros with yen and sell yen for euros.

Similarity #2: Spreads

When you bought your currency at the exchange booth, you probably saw a board with two sets of numbers, sometimes in red lights, offering exchange rates for the local currency against various other currencies. The first you probably noticed is that there are two different prices for each currency, sometimes identified as "We Sell" and "We Buy." The "We Buy" price is always lower than the "We Sell" price. In other words, if you've just arrived in Paris and you're selling dollars (and thus, he's buying them), the man behind the counter will give you 72 euros in exchange for your $100 bill. But what if your vacation is over and you're heading home, so you want to change your euros back into dollars? Your 72 euros won't buy you that $100 bill back. You'll need to pay him 77 euros to get it.

Why? Well obviously, the man isn't standing there for fun; he and the bank he works for need to be paid for their work making currency exchanges. The difference between his buy price and sell price, or *spread*, is how the man and the bank earn money for making exchanges.

Out in the vast forex market, the brokers who handle trades make their money precisely the same way—with a spread between their buy and sell price, not with commissions or transaction fees. This spread is usually less than a penny per dollar of currency traded. However, with leverage you're trading large sums of money (more about this later) so those small amounts can add up very quickly.

What this means is, when you first make a trade, you start out at a small loss position. The currencies need to move in the direction you favor enough to make up the spread, before you can start earning money on your trade.

Similarity #3: Values change over time

Meanwhile, back at the exchange booth in Paris, you've bought your 72 euros, and gone off to have a lovely lunch with a carafe of wine. You followed this up with a shopping expedition among the antique prints by the Seine, and a restful cup of coffee in a sidewalk café. Then you look in your wallet and notice your euros are nearly all spent.

The next morning, you go back to the exchange booth to get yourself some more euros. But things have changed. Now the "buy" price for dollars is not 72 euros, but 74. What happened? Out in the foreign exchange markets, the dollar gained value against the euro. You can make more from your $100 today than you could yesterday. And if you had sold them at yesterday's price to a French acquaintance instead of the guy at the exchange booth, your acquaintance could make a 2 euro profit by going to the exchange booth today.

This is the essence of currency trading: you profit—or lose—when one currency changes value in comparison with another. As with your friend's 2 euro profit, all you have to do to make money is guess which direction things are going to move—which currency gains value in a transaction while the opposite currency loses. And, as with your friend's transaction, you can't make or lose money if the two currencies' exchange rate remains unchanged. This is why expert traders sometimes describe what they do as sitting in front of the computer screen, waiting for the trade they want. If nothing moves, no one makes money in the foreign exchange world.

Getting to Know the World of Forex

If trading currencies in the foreign exchange markets seems similar to buying euros on vacation, there are also some very significant differences, many of which make the foreign exchange world much more exciting. Here are a few of them:

Difference #1: Limited currency choices

What currencies do investors trade? It turns out to be a surprisingly short list. The reason is market liquidity—you want to trade currencies that are in the market in enough quantities that brokerages "make a market" in them—which is to say there will always be a seller available when you want to buy, and a buyer available when you want to sell. (Other financial markets work this way too: If you're holding a stock whose price has fallen dramatically, obviously most investors are selling, not buying it. Yet, you can always sell at any moment, though perhaps not at the price you would prefer. This is because there is a financial company on the other side of the trade responsible for "making a market" in that stock—picking up the slack so that demand never overwhelms supply, or vice versa.)

Major currencies used by most forex trading systems include: the U.S. dollar (USD), the Japanese yen (JPY), the Swiss franc (CHF), the euro (EU), the British pound (GBP), the Canadian dollar (CAD), the Australian dollar (AUD), and the New Zealand dollar (NZD).

I should note that, at this writing, there is another currency that could potentially join the list of majors at some point: the Chinese yuan (CNY). Until recently, the yuan was pegged by Chinese government decree to the U.S. dollar at a fixed exchange rate, which obviously made buying and selling yuan for investment purposes pointless. In 2005, the Chinese government decreed instead that the yuan would be pegged to a "basket" of several major currencies and allowed to fluctuate only slightly in relation to these. More recently, the Chinese government has announced it will allow the yuan to float a bit more freely and will gradually loosen its restrictions on the yuan. This is in part a response to pressure from the U.S. and European Union—because an unnaturally cheap yuan makes Chinese goods sold in other countries unnaturally cheap as well.

If the Chinese ever allow their currency to float freely, and if they continue to be the economic powerhouse they have become, the forex world will have to take note of the yuan.

Some brokerages may give you the opportunity to trade currencies other than the majors—called "exotics." However, unless you're an experienced currency trader, I suggest you stick to the majors for now, as there is plenty to learn and plenty of excitement to be had trading just within this group.

Difference #2: You're trading pairs, not individual currencies

After you bought your euros at the exchange booth, you could do whatever you wanted with them. You could trade them in again for Swiss francs or British pounds, or take them to a store and buy things with them. But in foreign exchange, you trade not single currencies, but currency pairs. Since all profits and losses in currency exchange are the result of movement (change in value) between two currencies, rather than buying an individual currency, you take a position in one currency relative to another. If your currency gains value in relation to the other, you make money. If it loses value against the other, you lose money. Sounds very simple, and it is. Guessing ahead of time which currency will gain value in any pair, and which will lose value, is the entire challenge of foreign exchange investing.

Trading currency pairs can be confusing when you're just starting out, because of the conventions associated with doing so. Currency pairs are always expressed as abbreviations for the two currencies, separated by a slash like this: EU/USD. By convention, the same currency is always first, and the price of the currency pair is denominated in the second. For instance, as I write this EU/USD is 1.3369, meaning it takes 1.3369 dollars to buy a euro (more about those fractions of a cent in a moment).

If you think the dollar is going to weaken against the euro, then it makes sense to buy this currency pair (buy euros), which will be worth more dollars over time. This is also called being "long" in euros and "short" in dollars. On the other hand, if you think the dollar will gain strength against the euro, then you should sell this currency pair, becoming long in dollars and short in euros. It's worth noting that in currency trading, you don't need to own a currency pair in order to "sell" it.

Difference #3: Pips, not pennies

Okay, about that 1.3369 dollars. Foreign currency exchange works in much smaller denominations than currency does in real life. The smallest denomination for any currency pair has the cheery-sounding name of "pip." For instance, in the EU/USD currency pair, $.0001 equals one pip.

Pips are a commonly used measurement in forex. For instance a spread (the difference between a broker's buying and asking price for a currency pair) is usually somewhere between 3 and 5 pips. Movement in a currency pair is usually expressed in pips as well.

Why the heck would anyone care if their investment went up or down by $.0001? That brings us to the next big difference between buying currency at an exchange booth and investing in the forex market.

Difference #4: Leverage

For most investors, the decision to use leverage—buying equities on margin, for instance, involves weighing risks and making difficult decisions about how much risk they want to assume. In foreign exchange, leverage is so commonly used that most brokers provide it automatically at 50 to 1, 100 to 1, 200 to 1, or even 400 to 1. Forex.com, to use just one example, automatically gives you 200 to 1 leverage if your account contains less than $2,500, and 100 to 1 if it contains $2,500 or more. In other words, having $1,000 in your account allows you to control $200,000 in the forex market.

BUYING FOREIGN CURRENCY ON MARGIN

You've heard it a thousand times: The wise investor doesn't buy on margin. Buy on margin, and you could be asking for trouble. You could wind up in debt for years paying off a single investing mistake. Make a traditional investment, and the worst that can happen if things go very wrong is that you lose all you've invested. Invest on margin, and you could wind up having to pay many times more.

All this is very sound advice when it comes to other types of investments, but you need to forget this rule if you want to invest in foreign exchange. For two reasons:

1. *You have no choice.* Remember that currency changes are measured in pips. In the case of the dollar against the euro, one pip equals $.0001. So, without leverage, if you invest $1,000 and your currency pair gains 10 pips—which would be an extraordinarily large gain—you stand to earn less than $1. The only way investing makes sense is if you use that $1,000 to control, say, $100,000. Now if your currency pair gains 10 pips, you stand to earn $100, which makes a lot more sense.

2. *You can invest on margin* without *risking more than your investment.* That's right: The biggest risk of margin investing for equity portfolios— that you could wind up owing more than you originally invested—need

continued

not be a concern when investing in foreign exchange. Why not? Most reputable forex trading systems offer a guarantee that, whatever happens in the market, you will never owe more than the full value of your account. (You should find out exactly what the rules are, and get them in writing, *before* investing with any forex system or broker.) This means that even if you make the most terrible of mistakes, the most you can lose is whatever is in your account.

But just because you have this built-in protection does not mean it's okay to make big risky investments on margin, because you can be forced to take losses you otherwise might have been able to avoid. A brokerage may agree not to demand payment from you if your account balance goes into negative numbers, but chances are it will immediately liquidate the account if this happens. If the currency you lost on were to bounce back the following day, you would miss your chance to recoup those losses, and possibly even make money in this volatile market.

For this reason, you should avoid very high amounts of leverage (such as 400 to 1) even if a brokerage is willing to offer them. Remember, all forex investors make at least some losing trades, and with very high leverage it's too easy to get wiped out too quickly.

Getting into the Forex Game

The quickest and easiest way to try out foreign currency exchange is to open an account with an online trading service. (I am assuming you have a reasonably up-to-date computer and an Internet connection, otherwise you will have trouble using this strategy.) You will find a few such retail services (sometimes called "platforms") listed in the Resources section of this chapter, and there are many more out on the World Wide Web. Whichever one you choose, look for the following features:

Regulation

Unlike other financial markets, the foreign exchange market is unregulated, and since it happens simultaneously all over the world, it would be very difficult to police. However, there is some oversight in the United

States, and any U.S. firm you sign on with should be registered with the National Futures Association, the agency that supervises foreign exchange trading in this country.

Reasonable Spreads

Most experts advise using firms with spreads of no more than 5 pips. A wider spread can cramp your style, especially if you're looking to profit off small currency movements. (As a reminder, the spread is the difference between a buy price and a sell price, and is how most trading firms make their money.)

Minimum Investment Requirements Suited to Your Goals

Minimum investment to open an account varies tremendously, from $200 to $5,000 or more. So pick a firm whose minimum account requirements are appropriate to the amount you want to invest in foreign exchange.

Mini Lots

Since standard forex trading is leveraged 100 to 1, standard lots are $1,000 units controlling $100,000 worth of currency. Some companies also allow you to trade mini lots, which are $100 units controlling $10,000 of currency. Some systems even offer micro lots, in which $10 controls $1,000 of currency. The beauty of micro lots is that they allow you to trade nearly inconsequential sums (think $100), and still learn by doing how the market works. Mini lots or micro lots are both great ways for a forex beginner to start out investing.

Free Practice Accounts

The best way to learn something is to do it. But when it comes to foreign exchange, making a mistake while you're learning could be expensive. The solution is to start out trading "paper money"—making imaginary trades, and seeing how they would fare if you had really made them. Most online trading systems allow you to do this, and will track your fake positions for you, just as if you had really bought them. It's a great training tool.

Choosing a Forex Strategy

Once you've selected a platform (the system you'll use for trading), your next task will be to decide what strategy to follow when trading forex—that is, how you will decide where to place your bets on whether one currency will rise or fall against another. The best way to start learning forex strategy is to take some courses, read some books, try out what you learn in your practice account, and determine which strategy makes the most sense for you.

You'll find suggestions for further study in the Resources section. Meanwhile, here's a quick look at the basic concepts behind forex trading:

Fundamental vs. Technical

Fundamental traders use information about the nations whose currencies they trade to make predictions about which way those currencies will move. They're the ones who are constantly checking the currency headlines, and schedules for such things as gross domestic product (GDP) reports, trade deficits, and inflation.

While this is a good approach to determining how a currency will do (especially in the longer term), it's important to remember that there's a certain amount of information overload when you try to follow all the news that might affect a currency, especially if you're looking at more than one currency pair. Therefore, part of learning fundamental trading is learning which pieces of news will likely affect a currency's price and which you can safely ignore.

Technical trading, on the other hand, at its most pure, completely ignores all news about such things as economic indicators and national debt, and instead operates on the principle of pattern recognition. The idea is that currency pairs move in predictable ways, following patterns that traders can profit from. Many of the technical trading formulas are highly mathematical in nature, but you don't necessarily have to do the math yourself. Popular technical trading formulas include Fibonacci numbers, which are used to predict "retracement"—how much a price will retreat or rebound from a high or low, comparing moving averages from various timespans, and stochastics, which holds that during an up trend, a currency will tend to close a major trading period at the high, and during a down trend will close it at the low. When the opposite begins to occur, it signals that the trend is about to reverse itself.

Both technical and fundamental trading have their adherents, with most sophisticated traders using some combination of both.

Trend Trading

Trend trading is a trading philosophy that seeks to "leave money on the table" by getting in after the beginning and before the end of a trend, rather than trying to capture the high and low. "Most traders don't realize the majority of money is made between the high and the low," explains Blake Morrow, president of 4X Made Easy software, which is designed to facilitate trend trading. "Trend traders don't care where the top or the bottom is, and they may get in late and get out early. But 60 percent of the meat is in the middle of the trend, which is why some of the most successful investors are trend traders."

Though it's used by very experienced traders, trend trading is a good strategy for beginners to try to master as well. How do you recognize trends? That does require some study, and 4X Made Easy has both software and training to help investors recognize forex trends so they can take advantage of them. Whatever system you use, some training and/or book learning on how foreign exchange markets work is a useful first step before you start investing.

Whichever trading strategy you choose, it's important to approach it with as little emotion as possible. In fact, forex experts actually recommend writing down what your strategy will be before you start trading. Having a strategy in place before you start, and putting stop-loss orders in place to automatically liquidate a position before losses get out of control, will put you in a position to build wealth with your currency trades.

Lower Your Risk—Forex

1. Find a trading platform (the system you will use for trading) that limits your losses to what's actually in your account (leveraged

accounts—standard in foreign exchange trading—mean your account could have a negative balance, meaning you would owe more money to make up the shortfall).

2. Even so, try to use less leverage, rather than more, preferably no more than 100 to 1, thus reducing the risk that a huge loss will cause the brokerage to close out your account prematurely.

3. Trade mini lots of $10,000 or micro lots of $1,000, rather than standard lots of $100,000.

4. NEVER post a trade without also posting a stop-loss trade—that is, a trade that will trigger automatically to cut your losses if the market moves against you. You can also create a stop order to "take your profit" after you've made a certain amount on your trade. Both types of stops have the potential to prevent you from making the maximum amount possible on the trade, but a stop-loss will protect you from catastrophic losses and a profit-taking stop will make sure you take profits before they turn to losses.

5. Choose a trading platform with a minimum account balance compatible with your investment goals. Don't invest more than you want to just to meet the minimum—there are many different choices out there.

6. Before you really begin trading forex, spend some time trading currency in a paper account.

Foreign Exchange Action Plan

1. **Learn about foreign exchange.** Use the Resources section of this chapter to find books and courses that will expand your knowledge of this complex market. Use them to decide how foreign exchange fits into your investment goals, and what trading strategy or strategies you should use.

2. **Choose a trading platform.** Use the information in this chapter as a starting point for selecting the best Internet interface for you.

3. **Get a practice account.** Sign up for a practice account that lets you trade imaginary currency to learn how the markets work. In fact, you should probably try a few different practice accounts on different platforms to see which one you like best.

4. **Start small.** When you're ready to actually start trading, choose a

platform with a minimum account balance that suits your investment goals. Fund your account.

5. Make a plan before you start trading. Before you begin trading, you should have a specific strategy in place. You should know which currency pair or pairs you will buy (or sell) and when you will exit the deal in order to cut your losses, on the downside, or take a profit, on the upside. Many experts believe you should write your plan before you start, and I agree this is a good idea.

6. Start small. Your early trades should be in smaller amounts, and you should exit early rather than late, taking smaller profits, or smaller losses, as the case may be, while you deepen your understanding of the forex markets.

7. Keep calm. The forex markets can be exciting, and also nerve-wracking. Try to set your emotions aside, and try to stick to your strategy and follow the numbers through every trade.

8. Reevaluate. After a few weeks or a few months of trading, review your performance and your trading strategy. Is your strategy working for you? If yes, then keep doing what you're doing. If no, consider adjusting your strategy or learning some alternate ones. There are many different approaches to trading foreign exchange, and different ones work best for different investors.

Case Studies

To help show you how these strategies actually work, I've provided two real case studies. The names and locations have been changed.

Greg Burton's job came with a decent salary, but many frustrations. Chief among them was the many nights he had to spend on business trips, away from his wife and young daughter. He thought he could have a happier time working from home, and began looking into ways to invest over the Internet.

Greg started out trading in the stock market, and, he says, he made money. But his 9:00 A.M. to 4:30 P.M. schedule was too constraining. Soon he began studying trading foreign exchange pairs. He invested in the 4X Made Easy software, and paid the monthly charge for the ongoing training, and began trading foreign exchange pairs.

The system seemed promising, and he and his wife decided on a plan for him to leave his job and begin studying and trading full-time. But before their target date for him to resign, Greg's job was eliminated as part of a downsizing. It was, in a way, a stroke of luck. "They gave me a four-month severance package," he says. "They gave me vacation time and access to my 401(k). And so I had enough time to learn the system."

And—make no mistake—it was a learning experience. "I destroyed a $5,000 account—traded and lost it," he says. "Then I went through another $1,000 account, and lost that. Then I took a third $1,000 account down to $200, back up to $1,200, and back down again to $300. I probably yo-yoed about three more times—but then I started making money, and I never looked back."

Today, he says, he makes about $7,500 a month trading foreign exchange. "Success is 75 percent psychological," he says. "Another 15 percent is knowing how much to trade—not trying to hit the lotto on every trade. And the remaining 10 percent is knowing how to read entry and exit signals."

The real key, he says, lies in a strict stop-loss strategy. "You have to be willing to be wrong a lot of the time, maybe more often than you're right," he says. "When you're wrong, lose a little. When you're right, make a lot."

Joe Martinson spent years working in a Wall Street firm before he struck out on his own trading currency pairs. An expert on Japan, Joe likes trading the yen, and usually sits down at his desk right after dinner, when the Tokyo Stock Exchange is opening.

Unlike Greg Burton, Joe is a fundamental trader, and carefully follows financial information from a variety of online news feeds to help him decide which pairs to trade and how. He also has CNN on in the background while trading. He's constantly following the news and flagging anything that could affect currency.

"All these things together create a pattern, and you can see which way the market is headed," he says. When he's analyzed the events of the day, he waits for the market to start moving. "Sometimes you have to wait for it. You can't force it," he says. If things seem particularly quiet, he'll watch TV or even go out to a movie, then return a couple of hours later to see what the market is up to.

Joe makes about $2,000 a week trading forex, he says. Even though his financial background prepared him to be a trader, he thinks anyone can do it—if they have the right outlook. "It's not whether you've studied economics," he says. "It's a matter of having that instinct for jumping in at the right time and being willing to take risks."

Resources

Books

Getting Started in Currency Trading: Winning in Today's Hottest Marketplace by Michael Duane Archer and James Lauren Bickford (Wiley, 2005)

This is a good book that gives you an overview of the currency markets and how they work, and a start toward developing your own currency trading strategies.

Foreign Exchange: A Practical Guide to the FX Markets by Tim Weithers (Wiley Finance, 2006)

Weithers uses his many years of experience as an economics professor and international bank executive to help you navigate the Forex market successfully. He explains the basic elements of the foreign exchange market, including major currencies, bid-ask spreads, and the importance of interest rates. He helps you look beyond the noise of news reports when you are trading and avoid some of the most common mistakes made by investors.

Forex Conquered: High Probability Systems and Strategies for Active Traders by John L. Person (Wiley Trading, 2007)

Person has thirty years of experience in foreign exchange, and in this book he explains how to develop a winning trading system. He describes such technical trading tools as candlestick charting, Elliot wave theory, and Fibonacci price indicators to help you make profitable trades.

Forex Revolution: An Insider's Guide to the Real World of Foreign Exchange Trading by Peter Rosenstreich (Financial Times Prentice Hall Books, 2005)

Longtime trader Rosenstreich offers students and investors a complete, practical guide to Forex trading, including risks and pitfalls. He describes fundamental and technical trading strategies and tells you how to employ the discipline needed to make these strategies effective. He explains all of the different Forex investment possibilities, including currency futures, options, and swaps.

The Complete Idiot's Guide to Foreign Currency Trading by Gary Tilkin and Lita Epstein (Alpha, 2007)

The concise, easy-to-follow guide by foreign exchange expert Tilkin and journalist Epstein explains the Forex market and provides tips on successful trading strategies. An interactive instructional CD is included, which allows readers to log on to the Global foreign Trading Web site and learn the process of currency trading with virtual trading.

The 10 Essentials of Forex Trading by Jared Martinez (McGraw-Hill, 2007)

Trading expert Martinez reveals his forecasting methods and trading strategies so you can profitably relate market movements to trading patterns.

Software/Courses

Forex.com (44 Wall Street, New York, New York 10005; 877-367-3946) www.forex.com

Forex.com offers free practice accounts, mini-lots, and a user-friendly, easy-to-follow interface. It's a good way to get a handle on how Forex trading actually works.

4X Made Easy (15601 Dallas Parkway, Addison, Texas 75001; 888-304-8881) www.4x.wizetrade.com

In addition to providing an interface, 4X Made Easy software and training combined help you follow a trend trading strategy—short-, medium-, or long-term—with a system that makes it easy to spot trends and know when to get out. Ongoing streaming video over the Internet lets you connect with the experts, as well as other traders like yourself, to learn how to make the most of your account.

PremiereTrade Forex (Suite 1020, 220 East Central Parkway, Altamonte Springs, FL 32701; 800-821-7325 or 800-785-7423) www.premieretrade forex.com

PremiereTrade is a gateway to the spot Forex market and provides education and support for traders, including ongoing financial market reports and a daily radio show about the Forex market. The company offers the FXDD Trader platform to give you direct access to the Forex market.

CHAPTER

9

Tapping into Cash Flow

Investing in financial instruments such as stocks, stock options, and bonds is a great way to make a profit, especially if you're busy with your career or your family and can't devote much time to working on your investments. But if you do have the time, and you like the idea of working directly with people, selling your services, and putting deals together, then you should look into cash flow as a way of generating fast profits.

What is cash flow, exactly? We're all familiar with the term, as it relates to the day-to-day cash both businesses and families need to pay their bills and their employees, keep the lights turned on, and everyone fed.

That definition is a good starting place for understanding how the cash flow industry works. Investing in cash flow consists of buying the right to receive future payments today at a discounted price. The concept rests on the fundamental principle that, due to inflation and the opportunity cost of lost investment earnings, money gradually loses value over time.

What do I mean by "opportunity cost"? Let's say you know you can reliably invest your money at 5 percent per year (a modest return, compared to some investments in this book). If I owe you $1,000 and I pay you today, you can invest that money, and in six months you'll have $1,025. So if I make you wait six months for your $1,000, I've effectively cost you $25. Thus, $1,000 today is worth $25 more than $1,000 six months from now.

Now look at it from the opposite direction: What if I offer to pay you $980 today instead of $1,000 six months from now? You should take the deal, because if you invest at 5 percent, in six months my $980 will be worth $1004.50—not to mention saving you the trouble of finding me and collecting the money in the future. And, of course, if you are going to use that $1,000 to, say, pay off credit card debt accumulating at 20 percent or more per year, you might be willing to take an even bigger discount to get that money today.

That's the simple idea behind the growing cash flow industry. (Some in the industry refer to it as buying and/or selling, or brokering notes, rather than cash flow, but the idea is much the same.)

You should know right up front that cash flow is a much more complicated strategy to learn than the others in this book, and reading this chapter will not be enough to get you started making cash flow deals. Instead, I'm going to give you an introduction to this fascinating field, and tell you about some of the benefits and challenges it offers. And, of course, in the Resources section, I'll tell you how you can get a real education in creating cash flow deals, if you decide this strategy is right for you.

For this chapter, I've drawn on the expertise of Fred Rewey, president of the American Cash Flow Association and publisher of the *American Cash Flow Journal*. He has been engaged in buying and brokering cash flow deals for more than fifteen years, and in many ways has helped shape the cash flow industry and profession. Now, let's start with a snapshot:

SNAPSHOT: Cash Flow Investing and Brokering

How It Works:

Your task is to identify people or businesses with future payments they'd be willing to sell at a discount for ready cash. You profit either by buying the payments yourself, or by serving as broker for a third party, typically a large company, that provides the funds.

THE UPSIDE:

- Fast Profits: It can take a while to get a deal going. But once you do, you can make phenomenal returns investing in cash flow. And some kinds of deals (such as factoring) keep on paying indefinitely.
- Low Up-Front Investment: If you broker deals with third-party funding

sources, you can make money with no investment of your own. (You will need to invest time, however, and possibly some money in getting educated about cash flow deals.)

- It's Noncyclical: People and business need fast cash in both good times and bad.

THE DOWNSIDE:

- It's Hard Work: If you're looking for an easy or passive way to make money, this isn't it.
- Study Required: The world of cash flow is complex, and it takes some effort to learn how it works.
- Long Start-up Time: It may take several months or a year to get the hang of the business and start closing deals.

Who Should Invest:

If you have little free time and you want an investment that will make money for you without too much of your attention, then cash flow is the wrong choice. But if you have some free time and you're interested in an industry that could dramatically increase your income, then learning to invest in and broker cash flow deals may be just the thing to set you on your way to financial independence.

Who Needs Cash Flow?

A few years ago, I was listening to a friend of mine complain bitterly about her work. She was a physical therapist who worked in a busy medical practice, but rather than drawing a salary, she operated as an independent contractor. Every Friday, she'd submit an invoice for that week's appointments to the practice's business manager, who would forward them on to the patients' insurance companies.

Then my friend would wait. And wait. "It's ridiculous," she said. "I earn good money, but I'm always scrambling to pay my bills because I never have the money when I need it. Sometimes it takes three months before I get a check."

I didn't know about it at the time, but my friend would have been a perfect candidate to sell her future payments into the cash flow market. She might have been able to sell her $10,000 invoice for, say, $9,700. Yes, she'd be losing $300—but she was probably spending at least that much during her three-month wait on late fees and credit card interest, so getting the cash up front would be a better deal. The person who bought the invoice would be earning more than 3 percent on his or her money in three months—for an annualized yield of more than 12 percent. As in every good cash flow transaction, everyone walks away happy.

The above type of cash flow transaction—providing cash for businesses awaiting payment of an invoice—is called cash flow factoring. It's only one of many examples of how the cash industry works.

Another common scenario for cash flow has to do with owner-financed real estate deals. Imagine you own a house, but you and your spouse have recently found that the house of your dreams is available on the market. You need to sell your current home—at a good price—in order to afford the new one. But the real estate market in your community has cooled, and after several months, no one has made an offer at the kind of price you're looking for. You need at least $300,000 to pay off your mortgage and make a down payment for the new house, and the highest offer you've gotten for cash is $265,000.

Your real estate agent suggests that you offer owner financing as a way of widening the pool of potential buyers for your home. If you offer to hold the note on your house, buyers who may be recently divorced, or have bankruptcy in their past, or may simply be self-employed without a salary they can demonstrate, can now make an offer on the house without worrying that a bank's mortgage department won't find them creditworthy.

The strategy works: With owner financing as an added inducement, you get an offer of $314,000. You should be happy, but you've got a problem: The buyer is only paying $35,000 in cash, and making monthly payments of about $2,200 at 9 percent interest for the next thirty years on the remaining $279,000. You've sold your house, but you still don't have the cash you need to pay off your mortgage or make a down payment on the new house.

Cash flow to the rescue! You can sell the note on your former home to a funding source for cash at a discount off face value. The funding source will earn a good rate of return, with your house as collateral in case the buyers don't pay. The buyers move into your former house, and you get the house of your dreams. Again everyone walks away happy.

According to Rewey, transactions like this one are growing as bank interest rates are on the rise. "The reason privately held notes got big a few years ago is that interest rates were through the roof—14 or 15 percent," he says. "As rates got lower, many people refinanced those loans at lower interest rates with traditional mortgage lenders, so those notes went away. Now that rates are rising again, we're seeing more of those deals." Rising interest rates also mean that homeowners with adjustable rate mortgages may find themselves needing to sell fast. "If I have to sell, what will help my property sell faster and at a better price? Owner financing," he says.

Six Types of Cash Flow

The cash flow industry finances everything from aircraft leases and purchases to retail store layaway plans. Rewey says there are sixty different types of income streams (i.e., sources of future payment) that can be purchased for cash, but they all fall into the following six categories:

1. Business-Based

Cash flow factoring, as in the example of my friend's invoices, is one type of business-based cash flow. Typically, business owners use this cash for day-to-day expenses or to buy the materials to fill an order before the invoice is paid. But there are other types of cash streams to buy from businesses, often similar to small business loans, for expansion, purchase or lease of equipment, or letters of credit, for instance. Collectability (the likelihood that future payments will be made as planned) depends on the solidity of the business and its customers.

2. Collateral-Based

In these deals, the income stream is guaranteed by an asset of equal or greater value to the cash provided. A real estate mortgage is a classic example of a collateral-based income stream, but the collateral could also be a car, a boat, or pretty much anything that could be foreclosed on in case of nonpayment. Collateral-based cash flow is a good place to start for those new to the industry, because you have some built-in protection.

3. Consumer-Based

In this case, you're buying cash flow, usually without collateral, and the payor is an individual. One typical example is buying delinquent consumer debt, as collection agencies routinely do, at a deep discount, so as to try to collect from the debtor. Generally, because it is high in risk, consumer-based cash flow is not a good starting place for those new to the cash flow industry.

4. Contingency-Based

With contingency-based cash flow, the future payments are dependent (or *contingent*) on variables that make the amount of eventual payment uncertain. A typical example is lawsuit financing. A law firm takes on a case on a contingency basis (rather than billing the plaintiff by the hour) because it has a strong expectation of receiving a judgment or settlement. In the meantime, the law firm may need cash in hand to pay lawyers and others working on the case. In this instance, the funder provides cash, with future repayment dependent on when and how much the law firm receives if it wins, or the defendant settles. These can include such items as lawsuits and royalty payments.

5. Insurance-Based

In these deals, the source for future payments is some sort of insurance. Examples include annuities and structured settlements, an agreement by an insurance company to pay a designated person a specific sum of money in periodic payments instead of as a lump sum; and also "viaticals," in which the terminally ill cash in on their life insurance in advance. Because the companies providing payments are often very large and well-established insurance firms, insurance-based cash flow is one of the lower-risk areas for investment.

6. Government-Based

Government-based income streams include things like lottery winnings and military retirement. (Large lottery winnings are often parceled out to winners in structured payments rather than a lump sum. Often the winners would rather have cash up front—particularly since they may be taxed on the entire amount in the year they win it.) Needless to say, these are some of the safest cash flow investments, but at the same time, returns may not be as high as in other areas with more risk.

Getting in the Game

Okay, you're interested. How can a small investor get involved in cash flow? The challenge for anyone in this industry is finding appropriate notes or other income streams to buy, and persuading the owners to sell them at enough of a discount to make the transaction worthwhile. Thus, even though you're the buyer (or broker) in this exercise, it's helpful to think of it in terms of selling, because that's what you'll be doing. Successful cash flow investors and brokers drum up business a variety of ways, among them:

- Cold calling business prospects
- Reviewing months-old real estate ads to identify sellers who might be holding owner-financed notes, and want to sell
- Setting up Web sites
- Attending local chamber of commerce events
- Making presentations
- Handing out flyers

Being successful in the cash flow industry is all about marketing, and the first step in any effective marketing plan is deciding exactly who you're marketing to. The more precisely you can target your market, the more efficient you can be in your approach, Rewey advises. Thus, if you're interested in dealing with real estate notes, you might target homeowners who've sold homes with values of $200,000 to $500,000 in the county where you live and the three counties immediately around it. I'm guessing that, right off the bat, if you were looking for such home sellers, you'd have a good idea already how to find them.

As part of deciding what type of income you want to buy, you should also consider whether you'd be most comfortable selling your services to individuals or businesses. Would you rather meet an executive in his or her office, and deliver a well-practiced presentation complete with a written proposal? Or would you rather meet with one of your neighbors and chat about cash needs over the kitchen table? How you like to work will determine which approach is likely to work best for you.

At the same time, remember that personal contacts are like gold in this industry, so ask yourself whether the relationships you already have can help you launch a successful career in cash flow. Did you just spend several years working in administration at a law firm? Maybe your old employer needs cash on hand, and would be interested in having you help set up a factoring arrangement, or secure contingency financing for a lawsuit. Or have you noticed that many of your neighbors are selling their houses and playing the real estate market? Maybe you can offer to buy some of their owner-financed notes.

How Much Can You Earn?

There's no doubt about it: Investing in cash flow is very hard work, but if you do it well, the potential returns can be truly spectacular, especially if you're willing to buy some of the higher-risk income streams. Rewey recalls one investor he knows who bought a second note on a property for $12,000. (A second note is a note that has property as collateral, but the debt is second in line to another loan, typically a mortgage, that takes precedence.)

In this case, the note was for a fairly small sum—$12,000—and it was "behind" (that is, subordinate to) a much larger mortgage on a house. If the borrower were to default on the larger, first note, the holder of the second would likely collect nothing.

This is why, as Rewey says, "Nobody wants to buy seconds." Because of the risk, most cash flow investors would only pay about 50 cents on the dollar for a note such as this, which is why Rewey would have advised against selling it. But the note holder needed cash quickly, and the investor bought the note for $5,500. Since the note was for 120 monthly payments of $158.58, that amounted to a return of more than 34 percent.

Sometimes, he adds, it's possible to beat even these returns if the borrower is willing to trade a quick payoff for a discount off the amount owed. "You can go to the borrower and say, 'If you can give me $9,000 in the next thirty days, we'll cancel the note,'" he says. "To save $3,000, it might be worth it to them to put the money on their credit cards or borrow from a relative. If so, you've turned $5,500 into $9,000 in less than a month."

That's great, but before you go running off to seek out other deals like it, remember the reason for the low price on the note: It was a high-risk transaction, with little protection for the investor if the borrower defaulted on the first note. "The collateral isn't really there," Rewey says. "If the borrower can't pay the first note, the house will be sold at foreclosure auction and it's unlikely there'll be enough left over to cover your second note." However, he adds, "If the borrower defaults on the second note, but continues to pay the original mortgage, you'll have a lien on the property, and it will just sit there. Sooner or later, the borrower will want to sell the property, and then will have to deal with you."

This is why he advises caution when purchasing high-risk notes. "If I buy just one of these notes, it will likely go bad," he says. "That's just Murphy's Law. If I buy a pool of them—and I'm buying them right— then some will go bad, but most will be paid." Thus, he says, in the aggregate, instead of winding up with a return of 34 percent, it might be in the high teens or low 20s. "That's still a pretty strong return at the end of the day."

When deciding which high-risk notes to take a chance on, he adds, his most important consideration is the buyer's credit score, and he won't buy unless the borrower seems creditworthy. "You're going to pass on a lot more of these than you're going to buy."

If you want a safer investment, Rewey recommends buying income streams that are guaranteed by collateral, as well as those backed by large insurance companies (such as structured settlements or annuities) or by state funding (such as lottery winnings). As with all investments, there's a trade-off of risk to earnings: Safer investments will yield a lower rate of return, and you will also face more competition from other investors to buy them.

"If you buy a lottery winning, you probably will earn about 8 percent," Rewey says. "That's not huge, but you're absolutely sleep-at-night safe: The state has your name on record and will mail you the checks, just as if you'd won the lottery yourself. If you're investing in CDs, where the most you'll ever earn is 4 percent, this is just as safe."

Is the cash flow industry for you? Learning how to find and close these deals is complex and will probably require attending a course, either through Rewey's American Cash Flow Institute, or one of the other organizations that offer cash flow teaching, followed by a period of trial and error as you learn to put together deals. Many who take up cash flow do it with the intention that it will become their full-time occupation, and in some cases, this plan comes true. Others simply do a few deals to supplement their salaries or other income. Either way, once you get the hang of it, brokering and buying cash flow can be one of the most powerful ways to build long-term wealth—in both good times and bad.

Should You Broker or Buy?

There are two ways of making money in the cash flow industry. One way is to invest your own money, buying the right to collect future payments on your own behalf. In this case, your investment earns from the interest on the payments (if any), and by buying these financial obligations at a discount off their face value. The second way to make money in cash flow is by brokering deals between a person or business who wants to trade future payments for immediate cash, and a *funding source* that can provide ready cash and wants to earn a return on its investment.

Obviously, you can earn more by investing your own funds, and rather than getting a onetime payment for putting the deal together, you keep earning for as long as the payments keep coming. But there are some good reasons to consider brokering as well:

1. Your money is not at risk. You earn your fee or commission for brokering the deal whether or not future payment(s) are made as planned.

2. You can do bigger deals. Some notes available for purchase are in the millions of dollars. Chances are, you don't have that kind of money to invest, but, as a broker, you can still make money on these transactions.

3. Funding sources are easy to find. You might be surprised to see how many funding sources are eager to work with cash flow consultants/note brokers, but lending is big business and there are many companies eager to have you help them find customers for their loans and credit lines. Dozens of funding sources advertise in *Cash Flow Journal*, the American Cash Flow Association magazine, and also exhibit at its annual convention.

4. You can put your knowledge to good use. It takes time and money to learn how to do cash flow deals successfully. That study may not pay for itself if all you do is one or two deals on your own behalf. Brokering lets you earn money from your newfound knowledge over and over again.

5. You can learn the industry. How much discount should you get when you buy collateralized notes? What kind of fees are reasonable? How can you make sure the obligation you're buying will be paid on schedule? Funding sources have formulas for determining these things so it makes sense to broker a few deals for a well-established funding source before you start buying cash flow on your own. "We always tell people, even if you can afford to buy a note, broker a few deals first," Fred Rewey says. "That way, you learn the process."

6. You don't have to create legal documents. Another advantage to brokering is that you don't have to worry about creating binding contracts to make sure future payments are made, since the funding company will provide the contracts for you. However, any good cash flow course will include detailed information on how to create binding agreements—and will usually offer sample agreements you can use as models for your own.

Lower Your Risk—Cash Flow Investing

1. Broker deals, rather than putting up your own money, so your funds are not in play.
2. Buy notes that are backed by collateral (a house, car, piece of land) that you can claim if the debt is unpaid.
3. Buy insurance-backed cash flow, such as annuities or structured settlements. Most large insurance companies aren't going bankrupt, and they pay their debts.
4. Buy government-backed cash flow, such as providing cash for lottery winnings to be paid over time.
5. Buy risky cash flow in pools. If you're going to invest in a high-risk note or other obligation, don't make it the only one. Own several different notes with different parties making payment, and be prepared for the likelihood that one or two will default.

Cash Flow Action Plan

1. Decide whether you want to invest your own money, broker deals, or both. Fred Rewey recommends that those new to cash flow begin by brokering in order to learn common procedures and concerns of the cash flow deal.

2. Decide what type of cash flow makes the most sense for you. This means choosing not only what type of cash flow (insurance-based, contingency-based, and so on) you want to work with, but also in what industry, and perhaps in what region. Narrowing your sights is good— the idea is to help you target a specific market for your services.

3. Get educated about how cash flow deals work. In order to create successful cash flow transactions, in which everyone walks away happy, you need to learn how to structure these deals and what kind of discounts or interest are typical for different types of transactions, as well as how to make sure you're as protected as possible if payments don't come through. The Resources section of this chapter offers information on Web sites and courses that can help you get started learning about cash flow.

4. Look for prospects. You should try many different ways to market your cash flow services: cold calling, using your network of contacts, printing up flyers and brochures, using a Web site, making presentations, and so forth. Find out which ones are the most effective for you, and focus your efforts accordingly.

5. Close the deal! Whether you're brokering or investing your own money, the final and essential step is getting the prospect to agree to sell the cash flow at a price that works for both of you (and your funding source, if you're brokering the deal). This is the most difficult part of the cash flow process—and the most exciting, when it all comes together.

Resources

Books

Cash In on Cash Flow: How to Make Full Time Income with Part Time Effort in America's Hottest New Business by Laurence J. Pino (Simon & Schuster, 1998)

Pino, the father of the cash flow industry, explains how to tap into the multiple opportunities available in the cash flow business in this classic work. He gives detail on profiting from structured insurance settlements, lotteries, real estate notes, and much more.

Factoring Fundamentals: How You Can Make Large Returns in Small Receivables by Jeff Callender (Soundview Funding Corp., 2003)

Factoring (buying cash flow from invoices and accounts receivable) is only one aspect of the cash flow business, but if you think it might be right for you, this book can help you get started. It provides a detailed introduction on the benefits and risks of factoring, and how small investors can get started.

Winning the Cash Flow War: Your Ultimate Survival Guide to Making Money and Keeping It by Fred Rewey (Wiley, 2005)

Rewey, the president of the American Cash Flow Association, offers a practical guide to turning the corner from paying everyone all the time to getting paid instead. He discusses all the major ways to get involved in the cash flow business for maximum profit.

Web Sites/Courses

American Cash Flow Institute/American Cash Flow Association
American Cash Flow Corporation
255 South Orange Avenue
Suite 600
Orlando, FL 32801
800-253-1294
www.americancashflow.com

This is the Web site for Fred Rewey's American Cash Flow Institute and Association. Membership in the association is available to graduates of the institute's three-day (or home study) course. ACFA is the first and largest association for the cash flow industry, and holds an annual cash flow convention, where funding sources exhibit offering cash for brokered deals.

Dash Point Financial Services, Inc.
PO Box 25591
Federal Way, WA 98093-2591
253-925-1948
www.dashpointfinancial.com

Dash Point is owned by Jeff Callender, and specializes in factoring for very small businesses, and it might be a very good fit if you are interested in factoring and know or can meet many small business owners in your community.

Pinnacle Investing
575 West Chandler Boulevard

Suite 220

Chandler, AZ 85225

888-736-5353

www. pinnacle-investments.com

Pinnacle investments focuses on buying and selling mortgage notes, and in training consultants in this lucrative market. The firm is run by Troy Fullwood, and in addition to working with consultants on deals, also offers Troy's Power of Paper course, which regularly sells out in cities across the country and even abroad.

Pinnacle also publishes *Straight Talk,* a free e-mail newsletter for real estate investors, at www.straighttalkforrealestateinvestors.com.

Newsletters/Web Sites

NoteWorthy Newsletter

www.notweworthyusa.com or (800) 487-1864

Like ACFA, NoteWorthy offers classes, books, an annual convention, and an active Web site. You can sign up for individual courses, as well as the *NoteWorthy Newsletter.*

The Paper Source Journal

www.papersourceonline.com or (800) 487-1864

This journal offers a print and online listing of companies that buy notes and funding sources, as well as books and e-books, and home study courses to help brokers get started in the cash flow industry.

CHAPTER

10

Profit by Doing Nothing: Passive Income Strategies

Ever dream of doing nothing, sitting at home while money rolls in? That's the big secret behind the passive income strategies I'll be discussing in this chapter. Now, don't get me wrong. These may sound like the perfect moneymaking opportunities for lazy people, but actually, this is far from true. All these strategies take work—sometimes lots of work, especially at the beginning of the process. But the concept is to put a system in place that will continue generating revenue year after year, almost automatically.

How can you achieve this? There are many different ways of creating passive income with your investment. One of the most familiar, for instance, might be to buy a piece of real estate, such as apartment units or a store. If you can collect rent that brings in more than you have to pay out in loan payments and maintenance costs, you've created passive income. Yes, you will need to make sure the property remains in good shape, occasionally deal with tenants, address their concerns, write and enforce leases, and so on. But, for the most part, the rents will roll in and—unless a unit remains empty or some unexpected mishap befalls the property—you will keep on collecting that income for the foreseeable future.

The strategies in this chapter are designed to create ongoing income in a similar way—they will take some time and effort to put in place, as well as some ongoing work of one sort or another. But each will continue bringing in steady and automatic income for the long term, with as little effort as possible from you.

Which one is right for you? When comparing, consider the following factors:

1. *Up-front Investment.* Some strategies require a substantial investment in order to start bringing in income. Others require very little or none at all.

2. *Effort to Get Started.* Similarly, some passive income strategies take a lot of work to get off the ground, while some are easier. As a generalization, the less up-front investment is needed, the more work it takes to get a passive income source going.

3. *Ongoing Effort.* Once the passive income is in place, how much work/investment will it take to keep it going? Will you have to deal with it several times a year, or every week, or every month?

4. *Selling Required.* Some passive income streams, such as vending machines or subscription services, can require sales skills to get off the ground. If you're good at selling, these can be great opportunities. If selling isn't your thing, look for passive income opportunities that don't require a big sales effort.

Which passive income strategy is right for you? This chapter takes a look at five of the most effective methods for creating passive income. Compare the pros and cons of each to find the strategy that best meets your skills, interests, and investment goals. As always, I'll start each off with a snapshot, for easier comparison.

Passive Income Strategy 1: Vending Machines

SNAPSHOT:

How It Works:

Placing vending machines in high-traffic locations allows you to collect passive income whenever customers buy.

THE UPSIDE:

- Low Start-up Investment: A single bulk vending machine can cost a few hundred dollars or less.

- Flexibility: You can start with a single machine around the corner, and build up to many more, or keep your investment and commitment small.
- Noncyclical: People buy from vending machines in good times and bad.

THE DOWNSIDE:

- You're on Call: When there are problems with machines, you have the ultimate responsibility for solving them.
- Labor-Intensive: You will need to visit your machines on a regular basis for maintenance and to collect cash—or hire someone trustworthy to do so for you.
- Some Study Required: Anyone can do this business, but you will need to spend some time learning its ins and outs.

Who Should Invest:

Vending machines are the perfect investment if you like to get out of the house, and want to pick up some extra cash. You can make your own schedule—up to a point. If you're already working late every night at the office, though, and don't have time to put into a new venture, this probably isn't for you.

"It's a myth that you can get rich quickly with vending machines," says vending machine entrepreneur Terri Tierney. "The reality is, it can be a profitable business, with certain types of machines and locations, and if you have the right approach. But there are also many unscrupulous people, and many ways to lose your investment—for instance with companies that sell you a machine but don't provide any support." To lower your risk, Tierney recommends taking the time to study the industry— she herself spent three years at it—before jumping in with an investment.

If you do decide to try investing in vending machines, there are many options—different types of machines, different types of products, and different ways of working the business to choose from. However you approach it, remember that you are, in effect, starting a small business, and whether things go right or wrong, ultimately the buck will stop with you. Ask yourself the following questions, to help you find the approach that will work best for you:

1. What type of machine is right for my business? Vending machines can be incredibly simple, such as the familiar "bulk" turn-crank machines that dispense peanuts or bubble-gum balls, right up to sophisticated devices that can pop out a piping hot serving of French fries! Which one is right for you? Ultimately, it depends on what kind of products are right for your market, and how big and complex a business you want.

But, if you're starting out, and just want to experiment and see whether owning vending machines makes sense as a passive income source for you, you should seriously consider bulk machines for one simple reason: They're less expensive. You can get a bulk vending machine—with a stand—for $150 or less.

Buying bulk vending machines also allows you to affiliate with local or national charities, many of which will give you a sticker to put on your machine in return for a regular donation from your proceeds.

2. What products should I sell? Here again, the variety is enormous, but it may be easiest to start simple. Over time, however, you'll want to experiment, keeping what works, and replacing what doesn't. The vending world is competitive, and there are a lot of machines out there. So if you can find something out of the ordinary that fits a niche market you can identify, your vending business will be that much more successful.

3. Where should I buy my machines? Experts advise using extreme caution when purchasing from an 800 number or Internet merchant, especially one who promises you a whole vending machine program, requiring little effort on your part, for a large up-front investment.

Instead, experts advise buying from a local supplier you can easily find if anything goes wrong with your machine. There are also great deals on the Internet, but this probably isn't the right place to buy if you're new to the business—you want someone local, so try checking your local yellow pages instead.

By the way, don't be afraid to buy a used machine, especially if the seller is a local vending machine seller who will provide service for it. Most machines are sturdy enough to withstand years of use, and they often become available when the previous owner upgrades to a newer model.

Whatever you do, adds Dave Gileo, whose service VendingGuy.com places vending machines in appropriate locations, "Never buy a machine that you haven't actually seen first. And never buy a machine until you know exactly where it's going." Which leads us to the next question...

4. Where will I put my machines? This is the biggest challenge in the vending machine business. Industry experts caution against trying to steal a location from another vendor (it's a small industry, and the other vendors will tend to remember tactics like this and hold them against you for a long time). So you'll have to find new locations, or at least new ones for the type of product you're selling.

How do you get new locations? The time-honored way is to visit businesses in your area, introduce yourself to the owners, or whoever has decision-making power, tell them about the machine, and ask if they'd be interested in having it on their premises. If the machine is small enough, you can bring along a sample machine to show them how it works. In most cases, you will share the take in your machine with them, giving them 20 percent of your take, or possibly more.

Choose your locations with care, experts advise, not only because you want high traffic and people who are interested in the product you have to sell, but also because you want these machines to be reasonably close to where you live. Why? Because you will be on call to go to the location, use your key to open the machine and clear jams when they occur. This will be a real drag if the machine is a two-hour drive away.

Wherever you locate your machine, it's important to get a written agreement with the location owner as to exactly what his or her responsibilities are, and what yours are, in relation to the machine. The agreement can be a very simple letter, however. It's also important to make friends with the staff at each location—for one thing, they may become your best customers, and for another, they'll be the first line of defense if someone's money doesn't go through correctly and they take out their frustration by damaging the machine. Free samples can often go a long way toward building loyalty in a location's staff.

5. Do I have to do everything myself? In the beginning, doing everything on your own is probably a good approach, even if it means starting your business with only one or two machines. For one thing, it's difficult to teach an employee how to properly service your route if you don't have much experience at it yourself. Besides, you'll build a better relationship with your location owners if they see you on a regular basis and get to know you. Remember, you're a small business owner, building up two customer bases at the same time: the end users who actually drop money in your machines and the location owner who decides on a day-to-day basis whether your machines can stay and exactly how they'll be positioned. You need to keep both parties happy.

Once your business is established—and if it's generating enough cash flow—you can consider hiring someone to take over servicing the machines. You might also think about using a locator service to find new locations for you and sell the owners on the idea of having your machines on the premises. This can be especially useful for vending machine owners who get so busy refilling the machines they already have that they don't have time to go out scouting locations for new ones.

Hiring an employee or locator makes the most sense if your ultimate goal is to have a large vending machine business, bringing in a nonstop stream of cash. If you want something smaller and more modest, then doing it yourself might be the smartest way to go. Either way, it depends on what you want to get out of the deal, and your long-term goals for your vending machine business.

Case Study

Harry Godsall is a graphic artist (as with all case studies in the book, names, locations, and professions have been changed) who works at home and turned to vending machines to generate a little extra cash to supplement his income. He specializes in putting machines with nuts, M&Ms, and mints into restaurant and bar entryways in the mid-sized Vermont town where he lives.

"It doesn't take much," Harry says. At 25 cents a sale, his machines average about five sales a day. With 49 machines in restaurants and bars, his average daily take is $61.25 a day, or $1,837.50 a month. Of that, about 20 percent is product cost, another 20 percent goes back to the location owner, and another 10 percent or so represents his overhead costs, such as gas. That leaves him with a profit of about $919 a month. Not enough to make him wealthy, but a nice supplement to his graphics work, which can be irregular.

And it doesn't take much time to earn that $919. Harry says he spends about four hours a week servicing the machines, refilling the candy or nuts, and emptying out the quarters. He services about half his machines one week and the other half the following week, so that each is serviced once every two weeks. "My ultimate goal is to have at least 200 machines," he says.

WORKING WITH A LOCATOR

A *locator* is a person or company that will do the hard work of placing your vending machine for you—for a fee. Locators find locations, according to your specifications, that are appropriate for your type of vending machine, and secure agreement from the location owner to have the machine on site. They then pass this information on to you and all you have to do is place the machine on site, keep it up and running and properly serviced, and refill it with fresh product. In essence, the locator takes over the most difficult up-front sales portion of the business off your hands.

Sounds like a good idea—and it is, with a few caveats:

1. *Don't take claims at face value.* The National Automatic Merchandising Association warns its members to be wary of locators, noting, "If it seems too good to be true, then it probably is!" Make sure to speak with a few of the locator's satisfied customers before signing on, and try to keep your initial investment low, till you have some experience working with the locator.

2. *Ask "What if…?"* What happens if the locator finds you a location with zero traffic, or where the location owner banishes your machine after a week? You should know what remedies are available to you if things go wrong.

3. *Plan for quick follow-up.* Experts say the faster you get a machine on site, once the location owner's agreed to have it there, the better. Wait too long and the owner may forget the agreement, or contract for the same product with someone else. So plan to obtain locations only where you can get a machine in place within a few days, and don't take on more locations than you can use right away.

Resources: Vending Machines

Books

Cash Locations: A Step-by-Step Guide to Securing the Best Money-Making Locations for Your Vending Machine by Ronnie Talent (BooksOnStuff downloadable PDF file from Amazon.com, 2005)

Talent reveals a methodology to identify and secure the best locations for your vending machines. He describes how to "piggyback" locations, so when you get one machine placed, it can lead to several more lucrative locations. He also explains how to expand your vending machine company to include different types of vending equipment.

Entrepreneur Magazine's Start Up: Start Your Own Vending Business by Anne Rawland Gabriel (Entrepreneur Press, 2003)

This is a good guide for people starting out in the vending business, and covers such issues as whether to buy new or used machines, which types of products sell best, where to get supplies, and how to get the best placements for your machines.

Vending Success Secrets—How Anyone Can Grow Rich in America's Best Cash Business! by Bill Way (Freedom Technology Press, 2000)

Way is an expert in the vending business, and this book guides you on all the do's and don'ts to create your own successful vending business.

Locators

VendingGuy.com
www.vendingguy.com
604-839-2980

This is David Gileo's business, which specializes in finding locations for vending machines, freeing machine owners to concentrate on servicing existing accounts.

Your Vending Machine Locator
717 Lizzie Street
Taylor, TX 76574
512-352-7694

This is something of a pay-as-you-go locator that will find locations on a week-by-week basis, only collecting money for locations once they're found and awaiting your machine.

Association

National Automatic Merchandising Association
www.vending.org
20 North Wacker Drive
Suite 3500
Chicago, IL 60606
Phone: (312) 346-0370
Fax: (312) 704-4140

This organization covers every aspect of the vending industry and offers education, publications, and regular conferences and other events.

Passive Income Strategy 2: ATM and Point-of-Sale Machines

SNAPSHOT:

How It Works:

Placing ATMs or point-of-sale (credit/debit card swipe) machines in merchant locations earns you passive income whenever customers use the machines and are charged a small fee.

THE UPSIDE:

- High Potential Returns: A typical store may see a debit card transaction twenty times a day or more.
- Ease of Use: If you work with a company such as MonEx, you may earn passive income with little or no effort.
- Market Growth Potential: There's growing demand for point-of-sale machines at merchants throughout the United States and Canada.

THE DOWNSIDE:

- Higher Initial Investment: Getting started in ATMs or point-of-sale machines costs considerably more than getting started in vending machines.
- Caveat Emptor! There are many disreputable and semireputable ATM locators in the market. Due diligence is required before signing on.
- ATM Saturation: Although the market outlook remains good for point-of-sale, with ATMs in nearly every gas station and convenience store, the supply of new locations may be dwindling.

Who Should Invest:

ATMs and point-of-sale machines are a great investment if you have $10,000 or more to invest and want to earn higher profits than with vending machines.

While vending machines can be a great way to earn passive income, there are several merchant services that can bring in cash much faster. Here is some more detail about the different machines:

ATMs: Merchants are often happy to locate an automated teller machine in their stores, because customers who use the machines to draw cash for a transaction are paying a fee (and the merchant collects a cut). If that same customer used a credit card instead, the merchant would have to *pay* a fee to the credit card company instead. This is the logic behind placing ATM machines in convenience stores, gas stations, and even at county fairs across the country, and why ATMs have proliferated so rapidly in the past ten years or so.

Cashless ATMs: The idea is similar to a traditional ATM, only it's easier to install in most locations, since the machine itself can be as small as the typical credit card reader. These machines are also much less expensive to purchase than a traditional ATM; in addition, since it isn't full of cash, it requires less security than a traditional ATM would. The machine swipes an ATM card and relays the request to the customer's bank just as a traditional ATM does, but rather than dispense bills, it prints out a receipt that the customer presents to the merchant in exchange for cash. As with a traditional ATM, the customer pays a fee that the merchant and ATM owner can share.

Point-of-sale (debit swipe) card readers: These machines collect a transaction fee, usually $1 or less, from customers as they make their purchases. Again, the fee can be shared between the machine's owner and the merchant in question. Many merchants appreciate the opportunity to collect a fee from customers rather than pay a fee to a credit card company.

Use of ATMs and debit card swipe machines is rapidly growing, and generates billions of dollars in fees each year. But how does a small investor get into the game? One way is to research available devices, and use your sales skills to pitch them to merchants such as gas stations and convenience stores, offering to pay them a portion of the fees you earn with the machine. Obviously, welcoming an ATM or debit swipe card onto the premises will be a bigger decision for many merchants than letting you place a gumball machine in a corner of the entryway. So, once you've chosen the type of machine you want to own, be prepared to present a very detailed account of how the machine works, how transactions (debit card transactions especially) will go through, how much customers will be charged, and how much the merchant will receive.

Some advise that this is the best method of trying out the world of ATM or debit swipe investing. For one thing, you are paying only for the machine itself, rather than making a larger investment with a company that will place the ATMs or swipe devices for you. On the other hand, it will require your own time, sales skills, and expertise with the machine to make the sale to merchants, and may require your time to service the machine as well.

The other option is to invest with a company that will place ATMs for you. In this arrangement, all the work is done for you—the machines are placed and serviced, paper replaced and fees collected without any work on your part, and you receive a large portion of the fee for each use. (This differs from the typical arrangement with a vending machine locator, which will find locations for a onetime fee, leaving you to do the work of placing, refilling, and servicing the machine, collecting the money, and making any payments to location owners.)

Unfortunately, most ATM providers sell or lease machines directly to retailers and aren't looking for individual investors. I know of only one that's open to private investment, Money Express, which offers investment opportunities for both its ATM and point-of-sale (POS) machines. Investments start at $10,000 and require a multiyear commitment.

For more information:
Money Express
www.monexgroup.com
71 Silton Road, Unit 3
Woodbridge, Ontario L4L 7Z8
Canada
(866) 286-7787

In general, before investing with any ATM or POS company that will place machines for you, make sure to:

- Find out serial numbers of the machines you will own.
- Find out the address or addresses where the machine(s) will be placed.
- Find out how to track your machine's transactions online, in real time.
- Ask your state's Division of Securities or other financial regulator if there have been any complaints against the company.
- Talk to prior investors who have been pleased with the returns they received.
- Have an attorney carefully review all contracts and paperwork.

Resources: ATM and Point-of-Sale Machines

Web Site

ATMmarketplace.com

www.atmmarketplace.com

This Web site for industry insiders covers every aspect of the ATM industry, including how to operate an ATM successfully, a comparison guide for different brands of machines, and current news affecting banking and ATMs. There's also a classified section for buying (or selling) machines.

Passive Income Strategy 3: Investing in Timeshares

SNAPSHOT:

How It Works:

Timeshares can make great vacation spots, but a carefully selected timeshare can serve as a good investment too, creating passive income in the years when you don't use it, and even appreciating in value for resale.

THE UPSIDE:

- Ease of Use: Probably the least labor-intensive of all the passive income opportunities.
- Financing Available: If you find a timeshare at the right price, you can finance your purchase, putting relatively little money down.
- Great Vacations: One of the great benefits of timeshare ownership is that you can use your investment for a great getaway in the sun or snow. (Try that with a Treasury bill!)

THE DOWNSIDE:

- Caveat Emptor! This industry is rife with a lot of hard selling. Make sure you choose a timeshare that meets your goals.
- Uncertain Appreciation: Although many timeshares gain in value, they have not always appreciated as dependably as outright real estate purchases usually do. If you're buying purely for a projected increase in value, you're probably better off with traditional real estate (see Chapter 2).
- Planning Ahead Required: In order to rent or trade a timeshare, you will need to start well in advance. This means deciding many months ahead

of time whether you will use your vacation time, rent it for money, or trade it for another location.

Who Should Invest:

Timeshare investing is appropriate if you would like to spend an occasional vacation at your home resort, and you have enough up-front capital, typically $5,000 to $50,000, to buy a high-demand week in a high-demand resort. You also have to be willing to spend the time and effort involved in renting out your unit, either by placing ads in newspapers, online, or with timeshare rental agencies.

One of the things I like best about timeshares is they are a truly populist concept. Fancy vacation properties that would otherwise be available only to the very wealthy are now accessible to middle-class vacationers who can afford to buy a week or two, but would not be able to afford the property year-round. Timeshares have been available since the 1960s, and exist all over Europe, as well as the United States.

But wait, you say. I've heard so many stories about timeshare scams. Is this really a worthwhile investment? There's no denying that timeshares gained a deservedly bad reputation, especially in the 1980s and 1990s, when unsuspecting sales prospects were lured on site visits with promises of free or nearly free vacations, only to be subjected to a relentless hard sell, sometimes for properties of questionable quality. And it's certainly true that some who gave in and bought in those situations wound up regretting it.

Meanwhile, the industry continued to grow, reaching more than $5 billion, with more than four million U.S. households owning timeshares. In the last few years, timeshares have gained respectability, as more and more of the world's most respected hotel and vacation brands have gotten into the business. The underlying principle—giving a wider audience access to upscale resorts, and allowing them to make money on their investment—remains a sound one.

It's certainly possible to buy a timeshare and wind up sorry that you did. But if you choose wisely, evaluating both the financial investment and vacation value, a timeshare can be a very nice investment indeed, bringing both profits and vacation perks. Here's how:

1. Pick the right timeshare type for you. There are several different flavors of timeshare purchases. In the most classic arrangement, you own a specific week of every year. That is your week to do with as you please—use it, trade it, or rent it to someone else.

"Float" or "flex" ownership is a variation in which you select a week within a period. This type of ownership may be preferable to some who do not want to be tied down to the same specific week each year. However, you should find out what the resort's policies are for reserving floating weeks. You may need to book your preferred week as much as two years in advance. There are also some timeshares that rotate all owners through the year. This levels the playing field among weeks in the year, giving everyone a turn in the most popular and least popular times. A policy like this will affect the timeshare's value, so make sure you know what the rules are.

Another variation is the vacation club, which typically owns timeshare properties in a variety of locations. Like a timeshare, a club membership can be bought or sold, and may gain or lose value. Club members can reserve space at any of the club's properties, so the advantage is that you can visit a variety of locations without the bother of putting your timeshare up for exchange. A further variation on the club is the points program, in which club members receive a certain number of points they can exchange against vacation stays each year. In all cases—timeshare, right-to-use, vacation, and points—you will pay a yearly maintenance fee for your property, and the fee may change over time as prices increase.

2. Know exactly what you're buying. What does it mean to buy a timeshare? We all know it gives you the right to a week (or choice of weeks) at a given resort location. But what, exactly, do you wind up owning? And what are your rights if the resort should close?

The answers to these questions depend on what type of ownership you have. Deeded ownership is sometimes called "fractional" because that literally is how the deed is recorded—and filed with the local government: You own a fraction of the property, corresponding to a specific week of the year. In the event the resort closed, you would become one of fifty-two co-owners of the property. You could band together to sell it, to try to recoup your initial investment.

"Right-to-use" ownership, as its name suggests, gives you the right to use the property during a specific time period each year, for a specific period of time. At the end of that period (usually many years), you lose the right and ownership reverts to the resort. Obviously, the value of a right-to-use timeshare will diminish as the period of use goes on. However, there are some nations with strict laws forbidding foreigners to own property, and right-to-use makes it possible to buy timeshares in those locations.

Vacation club memberships and points programs are more problematic, because you are not buying a deed to a physical property. If you buy a points program, check the contract to make sure the developer cannot raise the number of points required for its travel offerings at will. If it does, the value of your points will erode.

3. Buy a big brand. Let's say you visit a gorgeous resort with top-quality amenities. Impressed, you buy a timeshare. But then, over the next few years, things start to slip. Things that break down aren't fixed right away. Carpets and furniture start looking worn. Your property is losing value, and there may be little you can do about it—especially if the cause of the deterioration is that the developer of the resort is having financial difficulty.

How do you protect yourself? The best way is to buy a well-known, long-established vacation travel brand. Fortunately, many of these brands, such as Disney, Marriott, and Westin, offer timeshares for sale. First of all, a company such as Disney, Hilton, Marriott, or Westin is unlikely to run out of ready cash. More importantly, they have a vested interest in keeping your facility in tip-top shape, because even one run-down property would hurt the reputation of the entire brand.

4. Buy a popular time. It can be tempting to go for the savings that come with buying a timeshare in the off-season or in-between "shoulder" season. Don't give in to that temptation! Remember that you are planning to rent, exchange, and perhaps eventually sell your timeshare, and your ability to do all these things will be curtailed if you own a time when no one wants to go to your resort.

If you love taking winter walks on a deserted beach, as some people do, then buy a high-season timeshare, rent it out, and use the proceeds to book an off-season stay at a beach hotel. You'll probably wind up pocketing a profit, and the value of your investment will be secure.

5. Buy at the right price. As with any other investment, you must do your due diligence to make sure the price of the investment makes sense when compared with its future value, and the income it can generate. Get familiar with timeshare values, both for resale and rental, by studying timeshare exchange Web sites such as www.tug2.net. Pay special attention to whichever exchange the resort you're interested in uses for its listings. Try to find out about actual cost at closing as well as for sale listings. If you're considering financing your purchase (which many resorts offer) make sure the cash flow will be positive, given loan payments and likely future maintenance fees, balanced against the income you can make from renting and projected resale value.

One of the best ways to get a good deal in timeshares is *not* to buy from the developer, but from an owner who, for whatever reason, wants to sell his or her unit. Think of it like buying a used car: Buying a car that is even a few months old will often save you 50 percent or more of the price if the car were new. The same kinds of discounts can apply to timesharing, but unlike the car, you don't lose any of the amenities when you buy a "used" timeshare.

Since most people buy timeshares direct from the developer, as a result of a site visit and well-crafted sales pitch, timeshare reselling is a buyer's market, and you should be able to find a good deal on the timeshare you want. Check user classifieds (such as www.tug2.net), ask at the resort in question if they have a listing of timeshares for resale, check the exchange the timeshare uses for classifieds. There are also licensed real estate brokers who handle timeshare resales (don't mess with any broker who isn't licensed to sell real estate) who may be able to find you what you want. And, don't forget to check the classified ads of local papers where the resort you want is located (these are often available online at the local paper's Web site). Timeshare owners who want to sell sometimes list their properties in the classifieds.

6. Learn to plan ahead. As your timeshare week elapses each year, you should already know what you plan to do with next year's week: use it yourself, exchange it for other travel, rent it out, or sell it. You can also trade in your timeshare for reward points that you can use at the hotel chain or for other travel.

If you're going to exchange, rent, or sell it, you should start the process right away. Timeshare owners often encounter frustration if they wait too long to put their week up for rent, exchange, or sale. But if you buy carefully, and plan well ahead of time, you'll reap profits from your timeshare investment for years to come.

Resources: Investing in Timeshares

Book

The Everything Family Guide to Timeshares: Buy Smart, Avoid Pitfalls, and Enjoy Your Vacations to the Max! by Kim Kavin (Adams Media, 2005)

This book offers readers detailed information on negotiating a timeshare contract, as well as how to exchange timeshares for other vacation travel.

Web Sites

Timeshare User's Group

www.tug2.net

This is a great place to learn everything about the timeshare industry—much of it from timeshare owners themselves. There are helpful articles on buying and selling timeshares, and everything in between. There are also classified listings for buying, selling, renting, or exchanging timeshares.

RedWeek.com

www.redweek.com

Huge listings of timeshares for sale, resale, rental, or exchange, along with user reviews of resorts.

Vacation Timeshares and Rentals

www.vacationtimesharerentals.com

Online marketplace for those who want to sell, buy, or rent timeshares.

Rii® Stroman Timeshare Reseller

www.stroman.com

Real Estate broker specializing in reselling timeshares, and one of the largest selections of timeshares for sale in the industry.

MY TIMESHARE EXPERIENCE

My own experience with timeshares started about ten years ago, when I bought six midsummer weeks at the Grande Ocean Marriott Resort on Hilton Head Island, South Carolina. At the time, part of the resort was still under construction, which made these weeks less expensive than they might otherwise have been. The price was about $25,000 per week for high-demand weeks in summer. My plan was both to use the property for

continued

vacations with my family and also use the timeshares as an investment, and over the years, we've done both.

Maintenance fees are about $500 a year, and I've found that whichever weeks we don't use or exchange ourselves, we can rent out for $2,500 to $3,500 each. If we wanted to sell these weeks—which we don't—I've been told I could now get about $50,000 each for them.

In Marriott's program, I also have the option of exchanging a week toward a huge number of Marriott travel points, allowing me to stay free in Marriotts all over the country. Recently, I took my son on a tour of colleges around the country, and we used our travel points to pay for all our hotel stays.

Passive Income Strategy 4: Investing in Payday Loans

SNAPSHOT:

How It Works:

When employed customers need money in advance of their next paycheck, they turn to payday loan stores (sometimes called community financial services) for a short-term loan at high interest and service fees. You can get in on that income by investing in (thus providing capital for) the payday loans.

THE UPSIDE:

- High Returns: Because the investment is in high-interest loans and service fees, you can get higher returns than with many other types of investments.
- Growing Market: More and more customers are using this type of short-term financing.
- Becoming Mainstream: More and more middle-class people are using these services.

THE DOWNSIDE:

- High Risk: Interest rates and service fees are high because the customers are "subprime." The ultimate default rate is about 3 percent of all loans made.

- Commitment Required: Currently, there is no easy way to invest in pay-day loans without committing to at least a two-year relationship.
- Only One Way In: The only easy way I know of to get in the game is by joining the Freedom Investment Club.

Who Should Invest:

If you're looking for a very passive way to earn high income paid quarterly on a substantial up-front investment, and are willing to accept some risk, this may be the perfect vehicle for you.

Short-term, high-interest loans with substantial service fees have gained legitimacy over the last several years, with more and more large institutions offering short-term payday loans and more and more consumers taking advantage of them. Critics of these loans tend to focus on their high interest rates, which can top 90 percent when measured in annual terms, counting the service fees. On the other hand, the industry points out, it doesn't make much sense to compare a two-week loan to a thirty-year mortgage in this manner—any more than it makes sense to "annualize" a hotel room rate, multiplying it by 365 and comparing it to local apartment rents. Besides, most people who use payday loans don't have the option of obtaining more traditional financing through banks or credit cards. Their other alternatives may be very unappealing, such as failing to pay the rent, or bouncing a check. If they do bounce a check, they will have to make good later, as well as pay extra fees that are typically higher than the interest rates payday loan stores charge.

Whatever the reason, payday loans are a rapidly growing business, and the demographics of customers include many in the middle class. In a survey by the Community Financial Services Association, more than 40 percent of payday loan customers owned their own homes, and well over half were college-educated. The old stereotype that immigrant workers and unwed mothers are the sole customers for payday loans is becoming less true every year.

How to Invest?

How can a small investor get into this $50 billion-plus industry? Unfortunately, I only know of one easy way in, and it requires that you join the Freedom Investment Club. I should tell you right up front that, after joining the club myself as an investor, I became president of FIC USA Financial Services. The 4,800-member club is the largest investment club in North America, and has shown spectacular returns with many of its investments over the years. There's a onetime fee of $1,000 to join the club, which gives you access to a lot of investment information and market analysis and a bond investment in the payday loan industry.

It works like this: You buy a bond at a high annual interest rate, with payments made to you every quarter. The most recent interest rate for these bonds was 13 percent. Thirteen percent is, obviously, an extraordinarily high rate for a bond in today's environment, and the only reason the interest is so high is because the investment is used to fund highly lucrative payday loans. Keep in mind, though, that payday loan investments are considered high-risk, since there's a greater-than-usual chance borrowers will default on their loans.

The club offers these bonds at regular intervals. At the last offering, the club offered $5,000, ten-year bonds, with the right to cash out once every two years. (As with any bond, if an investor needed cash before the two years were up, he or she would have to sell the bond to someone else.) Bonds were sold in lots of four, for a minimum investment of $20,000.

Resources: Investing in Payday Loan Stores

To learn more about investing in payday loan bonds, and other Freedom Investment Club offerings, contact:

Freedom Investment Club
www.ficinvestors.com
555 West Hastings Street
P.O. Box 12091
Vancouver, BC V6B 4N5
Canada
(877) 258-2342 ext. 2054

To learn more about the payday loan industry:
Community Financial Services Association of America
www.cfsa.net
515 King Street
Suite 300

Alexandria, VA 22314
(703) 684-1029

Passive Income Strategy 5: Profiting from Internet Advertising

SNAPSHOT:

How It Works:

If you have or can create a Web site or blog that draws regular traffic, you can earn passive income by signing up for an Internet affiliate advertising program such as Google AdSense and others.

THE UPSIDE:

- Little or No Up-front Investment: All you need is a Web site or blog—if you don't already have one.
- Ease of Use: Once you sign up, the program is completely passive: They send you the ads and the money they generate automatically.
- Unlimited Potential: If you can create a Web site or blog that the public finds compelling, you can make very substantial sums—and even earn a good living—this way.

THE DOWNSIDE:

- Imagination and Luck Required: It can be challenging to find a topic or service that will bring in meaningful ad revenues.
- It's Labor-Intensive: The ad revenues are passive, but you will need to constantly add new content to your site—and look for ways to drive traffic there.
- Little Content Control: Affiliate programs may give you limited veto power over the ads you receive, but you will not have complete control. Does this mean you could wind up with an ad for penis enlargement? Unlikely, but not impossible.

Who Should Invest:

"Invest" may not be the right word, since it costs virtually nothing to try this out. If you're part of a large club or have an interest in anything that can build a wide following—or can offer anything that many people want, from cooking tips to specialized medical info, then Internet advertising might be the way for you to build a revenue stream.

A few years ago, twenty-seven-year-old Matt Daimler, a Seattle networking engineer, got fed up with his airline seats. After getting stuck one time too many in an uncomfortable position for the long flight from Seattle to Eastern Europe, he decided to do something about it. He began collecting inside information from travelers and flight attendants about the worst and best seats on many types of commercial airplanes, and posted them online on a site named Seatguru (www.seatguru.com).

The information proved popular, and he began to think he could make some money off the site by selling ads to airlines and travel companies. But they turned him down, saying he was too small for their ads. Daimler turned to Google AdSense, an affiliate program that delivers ads directly to Web sites and pays the Web site owner every time someone clicks on an ad. Daimler hoped he might make $3,000 a month off AdSense. Instead, he was soon earning some $120,000 a year—enough, he says, to turn his hobby into a full-fledged business. As I write this, the company has just been acquired by TripAdvisor (www.tripadvisor), a site that collects and offers inside user information on hotels and other travel products all over the world—and is well worth checking before you head off to a new hotel for the first time. Coming full circle, TripAdvisor itself offers an affiliate program, and will send advertising to your Web site if you sign up with them.

I know: Not everyone can provide content as universally appealing as the inside scoop on good and bad airplane seats. But if you have a Web site or blog of any kind, there's no reason not to add one or more affiliate programs—there's nothing to stop you from using several—and see what your earning power might be.

MY INTERNET ADVERTISING EXPERIENCE

As "America's Money Answers Man," my Web site www.moneyanswers. com provides information on everything from how to check your credit score to money strategies for those over sixty. I post articles there on a reg-

continued

ular basis, to keep my readers and listeners coming back for more—which I would do, whether there were ads there or not.

My Web site gets about 10,000 visitors a month—in part because I frequently appear on television and the radio, but also because people want the useful information I have posted there. Google automatically pays me $0.10 every time someone clicks one of its ads, so the site generates income of about $200 to $300 a month—of completely passive income.

Resources: Profiting from Internet Advertising

Affiliate Programs

Google AdSense
www.google.com/adsense
The first and largest of the ad-based affiliate programs, AdSense is easily accessible to anyone, and perhaps the easiest program to use. It's a good starting place if you want to test out your Web site's earning potential.

Yahoo! Affiliate Program
http://advertising.yahoo.com/affiliate_programs/
Yahoo! is Google's chief competitor, and in its affiliate program, you provide links to its product across your Web site and earn commissions when users click through.

PPCProfitMachine
www.ppcprofitmachine.com
PPCProfitMachine integrates ad feeds from several pay-per-click advertisers and feeds them to your site in order of highest-paying commissions—and creates search-engine-friendly content on your site, making it easier for users to find you in the first place.

Amazon Associates
http://affiliate-program.amazon.com/gp/associates/join
Perhaps the oldest affiliate program on the Internet, Amazon Associates works when users click through the associates' link and buy products from Amazon. Amazon pays the site owner a commission of up to 10 percent.

eBay Affiliate Program
http://affiliates.ebay.com

Similar to Amazon's program, eBay will pay you for every "active" user that comes to its site through yours, and will also pay you commissions on products users buy after arriving from your site.

Informational Web Site and Newsletter:

AssociatePrograms.com

www.associateprograms.com

This site offers a wealth of information on everything you need to know about online affiliate programs, including special guides and articles aimed at beginners and listings of affiliate programs (there are many more than I've mentioned here).

Index

Page numbers in *italics* refer to charts.